SOPHIA SOTKE

MACK SAHARA

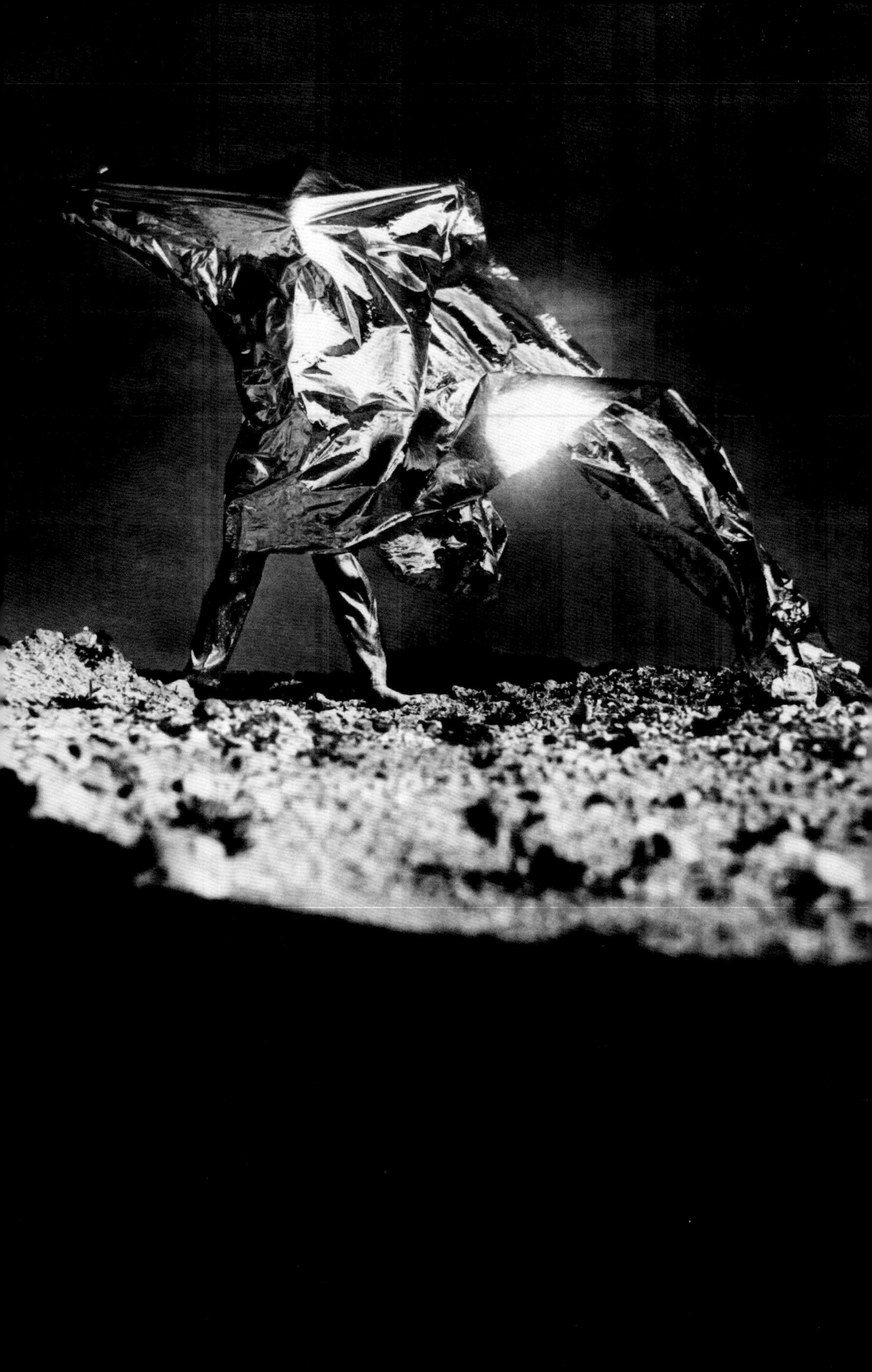

SOPHIA SOTKE

MACK SAHARA

From ZERO to Land Art
–
Heinz Mack's Sahara Project
1959–1997

HIRMER

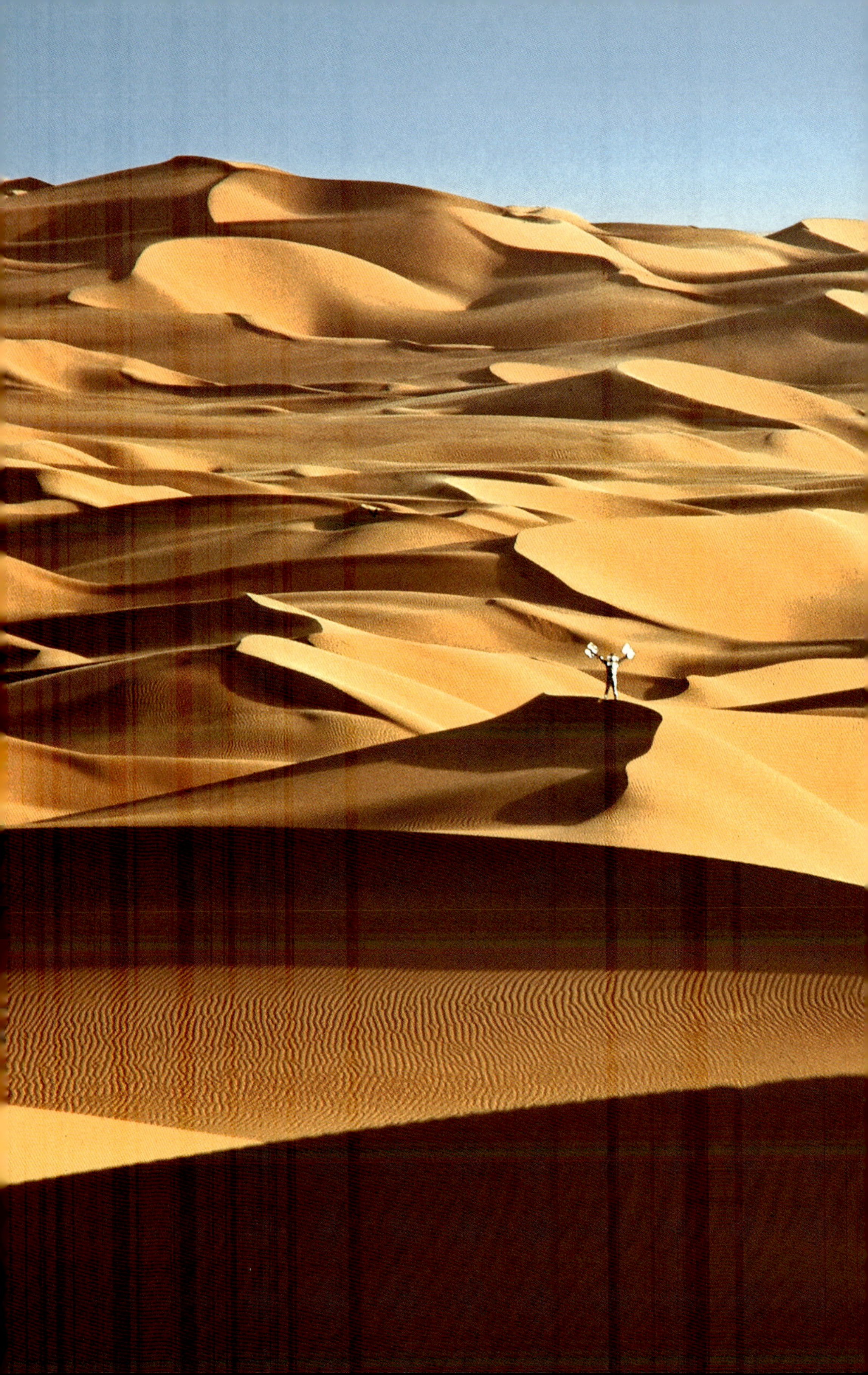

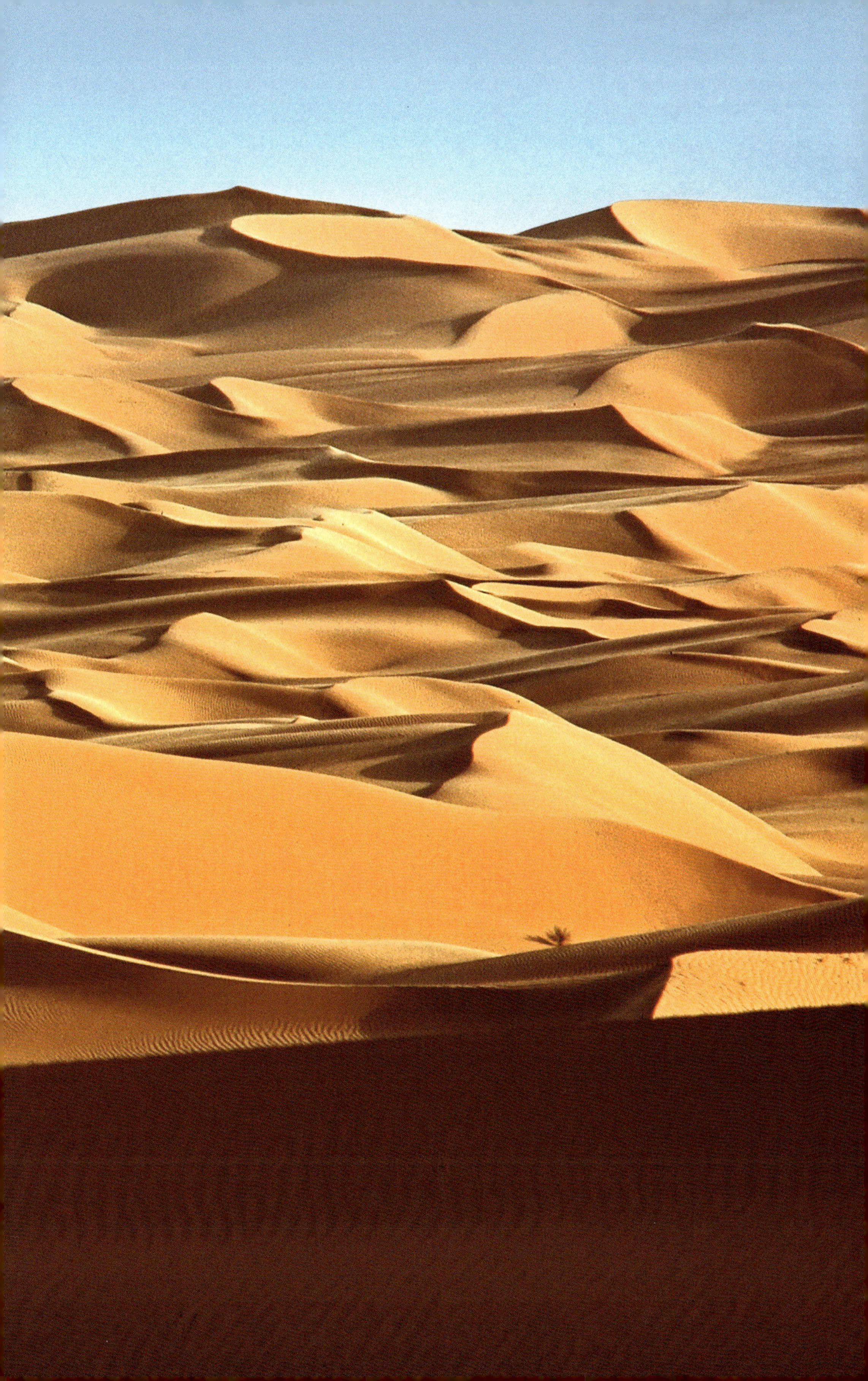

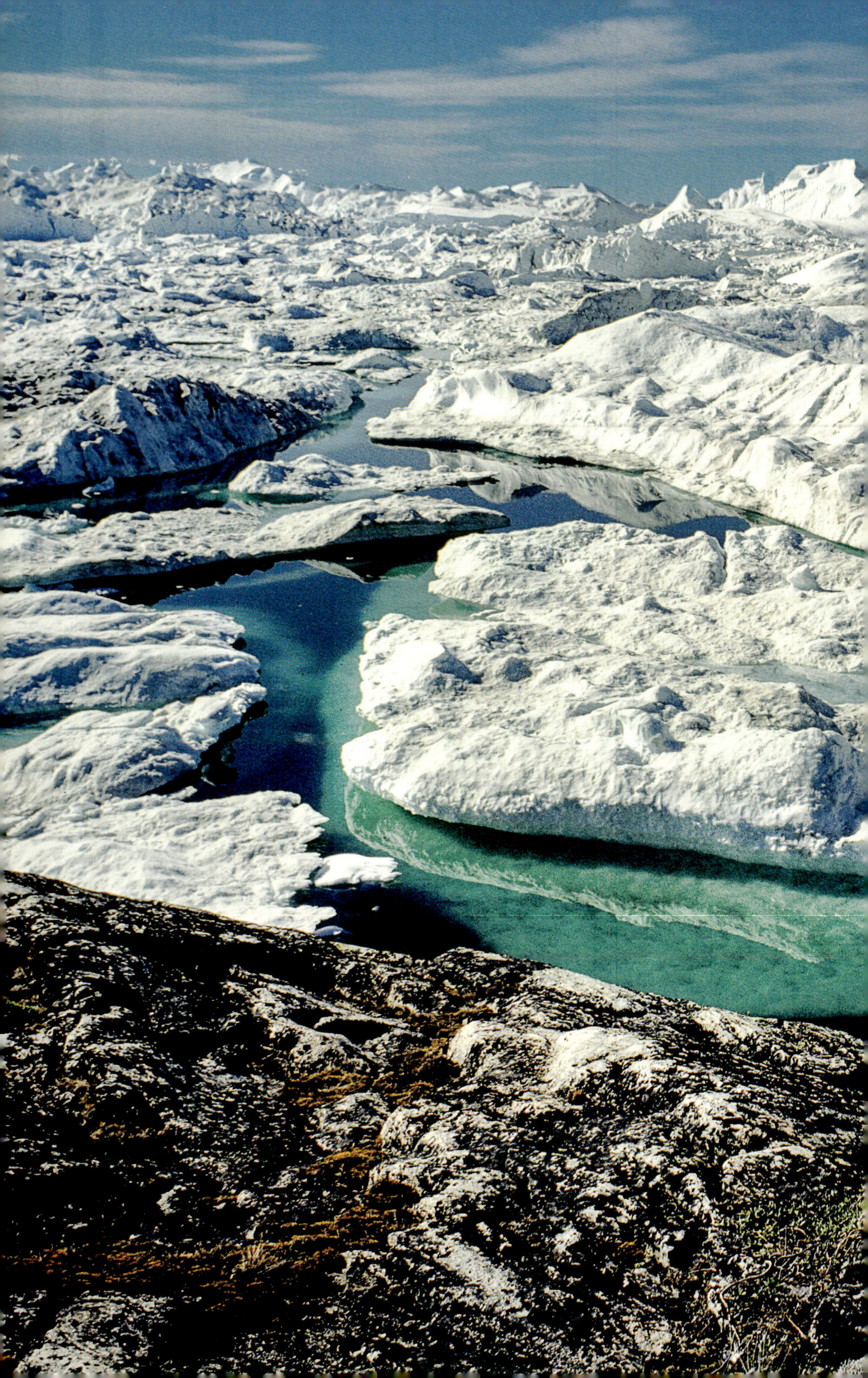

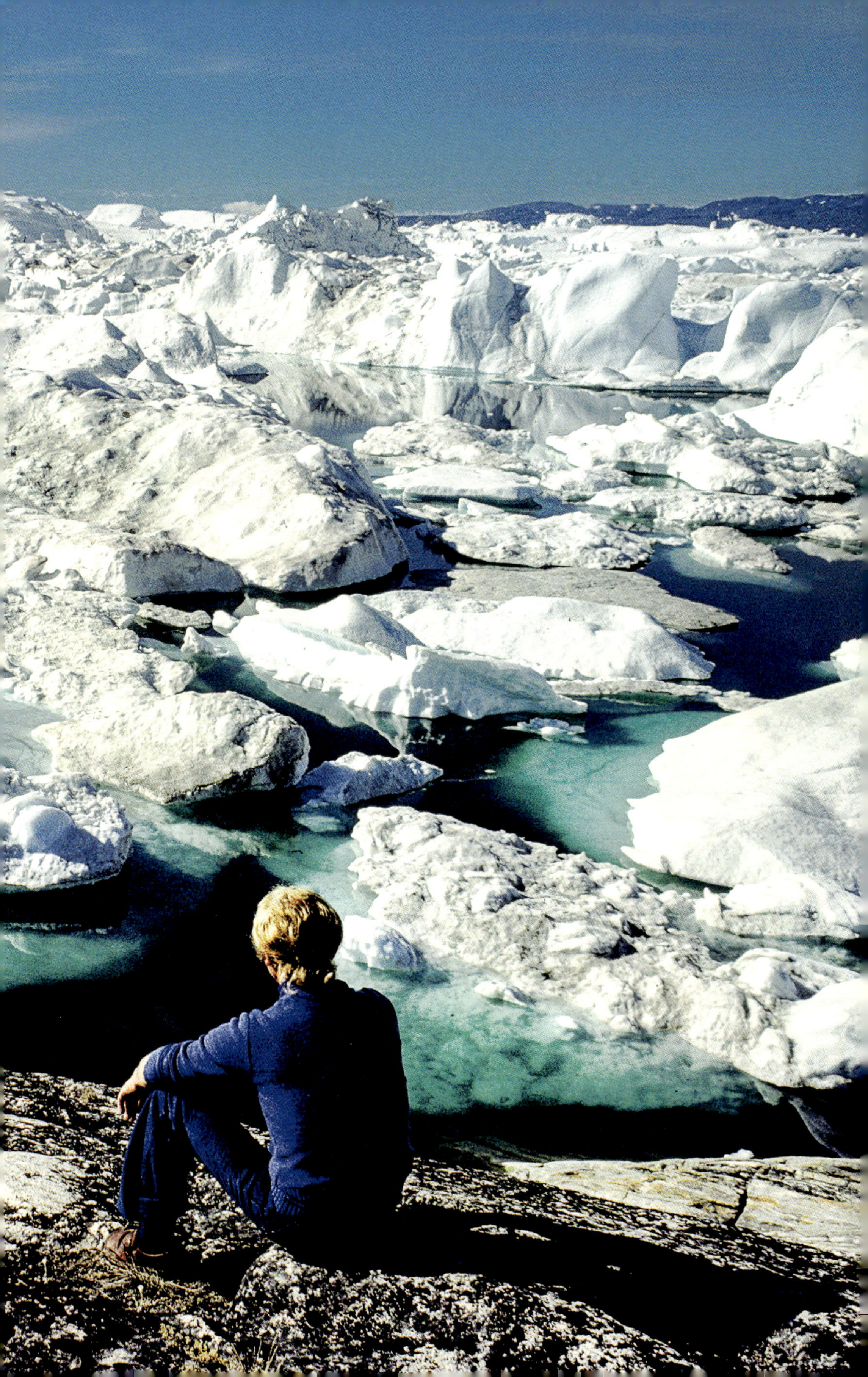

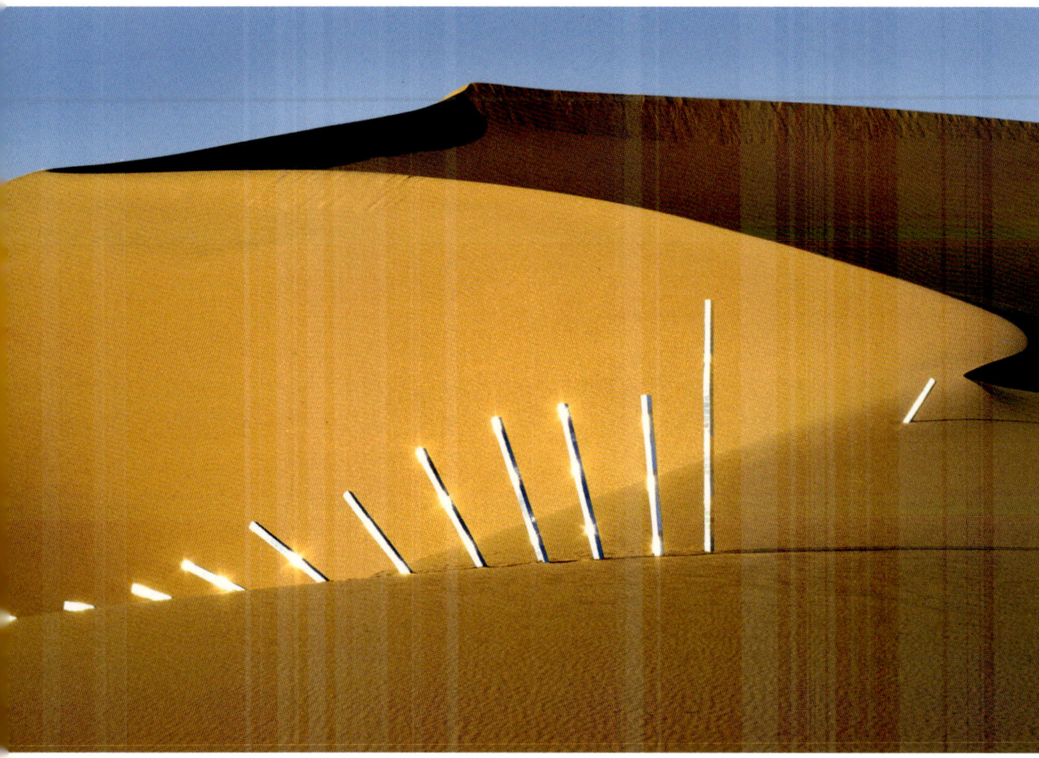

FOREWORD

ROBERT FLECK

This book introduces us to a living legend, the artist Heinz Mack, and does so through his *Sahara Project*. Formulated in 1959, first published in 1961, and experimentally implemented between 1967 and 1997, it is a major work of ZERO, the visionary art movement that manifested in Düsseldorf and the entire Western world between 1958 and 1966 and which has now been rediscovered. The *Sahara Project* is at the same time the magnum opus of 'utopian art', as one might call a large part of the avant-garde art of that time in its own vocabulary, comparable to the current of utopian architecture, which was constituted in the art of building at that time and which produced the Centre Pompidou in Paris (1977) as its most famous result. In a third respect, Heinz Mack's *Sahara Project* constitutes a hitherto unrivalled concept, namely working in the field of visual arts directly with the elements available through the planet: light, air, earth, fire, and water. In this context, the *Sahara Project* should be seen in relation to American Land Art, which it anticipated in many ways and modelled over time, in a constant dialogue across the years the artist spent in New York and beyond. Last but not least, the *Sahara Project* is, in retrospect – together with Christo's first landscape-related projects from the 1970s – the first visual art project that made us feel our planet as such, as well as its endangerment. This also makes it, by its very nature, one of the few 'unfinishable' works of visual art of the second half of the twentieth century that point to the future.

Sophia Sotke's book makes this accessible to us in a gripping and art-historically rigorous way. It is based on complete access to archive material, which, preserved in the artist's personal archive, as well as in public archives, was available to the author for the first time and in exemplary form. It is also based on numerous conversations with the artist and interviews with contemporary witnesses. Such universal source material is exemplary.

For the art historian, as well as for the historian of ideas – since Mack's *Sahara Project* is also highly relevant to the history of ideas, presenting a key moment from which history as a whole can be reconstructed – Sophia Sotke's book, which emerged from a brilliant doctoral thesis at the University of Cologne, contains a consistently rigorous coherence of facts and assessments. The author has reconstructed the *Sahara Project*, which was previously only rudimentarily examined, in a lasting way.

For the non-scholarly reader, this book offers even more: a gripping adventure novel about how an artist who, at not even thirty years of age, sets his mind on making the desert his studio and achieves this, albeit only partially, but highly significantly for other art of his time and art of the future. When the magazine *Stern* – at that time in West Germany, as important a medium as Instagram is today – published a report on the second partial realisation of the *Sahara Project* in 1976, I was an A-levels student and understood nothing when I encountered visual art. But this magazine was passed through all the rows: 'There's someone working directly with the planet, and respectfully dismantling everything again. Check it out!'

ON THE PREHISTORY OF THE SAHARA PROJECT

1950–1958

□01
Heinz Mack on his first visit to the Sahara
Tunisia, 1955

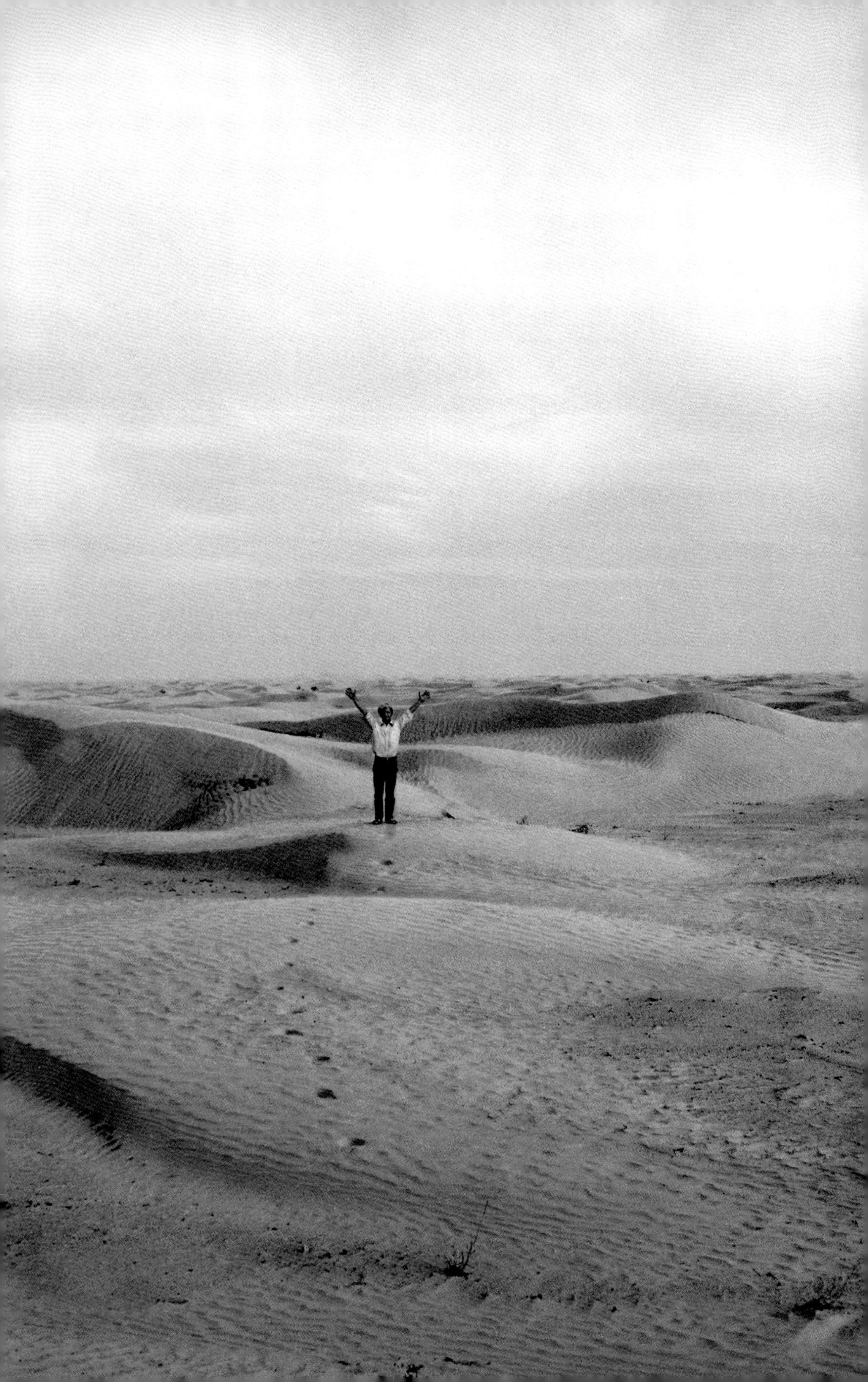

Dunes of light sand – as far as the eye can see. The hills stretch to the horizon with their fine relief, the wave forms created by the wind, sporadically interrupted by stones, boulders, and sparse vegetation. Above them: the wide sky, only rarely cloudy. It is warm when Heinz Mack sets foot in the desert for the first time. He feels the sand under his feet, the wind on his skin as he climbs a smaller dune. There, he turns around, directs his gaze towards the camera and stretches his arms in the air: Victory! – a sign of triumph and joy at seeing this longed for place for the first time. ↖□01

In 1955, the twenty-four-year-old Heinz Mack found himself not far from the oasis of Tozeur on the eastern edge of the Grand Erg Oriental, the largest sand sea in the Sahara. He had come to Tunisia via Morocco in his old Volkswagen to drive out into the desert. Mack remembers that he had brought a tent with him, which he pitched near a dry riverbed. Next to flowering oleander bushes, he dug a hole in the sand of the riverbed and found water enough for a bath. The bathtub in the desert, Mack says, was a luxury that did not come easily; it did not exist without a shovel. At the time, he was prepared to forego any comfort on this journey that seemed so important to him.[1] For during his first encounter with the Sahara, the young artist felt something that could be described as the opposite of *horror vacui*.[2] In the vastness of nature, which spread out before him like an endless blank canvas, Mack found a new freedom. 'I must confess: such spaces fill my imagination, and I admire not least of all the serenity of their unremitting expanse,' he wrote four years later in his text *The Sahara Project*. The open and deep space, which finds no limit even in the horizon, had formed the free sphere for his gaze, which hurried through proximity and distance without direction, without intention, and without weight. 'The experience of vastness stays with me.'[3]

The Sahara – 'queen of all deserts'[4] – stretches 6,000 kilometres in northern Africa from the Atlantic Ocean in the west to the Red Sea in the east; its north-south extension is 2,000 kilometres. With an area of nine million square kilometres, it is the largest desert on earth.[5] A space of ocean-like vastness, it is called *bahr bela ma* in Arabic: 'sea without water'. Here, size and vastness, space and time do not correspond to the experience that a Central European like Mack generally has of the world.[6]

Imagining this dimension, which was completely new for him, had motivated Mack to make his first trip to the Sahara. Since childhood, he had harboured hopes of one day being able to visit the desert. He had discovered his preference for solitary and wide-open spaces as a boy in Lollar, Hesse. There, outside the village, was a plateau that the villagers called 'Russia' because of its great expanse.[7] Born in 1931, Mack had initially grown up in Krefeld, but during the Second World War was evacuated to relatives in Hesse. The cramped domestic conditions there awakened in him a longing for places free of the 'fingerprints of human civilisation', as the artist puts it today.[8] Fortunately, as he had written in *The Sahara Project* in 1959, 'the nature of the earth does not yet allow the entire inventory of our world to spread out uniformly in space'. This is why he was interested in 'preserves of nature' of extraordinary size and dimension.[9] As a thirteen-year-old, he had found a small colour reproduction of a painting titled *Sandstorm in the Desert* in his father's Brockhaus encyclopaedia, which he immediately copied and then covered with liquid glass to make the colours glisten and glow – an artistic impulse that would later become extremely important for Mack's oeuvre as a whole, and especially for the *Sahara Project*.[10]

As a youth, Mack had intended to become a professional pianist, but a serious injury to his left hand forced him to abandon this career aspiration. The artist recalls, however, that the abstract drawings with which he then applied to the Düsseldorf Academy of Art resembled piano notes. In 1950, the nineteen-year-old began studying in the painting class for art teachers but was soon admitted as a guest student in the free sculpture class of Ewald Mataré, whose lessons he preferred.[11]

After his first semester, he received a scholarship of 150 marks, which allowed him to travel to Paris. There, he saw Henri Matisse's *Still Life with Oranges* (1898) in the Grand Palais.[12] He remembers visiting the painting every day for a whole week: 'It was my first great encounter with colour – with bright, pure, rich, mysterious colour.'[13] *Still Life with Oranges*, Mack realised, could only have been painted south of the Alps, and indeed Matisse had painted it in Morocco in 1912. Mack had grown up in the era of National Socialism, where 'the North' and the 'Nordic man' were idealised and where the world seemed grey or brown to him. When he encountered the work of Matisse, he felt the pictorial sensuality of Mediterranean culture as the epitome of colour and decided to become a painter.[14] Paris itself also impressed him immensely – not least of all because it was the first city in his life where there were no ruins or rubble. Here, he also saw works by Joan Miró, which inspired his own painting for a while. Back at the academy, however – much to Mack's astonishment – no one had ever heard of Miró. This reflected the informational gap left by Germany's long isolation from the international art world. In the sparsely stocked library, Mack and his fellow students could only inform themselves with great difficulty about the European art of the past decades, which had been considered 'degenerate' under the National Socialist regime.[15]

In 1953, he passed the state examination in art and crafts education with a thesis on 'Pietro Cavallini and his significance for monumental painting in Italy' at the Düsseldorf Academy of Art.[16] Mack's choice of this topic revolving around the medieval designer of large-scale frescoes and mosaics already expressed his preference for monumental dimensions, which was later to become a leitmotif of the *Sahara Project*. In 1956, he also passed the state examination in philosophy at the University of Cologne. These studies enabled him to reflect on his artistic work with the help of a profound knowledge of intellectual history and to write texts that have both artistic and poetic dimensions – one of these is *The Sahara Project*.

During his studies at the academy in Düsseldorf, Mack had become friends with Otto Piene. In 1955, they both rented a studio at Gladbacher Strasse 69 in Düsseldorf – a kind of 'poorhouse', as Mack later recalled – former factory rooms in a back building without heating or sanitary facilities. 'In a contrast – which is hard to convey today – to the spirit of optimism that had taken hold of us, there were the external, material, and existential conditions under which we worked.'[17] Moreover, in a cityscape marked by ruins, there was – at least at the beginning – a lack of any encouragement.[18] Mack, who had married in the meantime, taught art and philosophy at a secondary school.[19] He and Piene, who was also a teacher at the time, worked in the studio in the evenings and at night. There, three years later, they founded the ZERO movement, the influence of which on the *Sahara Project* is essential if only for its parallel development.

First however, in 1956, both artists joined Gruppe 53. The young artists united in this group, which also included Gerhard Hoehme and Peter Brüning, were largely dedicated to Tachism, a form of Art Informel.[20] This style of painting, which drew primarily from the irrational, the subconscious, and the coincidental, was decisively influenced by the German painter Wols, who had emigrated to France and died in 1951, and whose spontaneous, eruptive painting technique left amorphous spots (French: *taches*) on the canvas.[21] Mack and Piene took advantage of their membership in Gruppe 53 to present their works publicly by participating in a number of joint exhibitions. In 1957, however, they established their own exhibition format with the *Abendausstellung* (evening exhibition). For one evening at a time, they invited artist friends to exhibit their works with them in their studio. Initially, most of the participants were members of Gruppe 53, but Mack and Piene soon turned their backs on the group, as they no longer saw Tachism as a meaningful continuation of painting.[22]

Mack, who had also experimented with Art Informel, developed an aversion to the irrational, psychological element of Tachism and painted over many of his Tachist works. The realisation that everything he had learned and achieved thus far was not actually new plunged him into an existential crisis. When he learned that Kazimir Malevich had already painted a white square on a white ground in 1918,[23] he saw no way to contribute anything to painting himself. What could he add to this painterly expression reduced to the absolute minimum? He thought that the end of painting had been reached or, if he were ever to start painting again at some point, he would have to start from scratch.[24]

> Or – in musical terms – I knew very well that one could play a piano rhapsody with ten fingers; and since that is difficult, and one can make many mistakes, I began to strike simple notes with only one finger, accompanied by the thought: How can I forget everything I have learned thus far in order to discover something new, still unknown?[25]

Mack was able to overcome this inner crisis through the discovery of a new artistic language that was to have a decisive influence on the art of ZERO. Characteristic of his painting in the ZERO period was the depiction of 'dynamic structures', which were created by an open serial sequence of brushstrokes. In this way, Mack invented a new form of painterly expression which, through serially strung structural zones, triggers an optical vibration on the surface of the painting and a calm, pictorial movement in the eye of the viewer – a 'virtual vibration', as he put it.[26] His text 'Die neue dynamische Struktur' (The New Dynamic

Structure) appeared in the first issue of the magazine *ZERO*, which Mack and Piene published on the occasion of the seventh *Abendausstellung* in April 1958.[27] Titled *The Red Picture*, it was the most extensive of their exhibitions to date, with a total of forty-five participating artists, including Yves Klein, Georges Mathieu, Almir Mavignier, and Günther Uecker. In 1961, the latter became the third core member, alongside Mack and Piene, of ZERO, an increasingly diverse art movement that transcended European national borders.[28]

Even more important for the genesis of the *Sahara Project* was the eighth *Abendausstellung* titled *Vibration*, for which the second issue of *ZERO* was published in October 1958. In this, Mack described the creation of his first *Light Relief* in the text 'Die Ruhe der Unruhe' (The Calm of Restlessness):

> An unexpected possibility of making aesthetic motion perceivable arose when I accidentally stepped on a thin piece of metal foil that was lying on a sisal mat. As I picked up the metal foil the light was set to vibrating. ... My metal reliefs, which I would call light reliefs, and which are formed by hand, only require light instead of colour in order to come alive.[29]

Through the formation of the *Light Relief* above the metal surface, Mack achieved a dematerialisation of the work that transcends the boundaries of the object and manifests itself in each moment of viewing. The metal relief became an articulating surface, and, with this, light became the artist's actual material.[30] The inclusion of light as an expressive factor in his reliefs and sculptures accompanies Mack's work to this day and, as will become apparent here later, was decisive for the *Sahara Project*. Furthermore, the use of materials foreign to art, such as polished metal for the *Light Reliefs*, was a characteristic feature of the art of ZERO. Mack and his artist friends integrated materials into their works that had previously only been used in industry: semi-transparent aluminium webs from aerospace technology, acrylic glass and optical lenses, nails, mirrors, lamps, spotlights, and motors are part of the sculptural oeuvre of the ZERO artists in general as well as of Heinz Mack's *Sahara Project* in particular.[31]

Over the years, Mack, Piene, and Uecker networked with international artists such as Lucio Fontana, Piero Manzoni, Enrico Castellani, Jean Tinguely, Yves Klein, and Jan Schonhooven, who had a significant influence on ZERO, but at the same time also received impulses and ideas from the movement. An important exhibition took place in Antwerp in 1959. There, the transnational network of the ZERO movement took on a concrete form for the first time, after which the joint activities of the participating artists intensified.[32] The Belgian artist group G58 had invited the artists to exhibit their works in the loft of a medieval storehouse – in addition to Mack and Piene, participants included Yves Klein, Jesús Rafael Soto, Daniel Spoerri, and others. The improvised hanging of the works on nylon threads from the roof beams did not distract from the fact that the tendencies towards structure, dynamics, and immateriality were a European phenomenon among young artists. 'Everyone was fascinated by the juxtaposition of the, on the one hand, diverse realisations, which, on the other, produced an astonishingly cohesive overall impression,' Mack and Piene said of the exhibition, which became known under the title *Vision in Motion*.[33] Artists from different parts of the world exhibited their works together for the first time. Although the participants had previously known each other hardly or not at all, their works revealed astonishing similarities in artistic intention.

During the ZERO period friendly relations developed between the young artists, who visited each other's studios in Düsseldorf, Milan, Antwerp, Amsterdam, and Paris. In 1958, Heinz Mack made his second trip to the French capital, where he visited Tinguely and Klein. Tinguely's studio was in Impasse Ronsin, immediately adjacent to that of Constantin Brâncuşi, who had died the previous year. After Tinguely had given Mack access to Brâncuşi's studio, the latter stayed alone for an hour in the legendary studio where the Romanian had arranged and photographed his sculptures throughout his life. Today's replica of the studio opposite the Centre Georges Pompidou is not comparable to the deserted working space Mack found in its original state, as he later recalled: 'Even today, I have the impression that I had not entered a workshop, but rather a self-contained space radiating a deep calm and sense of timelessness.' Brâncuşi had left the studio as a coherent ensemble; all the objects were inextricably connected to each other: 'a Gesamtkunstwerk as if from another, legendary culture.'[34] Already during his time at the academy, Mack had become aware of the potential that lay in the restriction to simple geometric bodies in sculpture. The direct encounter with Brâncuşi's work confirmed the then twenty-seven-year-old in his feeling that his steles, like the *Endless Column*,[35] could mediate between heaven and earth as a visible part of an invisible, infinite line.[36] A short time later, Mack designed the *Model of a Vibrating Light Stele*,[37] on which the *Sahara Project* is based.

Mack's first trip to Africa in 1955 had given the impulse to recognise the Sahara as a space in which art could find a new freedom. Until the project was formulated in 1959, however, artistic developments that were necessary in Mack's work also conditioned the genesis of both ZERO and the *Sahara Project*. Because they were developed at the same time, ZERO and the *Sahara Project* are inseparably intertwined. In the project, which consists of thirteen stations of a *Jardin artificiel* in the Sahara, Mack integrated the artworks of the ZERO period, for which his work stands as much as that of his contemporaries. On nine pages of manuscript, he sketched this 'artificial garden' with its synthetic vegetation in the desert. As a sculptor, Mack strove for a new kind of spatial experience beyond the cities and ruins left behind by the war in Europe. He consistently pursued the question as to what meaning the experience of the pathless, infinite space of the desert could exert on his own artistic work. He had to find out for himself how his work could exist at all in such monumental spaces, how it could assert itself and lead to artistic discoveries.[38]

In 1958, Mack undertook the next extended journey to North Africa, driving there by car via France, Spain, and Gibraltar. Following his model Matisse, he went to the oasis of Sidi Harazem near Fez in Morocco. Did his vision of the *Sahara Project* have a chance of actually being realised? When Mack went to the Sahara for the second time, he felt daunted by the unimaginably vast dimensions of the space, but nevertheless realised that his project was possible. Upon his return home, he began working on his typescript of *The Sahara Project* with all the optimism he had drawn from that trip:[39]

> ... You ask: Can the project also be realised?
> ... I answer: Yes![40]

THE SAHARA PROJECT

1959

□02
Heinz Mack next to his eleven-metre-high *Light Stele* in the desert
Tunisia, 1968

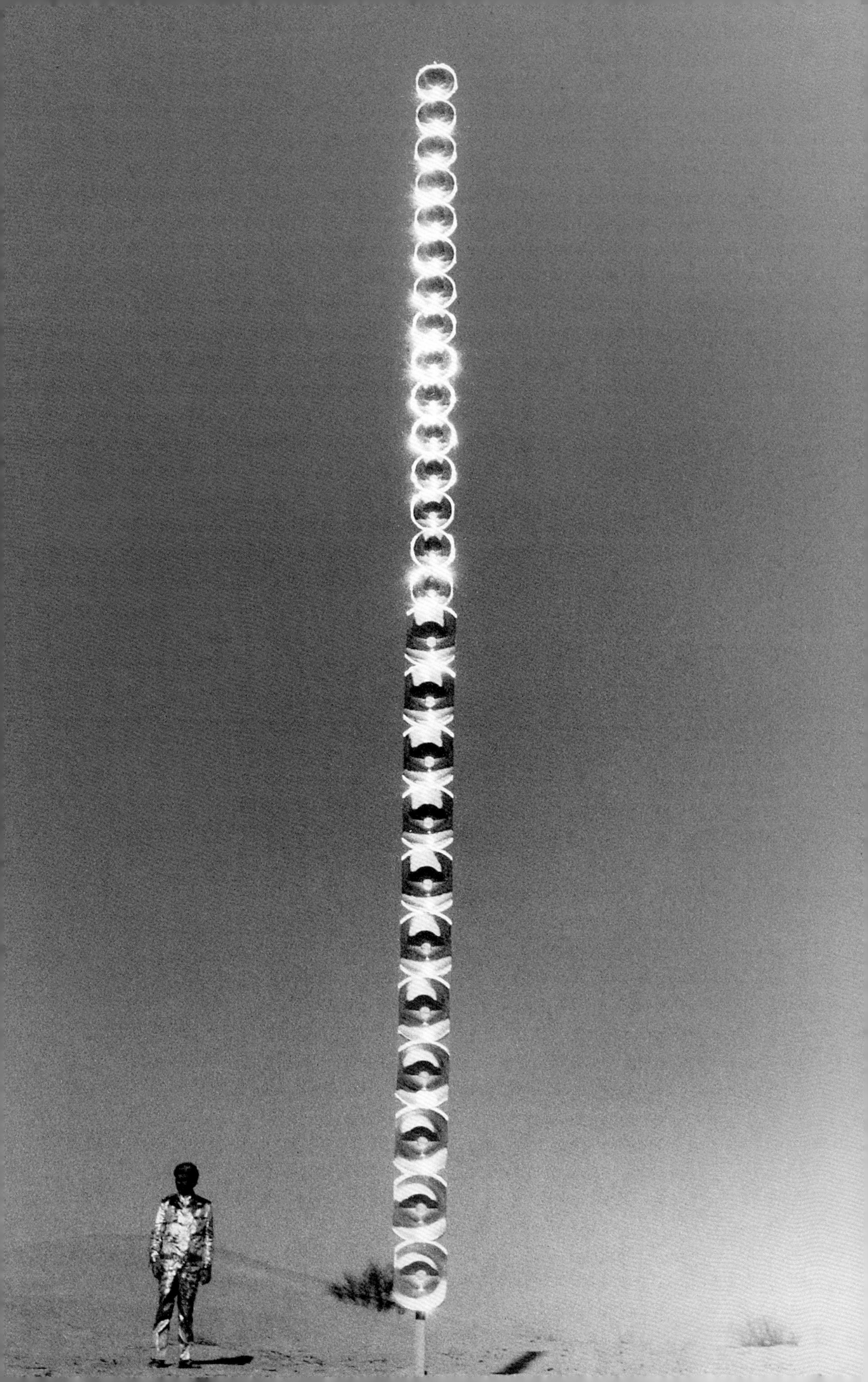

Heinz Mack conceived the *Sahara Project* in 1958, and the following year he documented it in writing. He designed a *Jardin artificiel* consisting of thirteen stations: an artificial garden in which his sculptural objects were to interact with the space and light of the desert. The artist understands his sculptures as 'objects of light in space' and light as a creative material, comparable to the paint of a painter.[41] The project is based on the idea that artistic works that capture, collect, and potentiate the light on their surface become vibrating 'apparitions of light' in an immense, light-flooded space such as the Sahara. Mack's *Sahara Project* refers to open natural spaces of great dimension in which the 'inventory' of the civilised world has not yet spread – the artist counts among these not only the desert, but also the Arctic, the sky, and the sea.[42]

> In such spaces, the clarity of light and the fullness of the silence are forever expanding. ... It is my wish that we should visit such immense natural spaces in order to realise that they have within them a second immense space, the space of art. I call this artificial space the preserve of art.[43]

In this 'preserve', art could find a new freedom, away from civilisation and cultural institutions that 'still showed the permanence of cemeteries'. With the stations of his *Jardin artificiel*, Mack describes the preserve as 'gardens that no gardener has yet dreamed of', and indeed the artificial vegetation initially appears as a dream that is hardly realisable.[44] The artificial garden is located in a place between utopia and reality. In this respect, the desert is to be understood as a 'non-place' in the sense of the ancient Greek *ou tópos*, from which the term utopia is derived.[45]

Mack explains the 'proximity of non-proximity' as the 'first principle of the total preserve': 'Just as the artificial space of the preserve reveals the relationship of the non-proximate proximity to natural space, the sculptural works of the preserve will also stand in this relationship to each other.'[46] The sculptural works in the preserve are therefore self-sufficient and have no direct relationship to each other. Although they form successive stations of the *Jardin artificiel*, they do not necessarily have to conform to the order set down in writing. It is thus possible that Station 1 is located in the Tunisian desert at a particular time, while Station 2 is realised in the icy desert of Greenland at a later date.

STATION 1
THE LIGHT STELES

In his statement regarding the first station of the *Sahara Project*, Mack describes his idea of the *Light Steles*. A stele is formed by an upright axis on which vertical mirror reflectors are mounted. A 'dress of intense light' covers the materiality of the technical construction. The *Light Steles* represent the starting point of the *Sahara Project* because the idea of an artificial garden in the Sahara is based on the design of 'a vibrating light stele in a desert'.

> Here, I am fascinated by one idea in particular: It must be possible to vibrate a powerful apparition of light in such a way that its intensity necessarily demands a new environ-

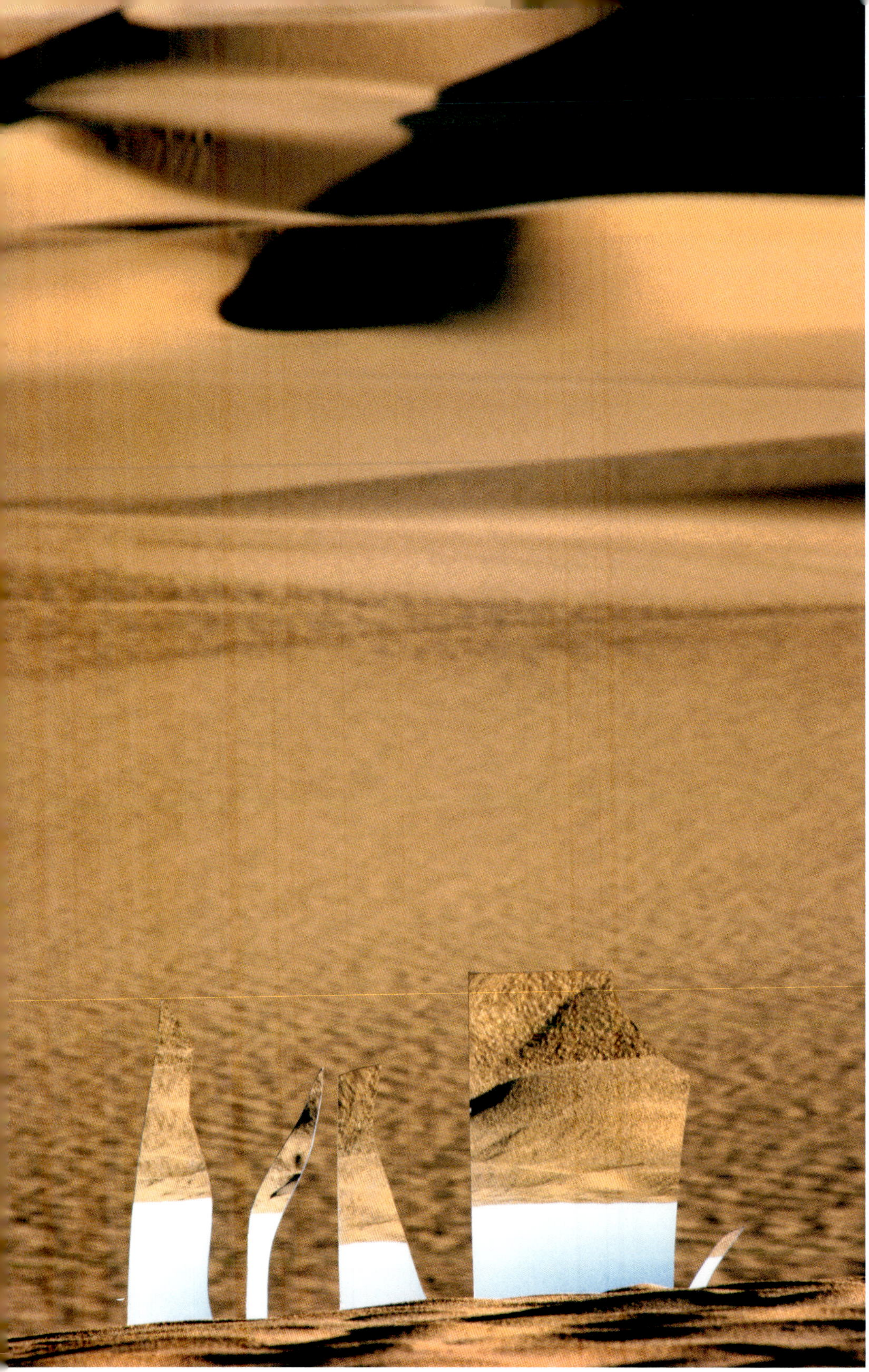

□03
Upside-Down **– mirror experiment**
Grand Erg Occidental, Algeria, 1976

ment, the expansion of which no longer conforms to the classical rules of measure, volume, and proportion.[47]

Mack's concrete *Model of a Vibrating Light Stele in the Desert* was first exhibited at Galerie Iris Clert in Paris in April 1959.[48] The surface of the human-sized, flat stele was made of textured metal on which an immaterial *Light Relief* revealed itself with the appropriate incidence of light. In a text on the gallery's invitation card, the artist Yves Klein praised the 'immaterial symphony that Mack presents to us with his aluminium reliefs'.[49] The artistic intention 'to make objects whose mode of appearance is immaterial'[50] emanated from the *Sahara Project* and accompanies Mack's work to this day.

Mack sees his steles as the equivalent of a person standing upright in space. The space is just as important as the sculpture he places in it. 'I can't think of one without the other,' Mack explains.[51] The artist had suspected as early as 1959 that the space of the desert would be particularly suitable for bringing about a vibrating 'apparition of light', but he only recognised the Sahara's own inherent spatial quality in 1967 during the first provisional and experimental installation of a bronze pillar in Tunisia.[52] He noticed that the light of the sun immediately 'took over' the sculpture and increased its visibility. The pillar became an incarnation of light, the material of which was dematerialised, as it were. Mack observed how the actual dimensions of the pillar changed due to the vastness of the desert; the optical dimensions no longer corresponded to the physical dimensions. With greater distance, the pillar occasionally appeared higher, or it appeared smaller when one approached it. In the Sahara, the artist noted in 1967, the balance of real, virtual, and optical scales was negated.[53]

In 1968, Mack travelled to the Tunisian desert again, this time with a film crew from Saarländischer Rundfunk to shoot the film *Tele-Mack*. East of Kebili, he installed an eleven-metre-high stele made of aluminium reflectors, which became an immaterial apparition of light in the glaring light of the sun. ↖□02

> It was only when the first silver stele, eleven metres high, was installed and the African sun got caught in the focus of its twenty-six light reflectors that our eyes saw more than even our boldest assumptions had expected; these are

those moments of pure fascination in which all thought is suspended.[54]

During the filming of *Tele-Mack* a group of eight other steles was installed around the eleven-metre-high *Light Stele.* cf. ↘□ 18 They seemed to glow from within, although their only source of light was the desert sun, which was reflected, refracted, focused, and dispersed on their metallic surfaces. Mack described this grouping of steles in the *Sahara Project* as 'widely visible beacons of the preserve'.[55] In 1966, he exhibited an ensemble of twenty steles at the Howard Wise Gallery in New York, arranged in the irregular structural order of a forest and titled *Forest of Light.*[56] The ensemble, which was also presented in modified form in the German Pavilion at the Venice Biennale in 1970, is one of Mack's major works. It is considered revolutionary in twentieth-century art history because it made light visible in space and thus expanded the understanding of what art is. The steles, made of hand-embossed aluminium, Fresnel lenses, and mirror and acrylic glass also conveyed an impression of astonishing novelty – the visual materials of the future.[57] To this day, the *Light Steles* are both an elementary component of Mack's work and a unique attribute – whether individually and monumentally, as with the forty-two-metre-high *Large Stele* in Stuttgart (1989/90),[58] or in an expansive ensemble such as *The Sky Over Nine Columns* with nine golden mosaic pillars, which was first shown in the Venetian lagoon in 2014 and later also entered into a dialogue with architecture and nature in Istanbul, Valencia, and St. Moritz.[59]

STATION 2
THE MIRROR WALL

As the second station of the *Jardin artificiel,* Mack planned the *Mirror Wall.* A continuous mirror surface, more than one hundred metres long and roughly five metres high, was to be installed in the sand of the desert. 'Approaching the mirror, viewers are confronted with a situation in which they inevitably encounter themselves.'[60] Although the *Mirror Wall* was never realised on this monumental scale, Mack's interest in questioning natural phenomena through mirror images was expressed in many experiments he carried out in the 1960s. In 1961, he began placing mirrors on the lawn of his garden, observing how nature encountered itself. Alongside factual reality, a virtual reality emerged that had the same optical presence. On the Mediterranean island of Ibiza, Mack placed a mirror on the beach in 1963. The photographs documenting the *Mirror Between Sky, Earth, and Sea* show an overlapping of the realms of reality. Images are created in the picture when the sky and sea are reflected by the mirror, which was placed in a stony beach landscape. Completely different elements – stones, sand, sea, and sky – become a collage of images.[61] In 1967, Mack extended the experiment during a stay on the island of Djerba in Tunisia. In the stone desert, he used coated glass that had a slightly concave curve. In the *Mirror Between Sky and Desert* (1967), the top was thus turned downwards, the sky was reflected onto the ground and the ground into the sky.[62] Mack repeated the upside-down experiment with concave mirrors several more times in the Sahara. ↖□03

For the realisation of the *Mirror Wall*, Mack also considered the use of large grid chains and structural surfaces of concave mirrors. The artistic intention of creating such *Mirror Plantations* lies in irritating and enhancing natural appearances. For the *Safrane Mirror Plantation*, Mack placed several crystal mirrors in the desert sands of Tunisia in the winter of 1967. cf. ↘□11 For the viewer, the work opened up a kaleidoscopic perception of the desert space, which was broken into a fragmentation of mirror images. The extraordinary fascination exerted by this monumental field of mirrors inspired Mack to create his largest *Mirror Plantation* to date, which he installed in 1970 on the occasion of the World Exposition in Osaka. Mack transformed the large entrance spiral with the rotating globe, via which visitors reached the cylindrically shaped rooms of the German Pavilion located underground, into a radial *Mirror Plantation*. In this, the images of the visitors were multiplied many times over, with the 'mirror images' displaying a kind of Cubist fragmentation. This was due to the fact that in this work the mirrors – each also one-by-one metre in size – were mirrored on both sides and thus doubled in their effect. The result was fascinating, but also irritating, broken mirror images of mirror images, a kind of mirror-image collage.[63]

STATION 3
THE SAILS

At some distance from the *Mirror Wall*, Mack imagined the third station to be 'several upright, tersely stretched, snow-white sails of varying sizes'. The sails 'show the exaggeration of a single human gesture

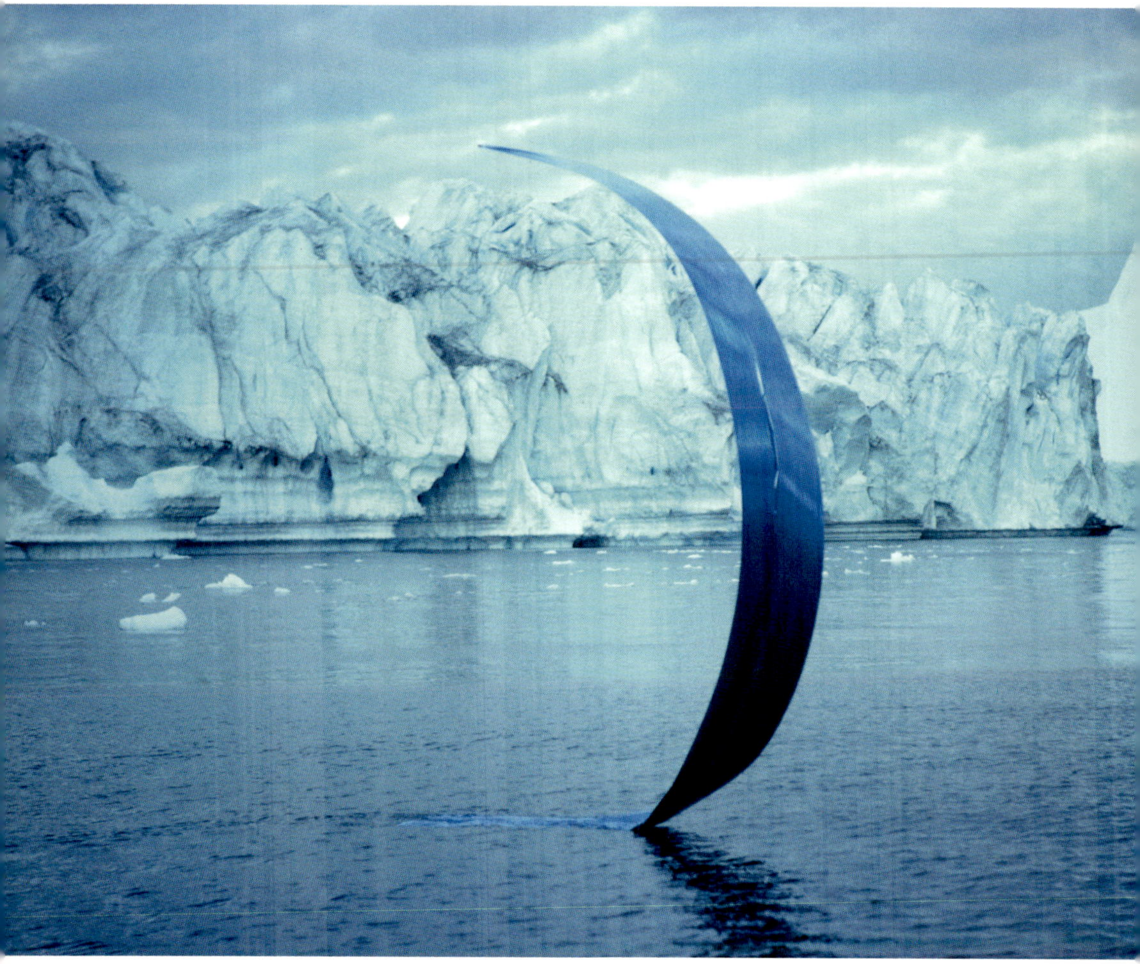

□04
Sail without Wind and Ship – The Secret of the Arctic
Greenland, 1976

that does not hesitate to violate the surface in order to provoke the space, the light, and the shadow'.[64] Hidden in this poetic description is a homage to Lucio Fontana, whose perforations of the canvas had for the first time articulated the space behind the previously sacrosanct surface. For the ZERO artists, Fontana's penetration of the pictorial ground was an act that made them like-minded, despite the fact that the Italian sculptor was a generation older. In his poem 'The Desert Lives' (1961), Mack described Fontana as his 'neighbour in the desert':

> ... Fontana's world
> is a world of emptiness.
> the phenomenology of emptiness
> is a paraphrase of the desert.
> Fontana, like me, is an inhabitant
> of emptiness. Only in the desert
> do our imaginations
> have that freedom of movement
> which I call the freedom
> of the artist.[65]

Mack proved that this freedom can also be found elsewhere in the world when he travelled to Greenland in 1976 to give his 'preserve of art' a new appearance in the Arctic desert of ice. In the cool blue light of the Arctic Circle, he added the element of water to the *Jardin artificiel* by floating the 'vegetation' of his 'garden' on the Arctic Ocean, including the *Sail without Wind and Ship* (1976) made of vapour-deposited mercury Ultraphan foil that reflected the blue of the water and the white of the surrounding icebergs. Mack gave the seven-metre-high work the poetic epithet *The Secret of the Arctic*: 'A white sailing vessel in the Arctic Ocean – those who encounter it will not guess its meaning, and any romantic conjecture would be a misunderstanding.'[66] ←□04

STATION 4
THE SAND RELIEFS

As a 'passepartout zone in the immediate vicinity of the preserve', ground-based *Sand Reliefs* were to be laid out over large areas in the desert sand. Through the resistance presented by glass discs set into

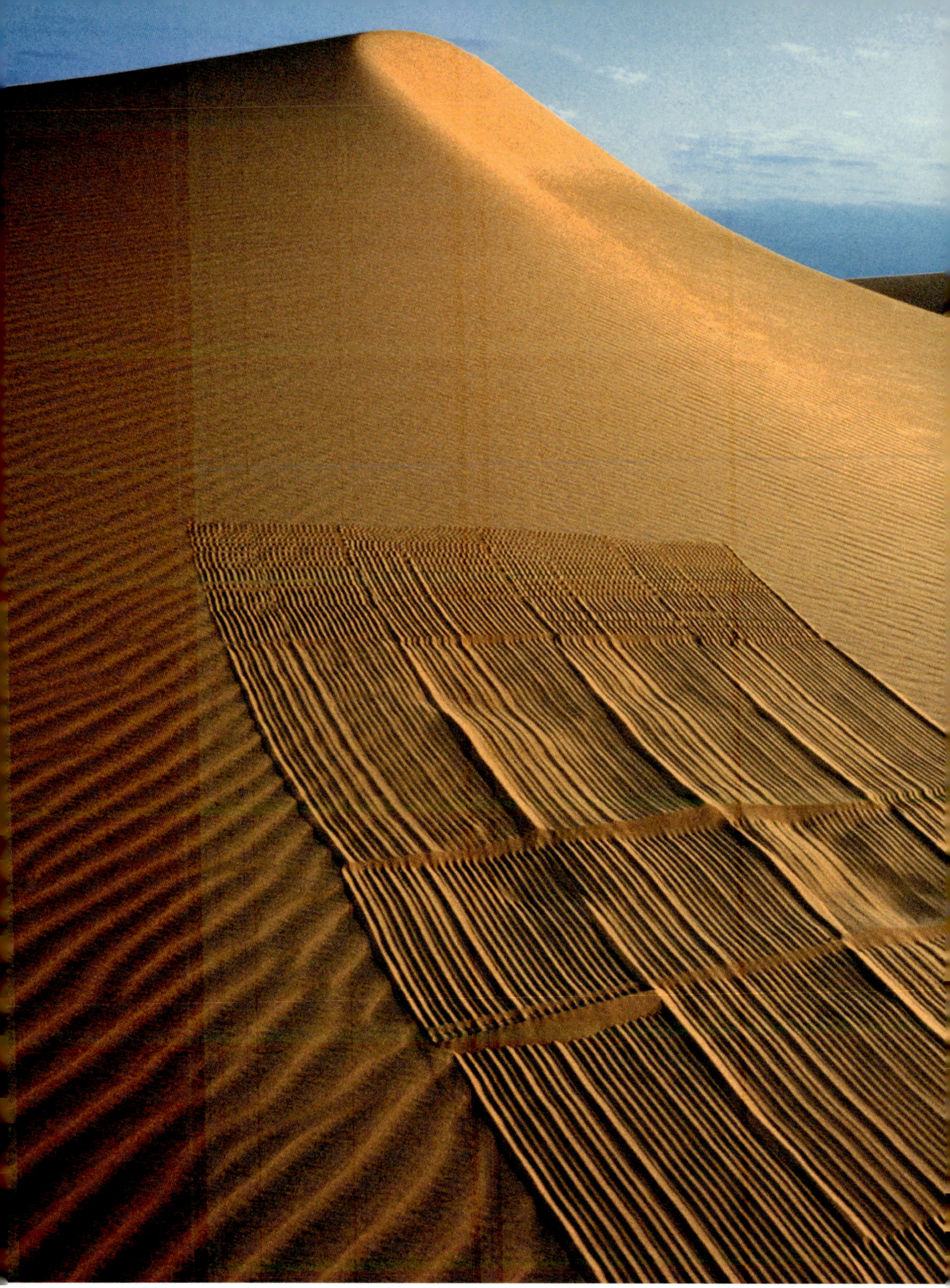

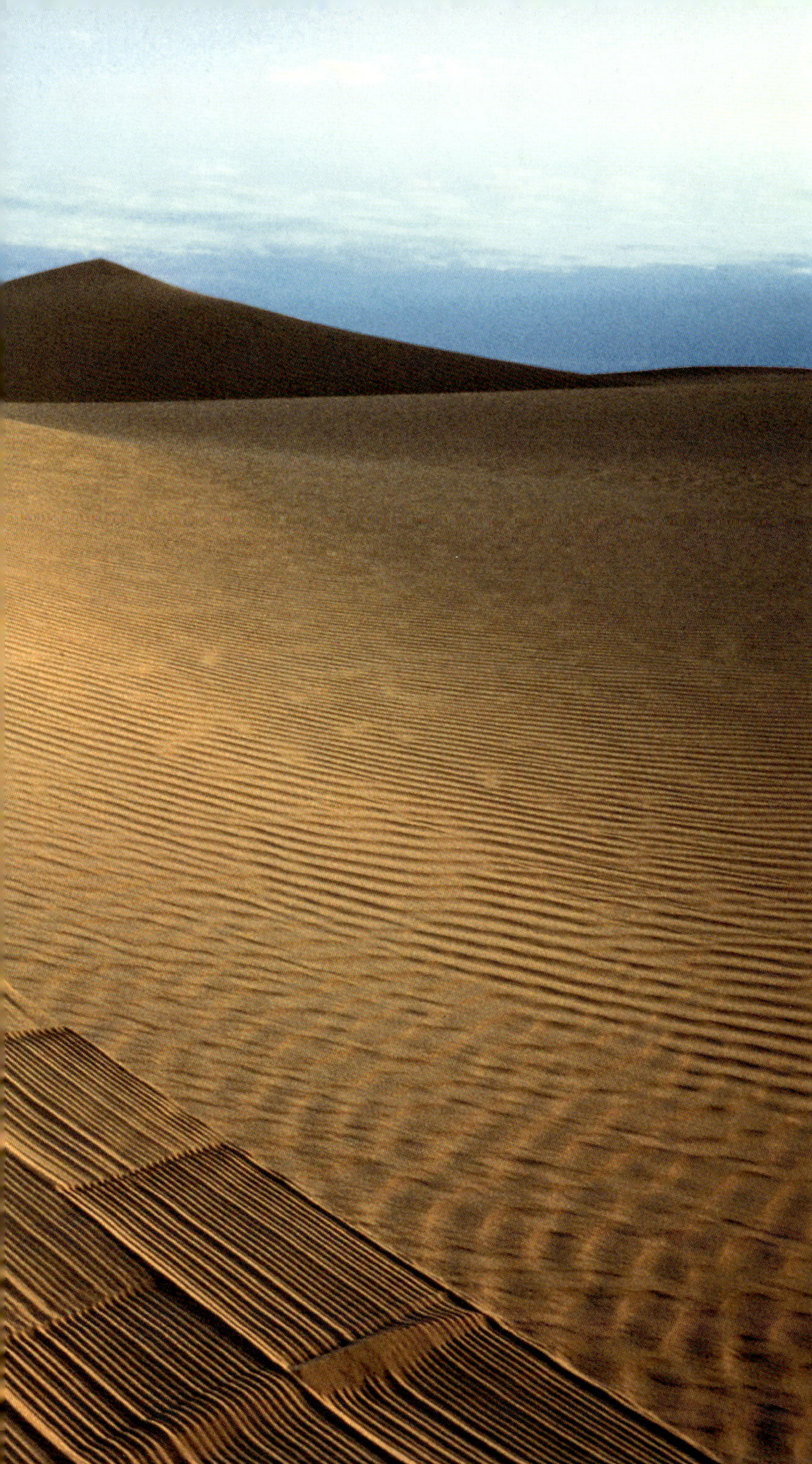

□05
Great Sand Relief in the Grand Erg Occidental
Algeria, 1976

the sand in a serial arrangement, the shifting sand would form 'artificial structures and modulations'. Mack succeeded in implementing this station in the Grand Erg Occidental in Algeria in 1976. On the slope of a sand dune, he laid out the *Large Sand Relief*, the twenty-five-metre-long and five-metre-wide furrows of which ran diagonally across the natural relief of the sand dunes.[67]

> In this sense, I make my sand drawings, which, in the light of the setting sun, become sand reliefs, spread out like artificial carpets, woven of light and shadow, ephemeral like traces in the sand.[68]

Of all the stations in the *Sahara Project*, the *Sand Reliefs* demonstrate most clearly how fleeting Mack's ephemeral experiments in the Sahara were. After being captured by a photograph, the traces in the sand could be instantly blown away by strong winds or dust storms, which are common in the Sahara. The artist never questioned the sanctity of the nature in which he stayed during his desert experiments. Accordingly, the aim was not to erect permanent works in the Sahara, but to experience a moment of pure fascination. ↖□05

STATION 5
ARTIFICIAL FORESTS AND GARDENS

The fifth station of the *Sahara Project* leads into an 'oasis of petrified and frozen reality'. In 'gardens that no gardener has yet dreamed of', we find a characteristic feature that links Mack's work to that of his contemporaries – the structure, which is preferred to figurative representation.

> Gardens, ... laid out like carpets of the earth, show the elements of our pictorial structures in perpetual plurality; the innumerable, the rigid passion of multiplication determine the layout of the plantation and forest grids.[69]

In addition to his *Dynamic Structures* and *Light Reliefs* of the ZERO period,[70] which trigger an optical vibration in the viewer's eye, structure is an essential component of Mack's oeuvre, which remains largely non-objective to this day. His paintings, which consist exclusively of structures, depict lines that are in tension with each other and describe a potentially unlimited space beyond the edge of the painting. In sculpture as well, Mack is, as Robert Fleck and Antonia Lehmann-Tolkmitt have formulated, the most consistent structuralist: 'The structure supersedes and overcomes composition, as well as the traditional painterly and sculptural act of creating illusionistic forms.'[71] This connects Mack's oeuvre with the works of other ZERO artists, to which the vegetation of the 'artificial forests and gardens' further alludes: 'Forests of sponges, nail reliefs, grids of rising columns of smoke, accumulations of factory materials, and catapults of light will form the desert forests.'[72]

Here, one is reminded of the *Éponges* by Yves Klein, who, in 1957, installed large-scale sponge reliefs in the foyer of the new theatre building in Gelsenkirchen.[73] The 'nail reliefs' refer to Günther Uecker, who also discovered the nail as a sculptural medium in 1957 and has since used it in a uniformly structuring way by creating planar nail reliefs.[74] The 'grids of rising columns of smoke' – in a later version of the text, Mack changed this to 'columns of smoke and fire'[75] – are related to several ZERO artists who used smoke and fire as media for their artworks, such as Otto Piene, Yves Klein, and Bernard Aubertin. The 'accumulations of factory materials' establish a link to Arman, who, with his *Accumulations* (1959–) created collage-like collections of similar objects. Finally, Mack's own works function as 'catapults of light' when they reflect the sun's rays, concentrate them, and reflect them back into the space of the desert.

STATION 6
THE MACHINE PARK

The sixth station of the *Sahara Project* 'shows the machines in a state of complete confusion, which is comprehensible because it is poetic'. This 'error in the system' fascinates the constructor who, with the courage of an animal trainer, 'programs his mechanical lion but forgets the programme in order to be able to present the unexpected confusions more dangerously'.[76] Here, Mack thematises the self-destructing machine art for which the Swiss sculptor Jean Tinguely also became famous with actions such as *Hommage à New York* (1960).[77] Mack's *Fire Ship* can be seen in this context, since it uses the equally luminous and destructive power of fire. Presented on a lake near Mönchengladbach in 1968 but developed as early as 1963,[78] it consisted of a raft with a truss-like wooden framework that floated on the water. cf. ↘□ 13 On this, fireworks were mounted. On the struts, elements soaked in phosphorus became fire gyroscopes, and on the ridge, tubs full of petrol ignited in a precisely prepared choreography to form a comb of fire. Mack's *Fire Ship* combined the elements of fire and water, with the water becoming the reflection surface of the fire. As a construction that first performed a light spectacle and finally destroyed itself, the *Fire Ship* belongs to the *Machine Park* in the sense of a light-aesthetic performance that overcomes the original materiality of the work.[79] The artist describes the striving for immateriality inherent in the machinery:

> It is my wish that its virtual volumes of rotation would stand in space like giant cyclones. As stable apparitions of spherical light and wind, they will appear to the viewer like a frozen mirage. This district is surrounded by clouds of coloured gas, the pneumatic pulsation of which can be controlled.[80]

Immateriality is often achieved by integrating natural elements, in this case air. On the one hand, the artist describes the winds generated by this destructive power as 'huge cyclones in space', which they can unleash as a storm. On the other hand, the element stands for breath, the 'breath of life', which Mack describes with the 'pneumatic pulsation' of clouds of coloured gas.[81] The use of breathing air to produce a work of art is also found in the oeuvre of the ZERO artist Piero Manzoni, whose *Corpi d'Aria* (1959/60) were exhibited at Galleria Azimut in Milan in 1960. His pneumatic sculptures were artistically shaped, inflated balloons that Manzoni sold with the slogan 'Breath for Sale!'[82]

STATION 7
THE PLATEAUS

> On levelled plateaus, lamellar grids spread out in endless succession until they finally end in their own horizon. Under the Saharan sky, they become resistors of the light caught by the constantly recurring elevations; shadows remain in inevitable proximity.[83]

The seventh station describes the duality of light and shadow evident in Mack's reliefs. Although conceived for the desert, the ideas of the *Sahara Project* were also realised in other places. For example, Mack applied the principle of plateaus in an architecturally related work in Leverkusen. The thirteen-metre-high *Sahara Reliefs*, which formed the

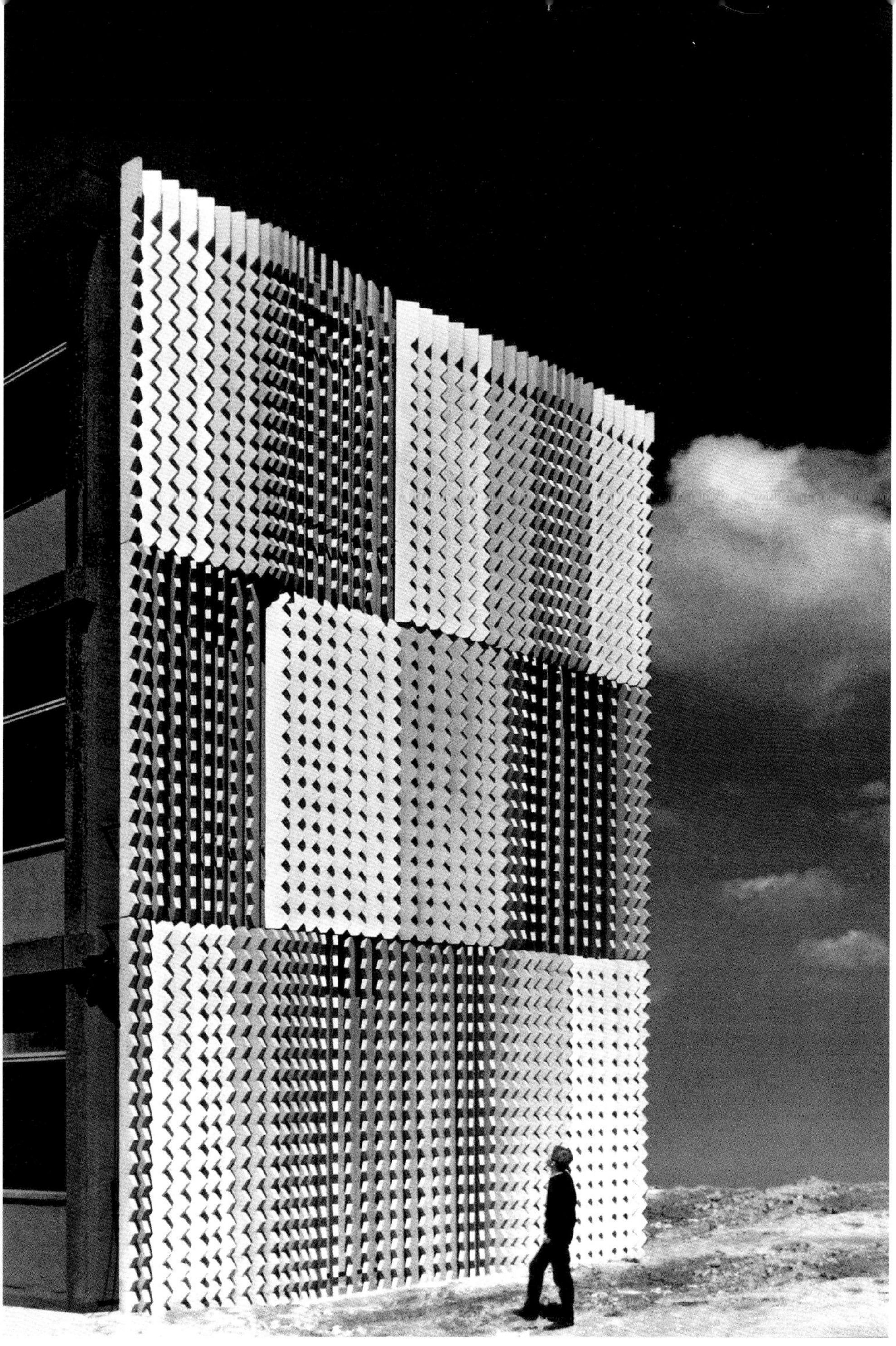

□06
Sahara Reliefs
Mathildenhof School, Leverkusen, 1960/61

façade of the Mathildenhof School (now the Astrid Lindgren School) from 1960/61 onwards, consisted of serially assembled concrete slats on an area of approximately two hundred square metres, arranged in horizontal rows. ↖□06 The angle of inclination of the slats to the wall surface varied, resulting in a radial fan, so that with changing incidence of light or depending on the position of the viewer, different light-shadow effects became visible on the surface, and the grey colour of the concrete slats was enlivened by diverse light-dark shades.[84]

STATION 8
THE CORSO

The *Corso* that Mack planned for the eighth station was to be 'longer than any street in the world' and extend 'from a blue monochrome wall to a wall covered by a single silver light'. Yves Klein's monochrome painting in so-called International Klein Blue (IKB)[85] and Mack's silver *Light Relief* made of metal form the opposite poles of the *Corso*, since the work of both artists – albeit in different ways – strives for immateriality.

> The Corso itself is made of mirrors; the costume that the one walking [on it] wears is a mirror fabric. It is thus not the earth that carries the walker, it is the mirror of the sky on which we walk.[86]

In accordance with this idea, Mack designed the futuristic costume in which he was to stride through the desert. cf. ↖□02 The silver-coloured suit made him well known as 'Silver Mack':[87] In 1968, an artist dressed as an astronaut explored the desert landscape of the Sahara – an analogy to the first manned moon landing that took place a year later.

STATION 9
THE SYMPOSIUM

The *Symposium* is located in the centre of the 'preserve' and is only accessible to the participating artists. Mack describes it as a hermetically sealed cube with outer walls of white marble, resting in the middle of an artificial lake of mercury. 'The interior: a white light-colour-space by Yves Klein.'[88] The ninth station thus opens up the possibility of other ZERO artists participating in the *Sahara Project*. Mack had already pointed out in the introduction to the text that 'my artist friends are

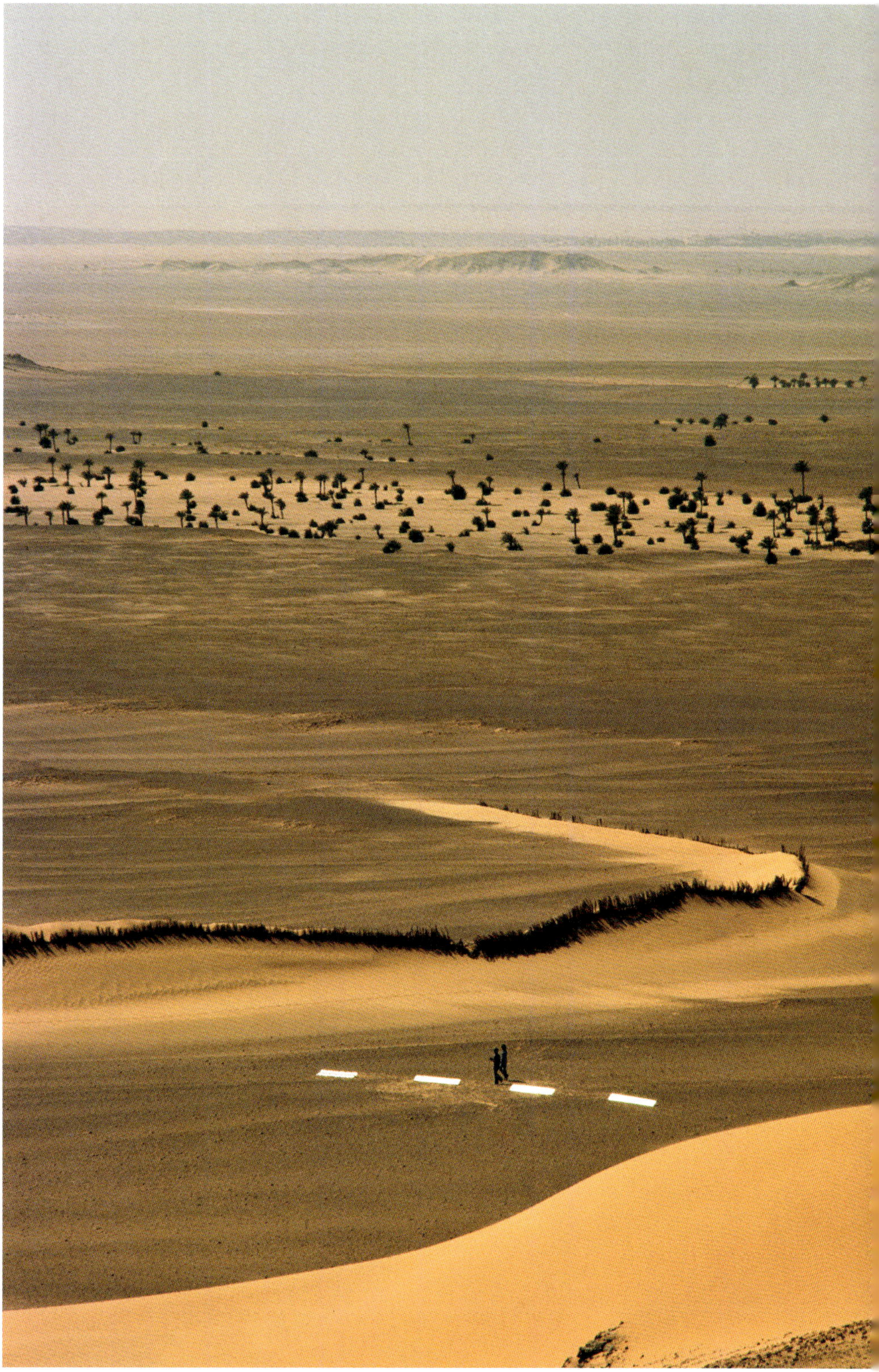

□07
The Scale of the Desert in the Grand Erg Occidental
Algeria, 1976

involved, as well as myself' in the stations of the *Jardin artificiel*.[89] Before the publication of the project text in 1961, Mack provided the various stations with footnotes containing references to the artists Arman, Enrico Castellani, Lucio Fontana, Yves Klein, Piero Manzoni, Almir Mavignier, Ira Moldow, Otto Piene, Jean Tinguely, and Günther Uecker.[90] Since the *Sahara Project* was first published in volume 3 of *ZERO* magazine, Mack was keen to refer here to the context of the ZERO movement. Although a collaboration with the aforementioned artists never came about in the desert, he did indeed speak with Piene and Klein about the project while they were driving to Antwerp together in 1959. Sitting crowded together in the car, they had a passionate discussion about the new possibilities that Mack's idea opened up. It should be possible to create an artistically generated mirage and thus spread out an ensemble of numerous light phenomena in the large, open natural environment, creating an entirely immaterial spatial image. In their enthusiastic spirit of optimism, the three artists considered realising an exhibition in Antarctica or the Sahara with large sculptures that would correspond to the dimensions of the landscape. They considered doing without an audience altogether in favour of an ideal, 'pure' situation – which Mack ultimately realised alone.[91] The *Sahara Project* was never a joint ZERO project, but an exchange of ideas between the artist friends marked its genesis.

STATION 10
THE LIGHT RELIEFS

The *Light Reliefs* of the tenth station are freely positioned panels facing upward into the sky. 'Their vibrating pulses of light are created by the reflections of light on their outermost surface.' On highly polished metals, the actual articulation of light unfolds through the relief structures embossed into them, as Mack continues to describe: 'It is thus not the metal relief that manifests itself, but rather the relief of light that outshines the materiality of the metal.'[92] In the immense sandy desert of the Grand Erg Occidental, which Mack visited in 1976, he achieved this optical effect with four elongated aluminium reflectors, the materiality of which was outshone by the intense sunlight. He called the work the *Scale of the Desert* (1976), since the four reflectors lay in the sand in serial order. ↖□07

Within Mack's oeuvre, the reliefs as a transitional form from painting to sculpture represent the most extensive group of works. As early as 1952, he had begun to form reliefs as sculpturally structured surfaces, initially from plaster or synthetic resin, occasionally also from wood. Since 1957, his *Light Reliefs* have been made of aluminium or stainless steel, whereby it is not the elegance of the material that is decisive for Mack, but rather its reflectivity.[93] 'Polished to a shining, mirror finish, a slight relief is sufficient to shake the calm of the light and set it vibrating,' Mack explained in 1958 in the text 'Die Ruhe der Unruhe' (The Calm of Restlessness). 'The possible beauty of these structures would be a pure expression of the beauty of light.'[94] Here, the pictorial surface no longer functions as a mere carrier of representation, but rather becomes the scene of an actual event that unfolds between the work and the viewer in the interaction with light and space.[95]

STATION 11
THE PALACES OF LIGHT

In the eleventh station, Mack describes his vision of monumental light cubes in the desert. Concrete cubes are to be covered with light reflectors in serial formation so that a *Light Cube* appears.

> As uninhabitable architectural structures, they [the light cubes] exhibit the same non-proximate proximity as the pyramids, surrounded by the boundless anonymity of the space of which they are the monumental expression. As pulsating, feverish volumes of light, however, these cubes gain a dynamism that is opposed to the stony static of the pyramids.[96]

Within Mack's oeuvre, the *Cubes* form a relatively small but important group of works that have been created since 1955. Dieter Honisch described them as 'small, self-contained worlds that have their own, often moving and coloured interior'.[97] Several *Light Cubes* are transparent and have a kinetic light programme in their interior. Others consist of nested acrylic glass cubes resting on a mirror surface. In 1976, Mack placed metallic cubes in the Grand Erg Occidental to create a *Topology of Space*.[98] The work consisted of a large, mirror-like metal cube, on the surface of which a second cube positioned at some distance was reflected. Its surface had a metallic structure and shone in the desert sun as a bright light object. The positional relationship between the two objects, the topology, could be determined on the basis of the reflection. When

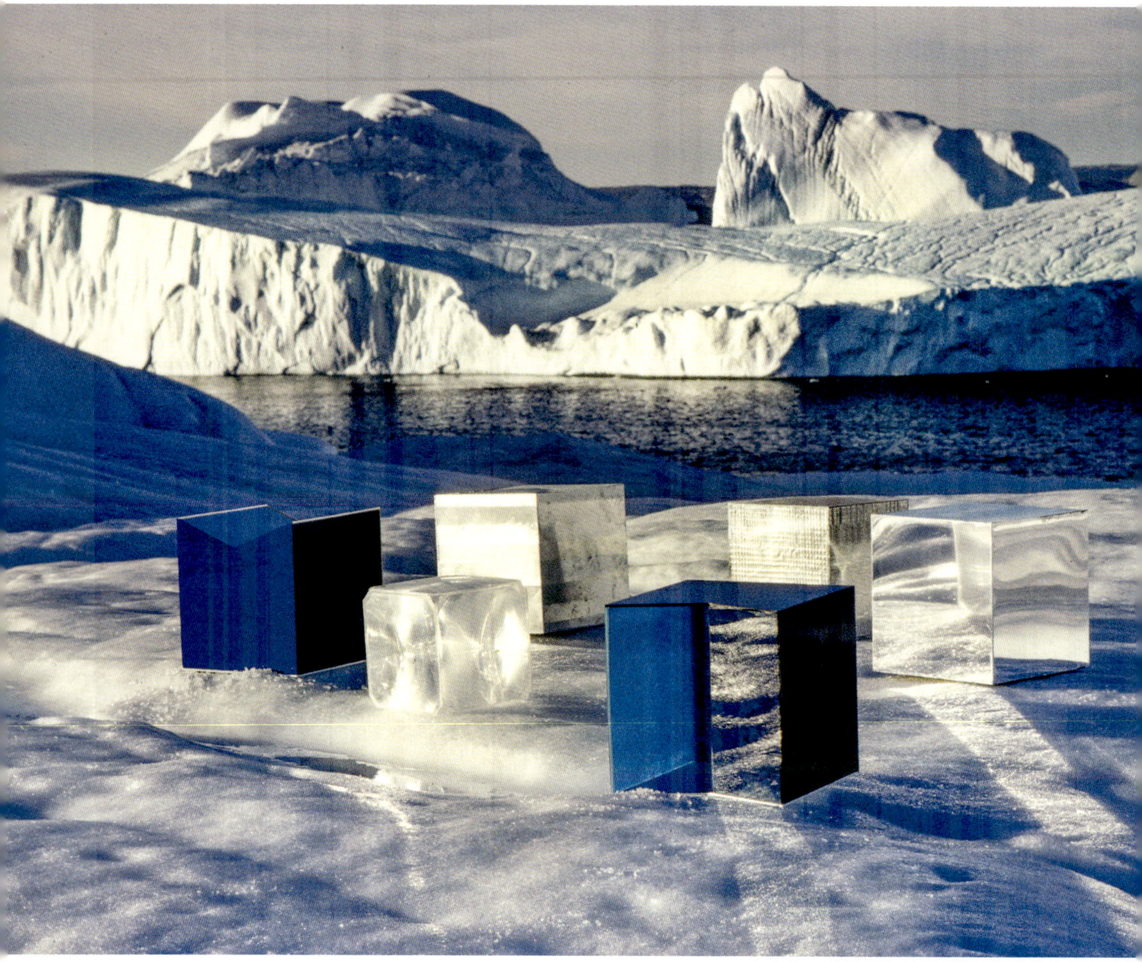

□08
Ensemble of *Cubes* in the Arctic
Greenland, 1976

Mack placed an ensemble of six *Cubes* in the Arctic that same year, the impression was different: On the bright white ice and in the bluish light of the polar sun, their surfaces appeared almost transparent. In many places, it is not obvious where the ice ends and the cube begins, because, here, areas of reality overlap in mirror images. ←□08

STATION 12
THE ARTIFICIAL SUNS

In the twelfth station, Mack wrote that the slowly rotating light formations of his *Dynamos* would only gain their actual energy when their disc diameter was fifty to one hundred metres. He strove for 'the open dimension of a large disc of light, the changing structures of movement of which continually exchange, lose, and find each other again, in a "state" of continuous transition'. Due to the phenomenon of the mirage, the impression should be created 'that these artificial suns become apparitions of the sky'.[99]

Circular, light-kinetic *Rotors* or *Dynamos* became the signet of the ZERO movement from 1958 onwards, and they remain part of Mack's sculptural oeuvre to this day. No other group of works visualises his idea of a dynamic, constantly changing appearance as clearly as this one.[100] The appearance of the *Rotors* is determined by one or more circular discs that rotate at a slow speed and at times in opposite directions behind a translucent, often grooved glass surface. The slow movement, together with the reflection of light, causes the emergence of constantly changing light phenomena; virtual images of the slow movement of light in constant transformation are created.[101] Here, movement takes the place of form, and in the continuum, beginning and end become interchangeable. 'Incidentally, the rotors have something of the equanimity and serenity of ancient Indian philosophy,' Mack explains. 'In the sense of the Buddhist doctrine of eternal recurrence as expressed in the circular form.'[102]

STATION 13
THE APPARITIONS IN THE SKY

'Silver balloons hovering in the sky carry invisible nets in which light-reflecting membranes are suspended,' Mack describes the last station of his *Sahara Project*. With *The Apparitions in the Sky*, he declares the sky to be a further sphere of his *Jardin artificiel*, which experiences an unexpected articulation through these 'immaterial light carriers'. 'The colour of the natural sun will be found in these new satellites of the sky. The preserve of art takes place not only on the Earth.'[103]

Here, Mack formulated for the first time his ambition to realise artistic projects in the sky and beyond in distant, unknown spheres. According to Mack, the ZERO period was also determined by the fascination that space travel exerted on the artists. The countdown of the rocket launch, in which the last ten seconds are read backwards until the call 'ZERO' indicates the beginning of a new sense of space, thus became synonymous with their ideas. Long before the first manned moon landing, Mack had already agreed with Piene on the term 'ZERO' as a name for their movement. This led Mack to paint the word 'ZERO' on a launching rocket in the form of a photomontage, which was published in the third volume of *ZERO* in 1961. At the time, he did not yet know that as early as 1948, Lucio Fontana had already declared in this sense that the architecture of the future would be a rocket.[104] When Mack and Piene held their first *Abendausstellungen* in Düsseldorf in 1957, the first satellite entered the Earth's orbit with Sputnik 1, and the longing for the 'final frontier' also gripped the artistic zeitgeist. Even before the first manned moon landing, Mack had already conceived of a project that envisaged the spreading of a large metal foil over the surface of the Earth's satellite. His *Moon Project* (1963–73) was intended to create 'a punctiform reflection of sunlight', 'a kind of beauty mark on the face of the moon'.[105] In the third volume of *ZERO*, Otto Piene presented a comparable idea, namely that of projecting a *Light Ballet* into the sky: 'My higher dream concerns the projection of light in the great nocturnal sky, the sensing of the universe as it presents itself to light, untouched, without obstacles.'[106]

When he visited the Arctic in 1976, Mack realised the vision of his *Apparitions in the Sky* by having red and white balloons hover over the icebergs. *Coloured Weather Balloons over an Iceberg* carried silver nets in which the Arctic sunlight was reflected. ↘□ 09

The text concludes by pointing out that the *Sahara Project* would be misunderstood 'if one assumes that the surreal effect of an alienation of the environmental is sought by transporting the art objects, as they are now, into the desert'. Mack included the objects in the description of the project, however, because in the desert they would gain their actual radiance as 'new manifestations of an as yet unseen artistic reality'.[107] This leads to the conclusion that Mack's *Light Steles* and *Light Reliefs*, as well as his *Rotors* and *Cubes*, were conceived with the *Sahara Project* in mind or on the basis of this. 'Not least of all, their destiny was to be installed in the desert and to make light and space perceptible as such or to cause them to vibrate by compaction, reflection, and rhythm.'[108] Mack's sculptural oeuvre of the ZERO period is inalienably intertwined with the *Sahara Project.*

If the 'expedition of our imagination' were to move inexorably away 'from the oppressive melancholy of old habits, the archaic oxidation of which we call the culture of Europe', the 'total preserve of art ... could mean a new sense of freedom'. As an 'expression of the Zero zone', a 'new collaboration of artists must bid farewell to the functionaries and consumers of art ... as well as to its utopians and prophets.'[109] In the concluding sentences of the *Sahara Project*, Mack declares the desert to be a place where art would find a new sense of freedom, because the usual parameters such as presentation, mediation, and audience would no longer be relevant. This turning away from the mechanisms of the art industry connects the *Sahara Project* with Land Art, which emerged during the 1960s not only in the United States, since Mack was one of its European pioneers.

THE DESERT AS A SITE FOR ART

The retreat into the desert as a metaphor for escapism and distancing oneself from humanity has a long tradition in spiritual history.[110] From as early as the third millennium BCE, the Gilgamesh epic describes the flight of the mythical king of the Babylonians 'to the great desert'. Gilgamesh mourns the death of his friend Enkidu, leaves the city of Uruk, and rushes lamenting 'out into the steppe', where he becomes the 'robber of the wilderness'.[111] In the Old Testament, going into the desert is symbolic of transformation: The Book of Exodus tells of the flight from Egypt, with which Moses led the Israelites out of slavery under the Pharaoh and into the desert. The New Testament describes how Jesus fasted in the desert for forty days and forty nights and resisted the temptations of the devil in order to find salvation.[112] The *Temptation of Jesus* in the desert became the 'proto-fiction' for later depictions of ascetics by the so-called Desert Fathers.[113] For example, St. Anthony, an early Christian monk, spent most of his life as a hermit in an abandoned fort on the edge of the Egyptian desert. According to the *Legenda aurea*, he was afflicted there by demons who tormented him with the 'temptations of hell'.[114] The *Torments* and *Temptations of St. Anthony* advanced to become a popular subject around 1500, depicted by artists such as Martin

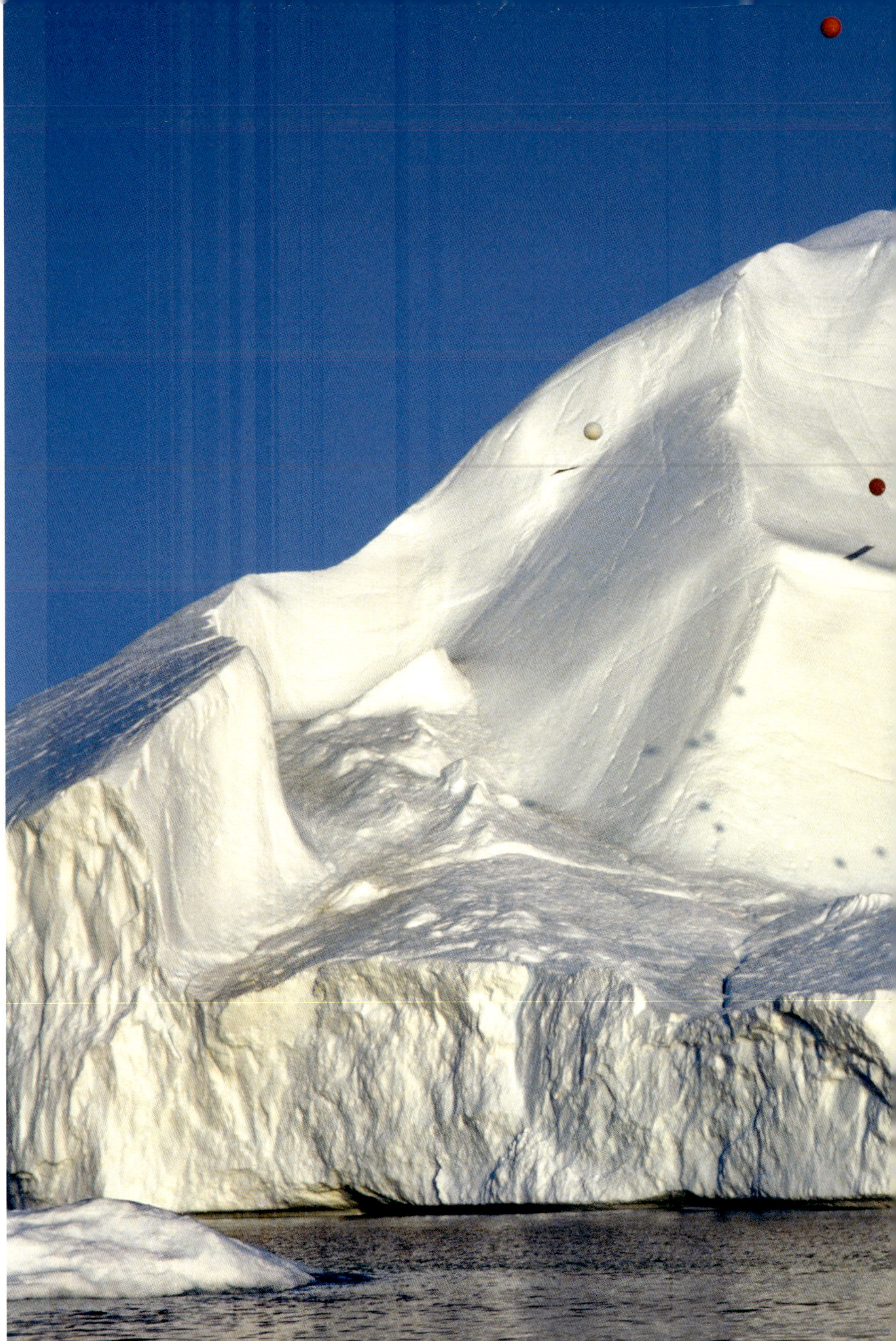

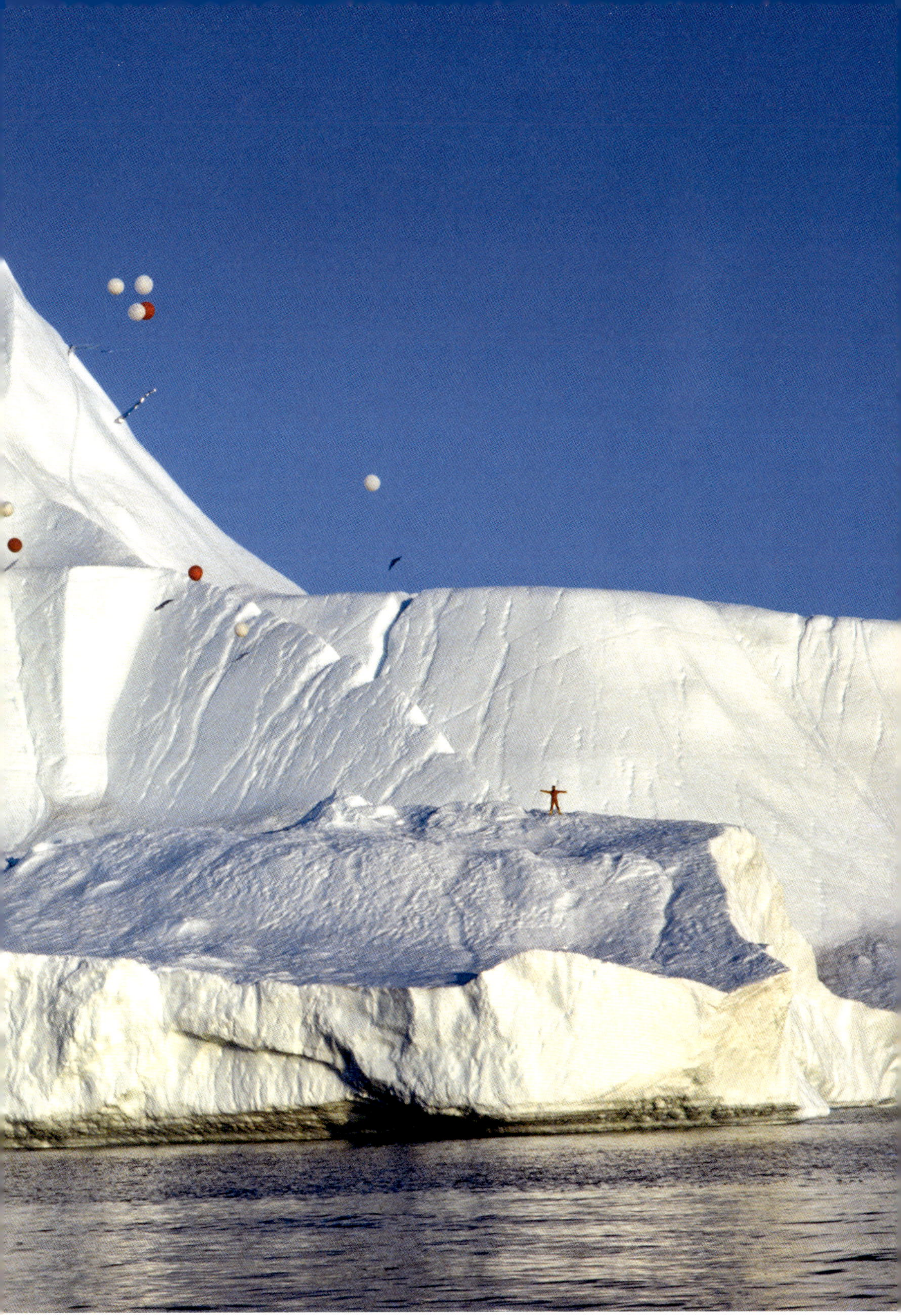

□09
Coloured Weather Balloons over an Iceberg
Greenland, 1976

Schongauer and Hieronymus Bosch.[115] Their pictures, however, focus on the imagination of horror – Satan presents Anthony with illusions in an effort to make him believe he is missing out on the earthly pleasures of life – while the desert as the site of the event is merely synonymous with the absence of civilisation. When Salvador Dalí also turned to the theme of St. Antony in 1946, he concentrated on the hermit's mirage: In Surrealist style, he painted the saint as he struggles against a long-legged parade of horses and elephants carrying beautiful women in golden riches. But the desert of endless sand and vast sky is clearly recognisable as the location of the occurrence.[116]

However, with his penchant for artistic emigration, Mack sees himself as being part of a different tradition. He refers to Henri Matisse, who painted *Still Life with Oranges* in Tangier, Morocco in 1912 in response to his encounter with Mediterranean light.[117] In North Africa, Matisse acquired a small African sculpture, whereupon he began to engage artistically with its formal language.[118] The endeavour of European visual artists to deal with works originating from Oceania and Africa had begun in the early twentieth century as 'Primitivism'. Pablo Picasso's *Demoiselles d'Avignon* (1907)[119] is considered a key work of this artistic appropriation, where the figures on the right side of the painting combine African sculptural qualities with Oceanic colouring.[120] Mack also collects masks, sculptures, and other objects from indigenous African cultures, the formal language of which is reflected in the abstract structures of his paintings and sculptures. During his numerous journeys through the continent of Africa, he repeatedly encountered nomadic and sedentary inhabitants. On his expedition to Morocco in 1958, Mack saw everyday objects carved out of wood and was amazed by their craftsmanship and creative quality. Through this experience, the so-called 'primitive' art of Africa revealed itself in a new dimension, and Mack recognised the artistic excellence of ethnological objects. Over the years, he had the opportunity to acquire several artefacts in the respective region of their origin. Counter-gifts were goods from the industrialised Western world, such as a Swiss army knife, razor blades, combs, mirrors, or a pair of scissors. 'The generosity of the people was impressive. Refusing gifts would have been dishonourable,' Mack recalls. 'Sometimes, however, an exchange resulted – if I gave painkillers, I received a counter-gift in return without being asked. One old man, for example, urged me to accept his quiver of poisoned arrows.' Mack did not, however, travel to Africa to buy or otherwise obtain works from

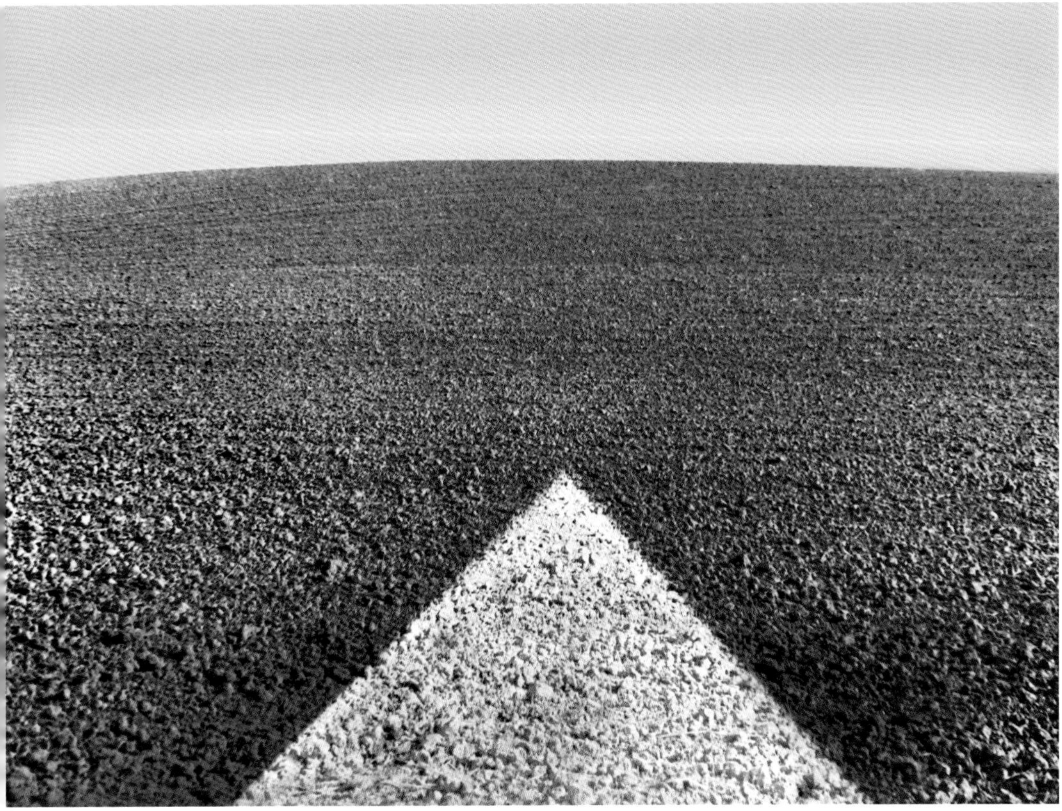

□ 10
Marking of the Earth
Hubbelrath near Düsseldorf, 1960

there. 'These were unpredictable moments when I acquired things.'[121] Although the realisation of artistic ideas and visions was paramount in his expeditions, Mack also learned about the culture and people of those regions during his travels through the African continent. Many journeys took him to Tunisia, Morocco, Egypt, Algeria, Mauritania, Namibia, Cameroon, and Senegal. In 1974/75, he took part in one of the first documented north-south crossings of the Ténéré, a particularly inhospitable desert of the southern Sahara in northern Niger.[122]

Mack's expeditions to the desert also place him in the tradition of August Macke, Paul Klee, and Louis Moilliet, who undertook their famous 'journey to Tunisia' in 1914. Like Matisse, the painters were inspired by the Mediterranean light of North Africa, since the intense luminosity of the light opened up a new kind of access to colour for them. Although they only stayed in Tunisia for about two weeks, the artists were highly productive, painting street scenes as well as watercolours of gardens and beaches. During the trip itself, Klee created only representational paintings; after his return, however, he derived several abstract works from the studies painted in Tunisia. On the basis of his watercolour *Hammamet with Its Mosque* (1914), he created a series of geometrically structured paintings, the abstracted reduction of representation of which marked Klee's first move towards abstract Colour Field painting.[123]

While these engagements with the desert and the impression of light in North Africa were still focused on rendering, in the 1960s artists associated with Land Art began to create works in direct contact with the landscape 'as small-format mark-making or as large-scale sculptures of excessive dimensions'.[124] Works made of Earth-based materials such as soil, sand, stones, turf, or wood are also known as 'earthworks'.[125] The protagonists of Land Art include, among others, the Americans Walter De Maria, Michael Heizer, Nancy Holt, and Robert Smithson. For this reason, the art movement was long described as a purely American phenomenon, until more recent observations came to the conclusion that it had emerged independently in many places around the world.[126] Robert Smithson's text 'Towards the Development of an Air Terminal Site' (1967) is considered a seminal contribution to the formulation of the earthwork aesthetic. Smithson writes that in remote areas such as the North or South Pole, art could emerge from the landscape ('the actual land as medium'). Instead of a paintbrush, artists should use a bulldozer. Smithson called for the consideration of a 'City of Ice' or 'City of Sand' made of amorphous sculptures.[127] Since Mack had already made similar proposals for the artistic integration of the landscape in 1959, he was often and correctly referred to as a pioneer of Land Art.[128]

This statement is confirmed when one compares the *Sahara Project* with works by American artists. In 1969, for example, Michael Heizer's *Munich Depression* was created on a construction site in Neuperlach near Munich.[129] To create it, the artist lifted one thousand tons of earth out of a four-metre-deep hole. The result was a crater with a diameter of roughly thirty-five metres. Like other 'earthworks' by the artist, *Munich Depression* was a 'negative sculpture' to be physically accessed and experienced by the viewer. Heizer had realised it with the help of the Munich-based gallerist Heiner Friedrich,[130] who had exhibited Walter De Maria's *Munich Earth Room* shortly before. For that installation, titled *Pure Dirt, Pure Earth, Pure Land,* fifty cubic metres of peat were spread out on the floor of Galerie Heiner Friedrich.[131] Brown garden soil, sixty centimetres high, lay in all the rooms. Visitors to the exhibition were thus only able to enter the hallway – they were not allowed to walk over or around the earth. Visitors had no overview of the entire exhibition space and simply had to trust that the gallery floor was indeed completely filled with earth. Both works belonged to the early projects of American Land Art / Earth Art, and Heiner Friedrich was one of the first gallerists to make them known in Germany.[132]

As early as 1960, however, one year after the conception of his 'preserve of art' in the Sahara, Mack had created his own first landscape sculpture. A vast, ploughed field stretching to the horizon had reminded the artist of the vastness of the Sahara, where he had stayed two years before. Intuitively, he realised that he could make an artistic mark in this barren landscape, a *Marking of the Earth.* Using light-coloured fertiliser lime, he formed an isosceles triangular on the arable land and positioned the 'marked earth' diagonally to the ploughed field soil. With simple means, the artist created a dynamic triangle, the apex of which points to the vanishing point of the photo taken of the work. ↖□ 10 *Marking of the Earth* thus verifies that Mack's works not only belong to Land Art, but also anticipated aspects of this art movement. Uwe Rüth called this 'reduced and simple minimalist ground relief' a 'classic work of Land Art'.[133] Although the works with earth do not form the centre of Mack's oeuvre, they do – in connection with the *Sahara Project* – represent a significant part of it. *Marking of the Earth* was not created

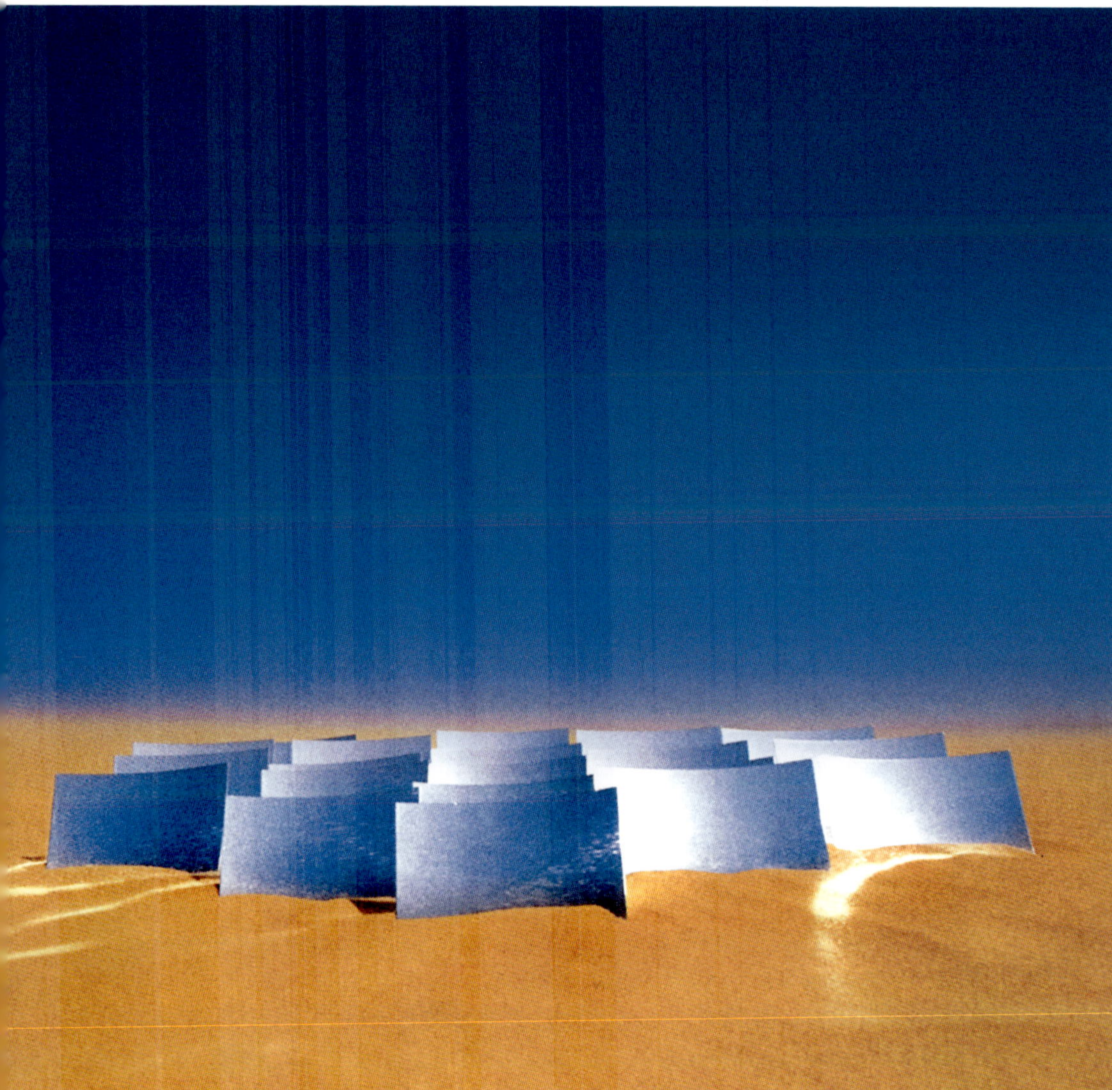

□ 11
Safrane Mirror Plantation
Tunisia, 1967

in the Sahara, however, but rather in a field near Düsseldorf. With this work from 1960, Mack's approach to the Earth as a sculptural medium can clearly be seen as pioneering.

In contrast to De Maria, whose *Earth Room* (1977) was installed in a gallery space, Mack in Düsseldorf and Heizer in Munich had created earth sculptures that were site specific – formed from the naturally occurring elements of the site and bound to it. The theory of site specificity originated with Robert Smithson. He defined his artistic works in the landscape as 'sites' and the documentary photographs, films, and texts that refer to them as 'non-sites'.[134] One of Smithson's major works is his *Spiral Jetty* (1970),[135] an approximately 450-metre-long spiral made of stones and other materials installed on site in the Great Salt Lake in Utah, which he documented in a film. In 1969, the artist had travelled to Yucatán in Mexico and carried out his *Mirror Displacements*, which he documented in the text 'Incidents of Mirror Travel in the Yucatan'.[136] He positioned small-format mirror plates in rows or groups in the earth or sand near the coast. The fact that a formal relationship exists here to Mack's mirror experiments has already been established.[137] Another common feature of the works is their ephemeral character, since both artists documented their mirror experiments in the landscape through photographs and subsequently deconstructed the resulting works. Mack had, however, already photographed *Marking of the Earth* near Düsseldorf in 1960, *Mirror between Sky, Earth and Sea* on Ibiza in 1963, and *Safrane Mirror Plantation* in the Tunisian desert in 1967. ← □ 11

The fact that Land Art was initially understood as a largely American phenomenon is also related to the North American tradition of the sublime. In the nineteenth century, painters of the Hudson River School had dedicated themselves to this theme by depicting the nature of their continent, perceived as sublime, in their landscape painting. As an aesthetic category, the adjective 'sublime' describes something that is of inspirational grace or grandeur that transcends ordinary beauty. Landscape painters such as Thomas Cole depicted scenes from the Hudson River Valley, Niagara Falls, and the American West. Their paintings reflected the pioneering spirit of the newly arrived settlers who discovered, explored, and inhabited the landscapes.[138] The Hudson River School was close to German Romantic painting, especially that of the Düsseldorf School. The depiction of weather phenomena and natural disasters was also a popular subject, for example with Albert Bierstadt, who painted *Storm in the Rocky Mountains* in 1859.[139] Walter

De Maria continued this tradition with his text 'On the Importance of Natural Disasters', written in 1960. This was published in 1963 in La Monte Young's book *An Anthology of Chance Operations.* Natural disasters are wrongly portrayed as something malign, De Maria wrote. For him, their grandeur and sublimity are superior to any form of art:

> I don't think art can stand up to nature. Put the best object you know next to the grand canyon, niagara falls, the red woods. The big things always win. Now just think of a flood, forest fire, tornado, earthquake, Typhoon, sand storm. Think of the breaking of the ice jams. Crunch. If all of the people who go to museums could just feel an earthquake ...[140]

The *Sahara Project*, published in volume 3 of *ZERO* in 1961, also refers to the sublimity of natural phenomena in that Mack expresses in it his wish that the virtual rotating volumes of the *Machine Park* should 'stand in space like giant cyclones'. These apparitions of 'spherical light and wind' would 'appear to the viewer like a frozen mirage'. In the station *The Apparitions in the Sky*, Mack points out that his apparitions of light were 'particularly sublime' – that is to say, intended to transcend ordinary beauty.[141] While De Maria emphasised the sublimity of nature's destructive forces, Mack took a more creative approach in the *Sahara Project*, highlighting the beauty of natural light and space. The sentence with which he ended his project text also bears witness to this: 'Only when we have the courage to realise the total preserve can we expect that beauty will gain a new radiance over the world.'[142]

TELE-MACK

1968

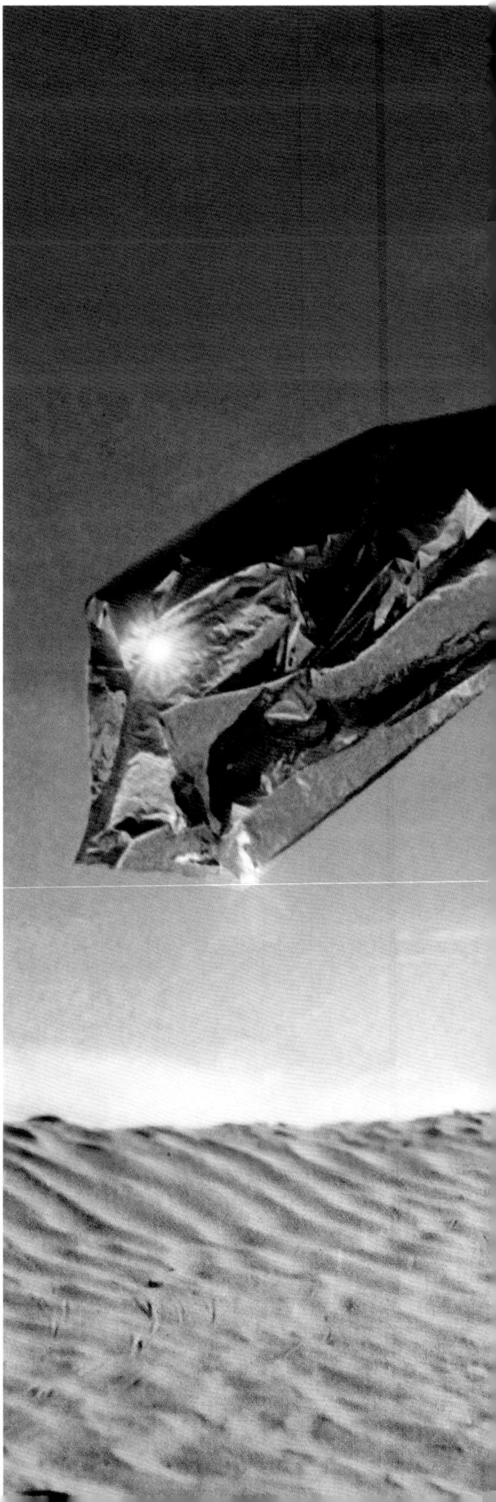

□ 12
The artist with a silver flag
near Kebili, Tunisia, 1968

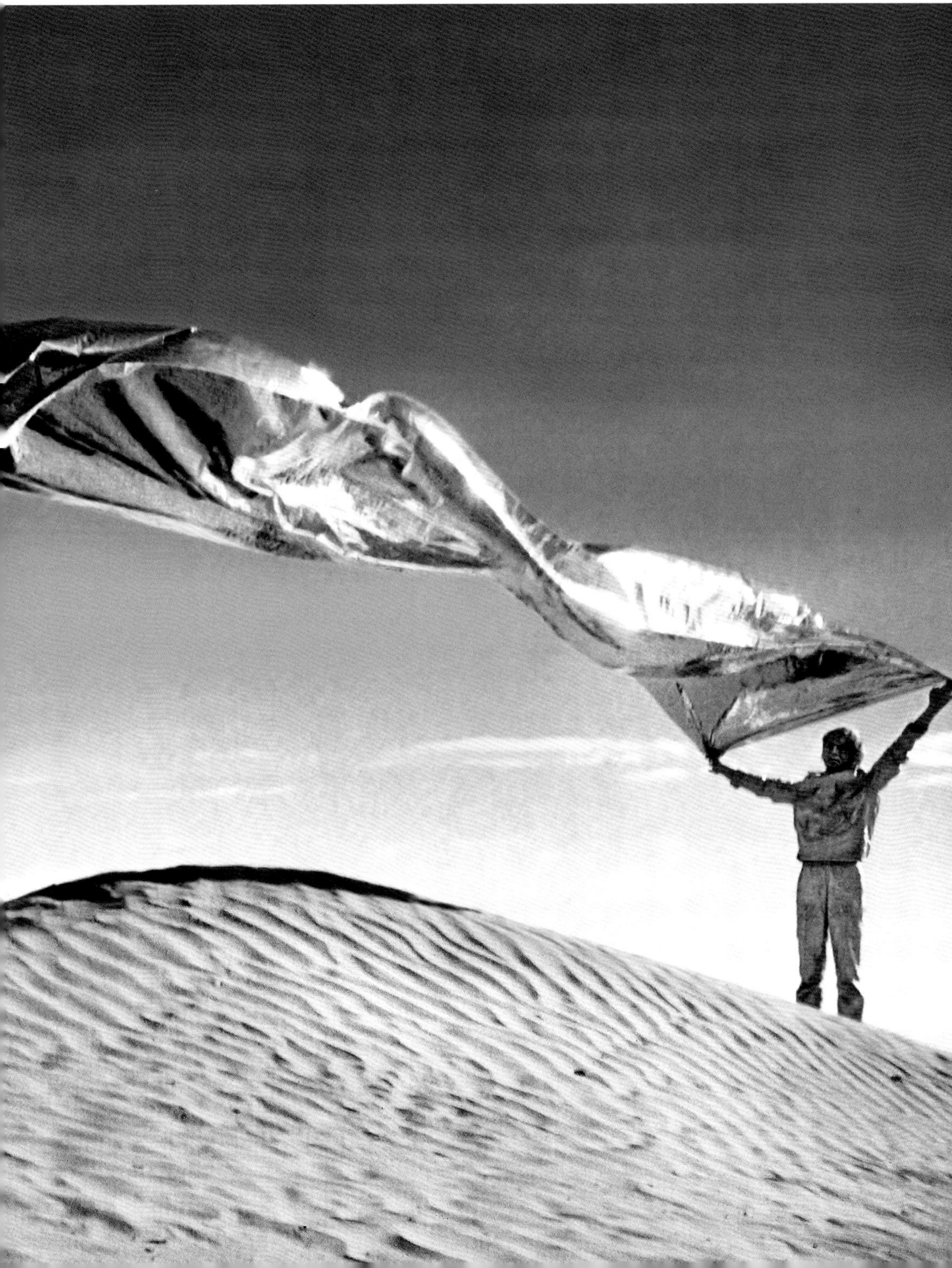

In the autumn of 1968, the press reported: 'There is turmoil in the house of the Düsseldorf-based sculptor Heinz Mack. Camera crews from the Saarländischer [SWR] and Westdeutscher Rundfunk [WDR] scurry through the rooms and across the courtyard: Since early October, television has been shooting a film about kinetic happenings by and with Heinz Mack.'[143] After the editorial staff of SWR had suggested producing a film about Heinz Mack in early 1968, the director Hans Emmerling contacted the artist. The two met and talked several times before Emmerling travelled to Mönchengladbach with a film crew in October 1968 to document Mack's daily work in the studio. The artist had come up with a few special ideas for the film. 'For example, he made a large disc, onto which he pasted tin foil,' Emmerling recalled. 'And then he put on a silver suit and said he would like to walk through the water with this suit and the disc.'[144] The team then drove to a flooded gravel pit near Mönchengladbach and shot the first scene of the film *Tele-Mack*. It shows the artist in a silver suit with the silver disc strapped to his back, wading through the water. 'He moved against the sun and kept bending over in gradations so the camera could pick up the different reflections,' Emmerling explained. 'That's why we called him the *Silver Mack*. The cameraman was always shouting: Reflection, reflection! And Mack moved about in the glittering jumpsuit. He wanted to make the reflections of the light manifest.'[145] Mack had designed the silver costume of aluminium fabric especially for the film; in it, he himself became a light object in front of the camera. The artist knew how to use the medium of film to stage his actions, which fascinated the director and his cameraman, Edwin Braun. For the first time, Emmerling explained, they had not filmed already completed art objects in a museum or gallery, but rather assisted in the creation of new objects and actions.[146]

Although *Tele-Mack* is mainly known for its desert scenes, the forty-five-minute colour film contains several scenes showing Mack in his studio and his actions in his local surroundings. During the opening credits, he drives briskly through the city of Düsseldorf in his Jaguar E-Type. 'Sometimes, I think a car is the best kinetic object,' the narrator quotes the artist as saying.[147] Scenes in the studio in which Mack demonstrates the principle of his *Rotors* with grooved glass panes make it clear that film is far better suited than photography to presenting kinetic works, since it is able to show them in motion. Other kinetic works are shown, such as the *Playing Wall* (1966-69) made of movable, coloured acrylic glass elements for the children's clinic of the Lukas Hospital in Neuss and the kinetic *Light Forest* (1966) for the Expo 67 in Montreal.[148] The viewer of the film 'enters' an installation with rotating aluminium nets swinging from the ceiling, between which the visitors of a vernissage move about. 'The images that Heinz Mack presents to us demand the medium of film,' says the speaker. 'Mack's concept for this film strove to show his world as only film can capture and reproduce it.'[149]

Other scenes show clear connections to the stations of the *Sahara Project*. These include a sequence showing the artist in the garden of the Huppertzhof on the outskirts of Mönchengladbach, where he has lived and worked since the 1960s. He fiddles around with large mirrors that he lays on the lawn. 'A collage of mirrors is created,' the speaker explains. 'In the composite mirror image, studio, house, and garden, concrete things, colours and light become artful elements.' The artist steps onto the mirror surface; it breaks under his feet. 'Mack wants to break it down into the smallest particles of mirrors. A mirror plantation emerges from the crushed glass.'[150] The artist then arranges upright shards of

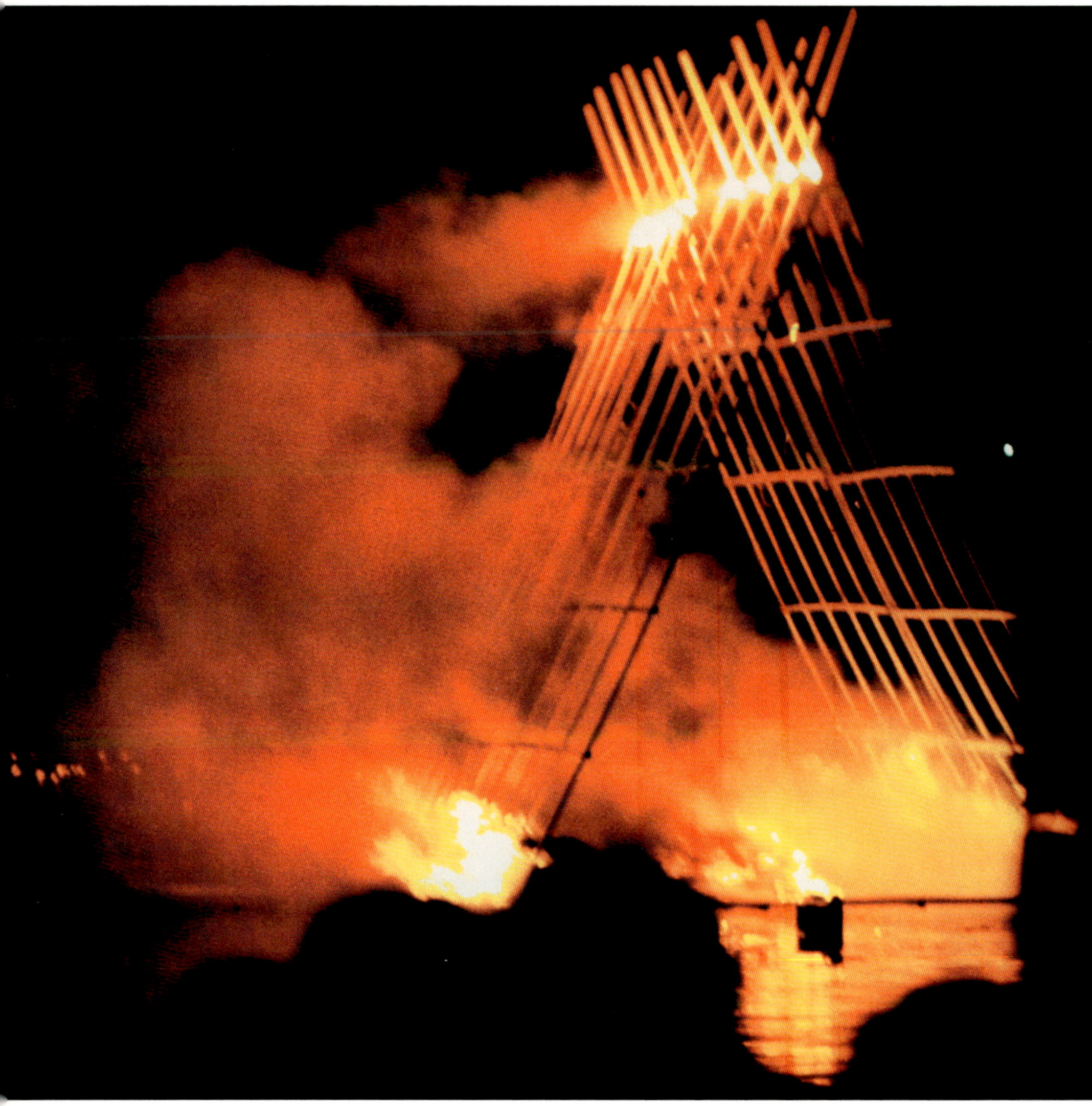

□13
Fire Ship on a lake near Mönchengladbach
1968

mirror glass on the lawn and in the vegetation surrounding it. Reality is dissolved into fragments; a fragmentation of space takes place. For Mack, this act meant the final destruction of the tradition of Western painting since the Renaissance. As with the *Mirror Wall*, in which viewers 'encounter themselves',[151] the mirrors in which humans and nature find each other again are part of this action that Mack carries out in the spirit of the *Sahara Project*.[152]

Mack's *Fire Ship*, already mentioned in connection with the *Machine Park*, can also be seen in the film: ←□13 After equipping the raft he built with a wooden framework with pyrotechnics as described above, the artist let his object glide onto a lake on a string to ignite the fireworks on it on an hourly basis. 'It was a wet evening, however, and the remote ignition didn't work,' Hans Emmerling recalled. 'We thus had to pull the ship back ashore and light it with a torch. When everything was burning, we recorded it with three cameras. A little later the fire brigade came with sirens blasting because they thought a house was on fire.'[153] The self-destructing *Fire Ship*, a component of the *Jardin artificiel*, was recorded for the first time in the film *Tele-Mack* – an intangible light event that combined the elements of fire and water.

For about four weeks, the team filmed in Mönchengladbach and the surrounding area before travelling to Tunisia together with the artist. Initially, there had been no assignment to travel to the Sahara; the idea arose during the filming. 'During our first days of shooting, Mack kept telling us how fantastic it would be to show and record the work in the Sahara, in this unspoiled region. He raved about the light and dark of the dunes and the waves of sand and the deep blue sky above,' Emmerling recalls. 'Then, one day in Düsseldorf, we simply booked the crossings from Marseille to Tunis at the travel agency.'[154]

'MOMENTS OF PURE FASCINATION'
SAHARA 1968

With a Hanomag loaded full of material, the film crew set off and took the ship to Tunis on 20 November 1968, followed one day later by Mack. On 22 November, they drove two cars along the coast via Hammamet, Sousse, El Djem, Sfax, and Gabès to Kebili on the edge of the Tunisian Sahara.[155] South of there lie the desert zones of the Grand Erg Oriental, where the second shooting phase of the film *Tele-Mack* began – a challenge for the whole team. 'It was new territory for all of us; only Heinz Mack had been there before,' Emmerling recalled. 'At night, it was freezing cold; until noon, we walked around in parkas. Then it got hot.'[156] Although Mack had prepared himself for the artistic adventure, as had the film technicians, the first days were dominated by uncertainty, because no one had planned and executed a similar undertaking before. But Mack was fortunate to be accompanied by cameramen whose empathy and sensitivity of vision made it possible to try many experiments that were risky for the artist. He recalled that all those involved were inspired by the idea of capturing the various light phenomena on film in all their uniqueness and rich variation. According to the artist, the pace of work was almost hectic during those few days, and yet he could have continued filming for weeks.[157] ↘□ 14 – 16

South of Kebili, they drove into the Sahara, into the sand dunes between the Douz and Zaafrane oases. 'These are not landscapes where you can go for a walk,' the artist states. 'The desert is also life-threatening.'[158] Mack found the space of the desert extremely elemental: There was nothing to see there except sky and sand. Moreover, there was great silence – not a sound to be heard. The inimitable beauty of the sand dunes, however, fascinated the film crew, who were enthralled by their untouched nature, the complete silence, and the extraordinarily beautiful shapes – as long as there was no sandstorm, of course. Mack had brought several aluminium plates with him, polished to a mirror finish and embossed with relief structures, reflectors made of metal and acrylic glass, silver foil, coloured acrylic glass panes, and tools for setting up the sculptures. The first action was to make a mark in the landscape. A cross was formed from five blank aluminium discs and placed in the yellow-brown dunes to mark the location, the border of which – the blue of the sky – was reflected in the polished aluminium.[159] In the process, all participants were careful to cover their footprints again. Any human intervention was to remain invisible, in order to show the untouched nature in the film.[160]

Following the stations of the *Sahara Project*, Mack installed his *Jardin artificiel* in the desert. Freely placed *Light Reliefs* formed the luminous vegetation of the artistic garden. The silver disc of a rotor, placed on the crest of a dune, shone like an 'Artificial Sun' in the intense light. A rotating wing sculpture made of shiny aluminium, the surface of which showed a delicate relief, rotated as a *Crown of Light* on the crest of the dune. The movement created ever-changing optical effects, the light overplaying and alienating the substance of the metal. Mack, wearing his silver suit, let an aluminium-vapourised reflective foil flutter in the wind of the Sahara. cf. ↖□12 The violent wind blew it up and unfolded a sail of light, in which the colours of the desert were reflected, constantly moving and changing. A phosphorescent disc made of red acrylic glass broke when he tried to hurl it into the sky. Mack then stuck the bizarrely shaped fragments into the sand so that they glowed red against the luminous evening sky.[161] Despite the difficult working conditions in the desert, there were no limits to the enthusiasm and ingenuity of the cameramen. According to Mack: 'Almost everything that we left to the light and the desert as an artistic challenge was transformed, became an expression of light, space, and time.'[162] It was thus a delightful surprise for him when he realised that, although space and time were stronger than his artificial works, these relatively small constructions could absorb the infinite expanse of space in miniature and articulate and intensify the all-encompassing brightness of light.[163]

The large *Light Steles* were assembled on site. For these, Mack mounted aluminium reflectors on long wooden poles. This strenuous work took place under harsh external conditions: High temperatures prevailed in the glaring sunshine, while a strong wind whipped grains of sand into the artist's face. He built a total of nine steles, each of which consisted of different elements, from small reflectors in horizontal rows and chequered, aluminium foil relief structures to diamond-shaped elements of anodised aluminium and the highest stele with circular reflectors at a height of eleven metres. Each stele thus produced its own light and had to be aligned at a different angle to the sun until the highest light intensity was reached and could be recorded by the camera.[164] When the first, eleven-metre-high silver stele was installed, and the sun caught the focus of its twenty-six light reflectors, the members of the expedition experienced 'moments of pure fascination'.[165] Mack recalled that all his concerns were resolved, since the result exceeded even his wildest expectations. And when the ensemble of nine steles finally stood in the desert, the artist realised that his 'concept formulated in the *Sahara Project* need not get lost in the vacuum of thought' but had a real chance of being realised. 'The incomparable light of the desert vibrated incandescently bright in my objects, which here – under this sky – can gain a unique appearance, since the light completely outshines their materiality.'[166] ↘□18

While the sight of the artefacts delighted the members of the expedition, the days and nights in the Sahara were marked by hardship and arduous conditions. Mack recalled that a record was kept of

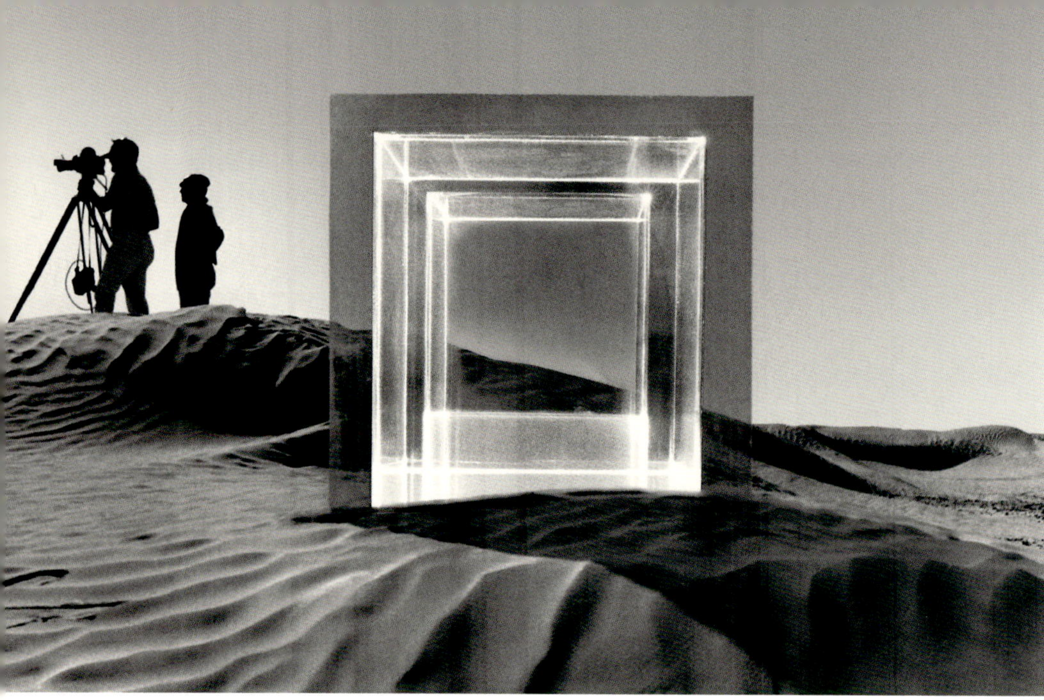

□ 14
Shooting for the film *Tele-Mack* in the Grand Erg Oriental
Tunisia, 1968

□ 15 & 16
Heinz Mack, Edwin Braun, Klaus Weber, and Hans Emmerling
during the installation of *Light Steles* in the desert
Tunisia, 1968

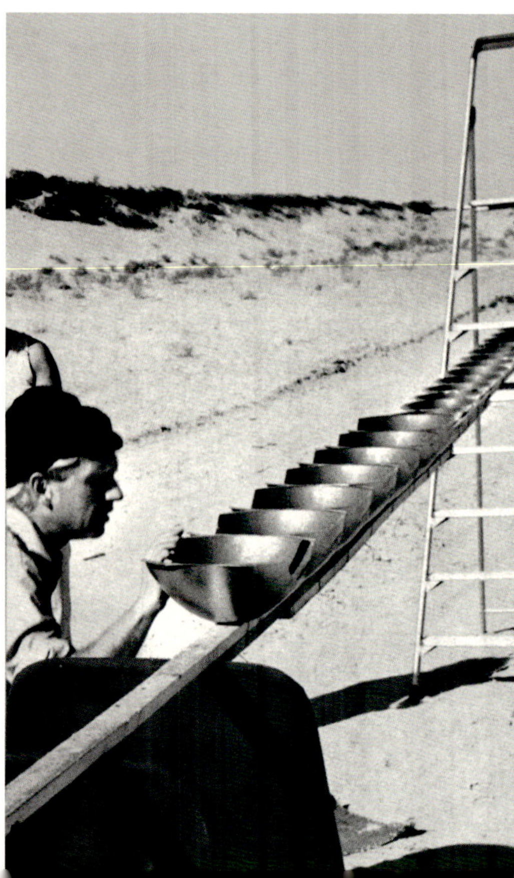

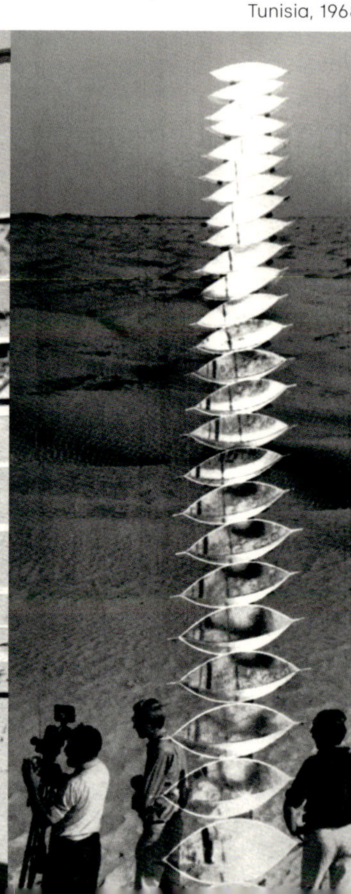

who ate an orange. And Emmerling recalled a chance encounter with a man on a mule who was carrying bags of dates left and right on the animal. As the man watched the unusual spectacle in the desert, he gave everyone a handful of dates – to the delight of the film crew.[167] On a bitterly cold night, the team piled brush and shrubs, so powder-dry that they appeared weightless, into a large heap. 'All it took was two matches and soon everything was burning like tinder, a metre-high inferno of flames that got lost in the night sky with furiously consuming energy,' Mack recalls.[168] The group experienced a particularly surreal phenomenon when the heated air wafted around the flames like the glassy glow of a mirage – here, a consequence of the completely dust-free coldness. As Mack watched this spectacle facing the fire, his back seemed even colder than before, and he felt himself on the borderline between two extremely contrasting temperatures. He could often observe the nomadic desert dwellers digging a small hollow in the sand with their hands as night fell, in order to light their charcoal in it so that they could make tea. If a larger fit pit was built, they would spread a thin layer of sand on the remaining embers after finishing their meal, on top of which they would lay camel hair blankets in which they would curl up to rest for the night. The embers not only warmed their sleeping bodies but could also be reignited the next morning by patiently fanning them so that they could make tea. 'Our propane cookers did not arouse the envy of our desert companions,' Mack recalled. 'After all, you can't lie down to sleep on such a device to warm yourself.'[169]

On the last evening in the Sahara, Mack installed an artificial garden of fan-like aluminium webs that shone like nets of thousands of small prisms in the red evening light. The material, which comes from the aircraft and aerospace industry, consists of closely meshed aluminium honeycombs modelled after the bee honeycomb. Mack had discovered the material in New York in the early 1960s and was the first ZERO artist to use it to create reliefs and sculptures in the form of fans and wings.[170] Easily mouldable by hand, the honeycombs were stretched and compressed by the artist, creating structures that closely resemble those found in nature, such as the cell structure of a plant leaf. Translucent and shiny, they showed a different colour and texture depending on the incidence of light and the viewer's standpoint, at times even appearing immaterial. The result was 'a perfect integration of artificial objects in a primeval landscape, the desert'.[171] ↘□ 17

Like the plants of an artificial garden, the aluminium structures blended effortlessly into the space of the desert. Here, Mack observed, to his own surprise, that his sculptures entered an astonishingly good relationship with nature, despite the fact that they were actually abstract. Nature, the artist realised, was not the enemy of his works, and technology was a condition for realising art. Everything he did in the desert, he said, did not violate its pristine nature, but rather confirmed it. At the best moments, his works became optical sensations that were themselves as untouchable as nature. 'Nature, which is boundless and rich in form, which does not have to obey any tradition of seeing, is not opposed to art if this is completely artificial and has a dynamic and thought-free quality,' Mack stated. Art must give nature a chance to manifest itself as nature within it – only then does art in turn gain a chance to manifest itself in nature.[172]

As the sun set over the Sahara, the fans had the appearance of a mirage in the evening light, and Mack asked the cameraman to film the unreal apparition once again. He replied that he had already used up all the film rolls – in fact the budget available for the production was relatively small.[173] The film was shot between 23 and 27 November 1968, after which the film crew and artist left the desert. 'For Heinz Mack, it was much more than an experience,' Hans Emmerling recalled. He said the film documented an important stage of his artistic journey and showed that his ideas about the *Sahara Project* were feasible. 'The idea of his artworks existing in such a space, in the desert, worked out fortunately. And the film documents that it was not presumptuous, but rather wonderful, to set out into the Sahara.'[174]

'ICARUS IN THE DESERT'
RECEPTION OF THE FILM

Tele-Mack received attention from the press even before the production of the film was completed. As early as December 1968, the newspaper *Rheinische Post* published a richly illustrated article: 'Works by Mack Made a Guest Appearance in North Africa – The Great Adventure'.[175] 'A colour television film of roughly three quarters of an hour aims to radically break with the practice of art exhibitions that has hitherto been practised all over the world,' wrote Heiner Stachelhaus in the *Neue Rhein Zeitung,* and continued: 'The film is not a reportage or document of an art exhibition; it is itself an exhibition.'[176] *Tele-Mack* was also announced in the national press. In March 1969, the *Frankfurter Allgemeine Zeitung*

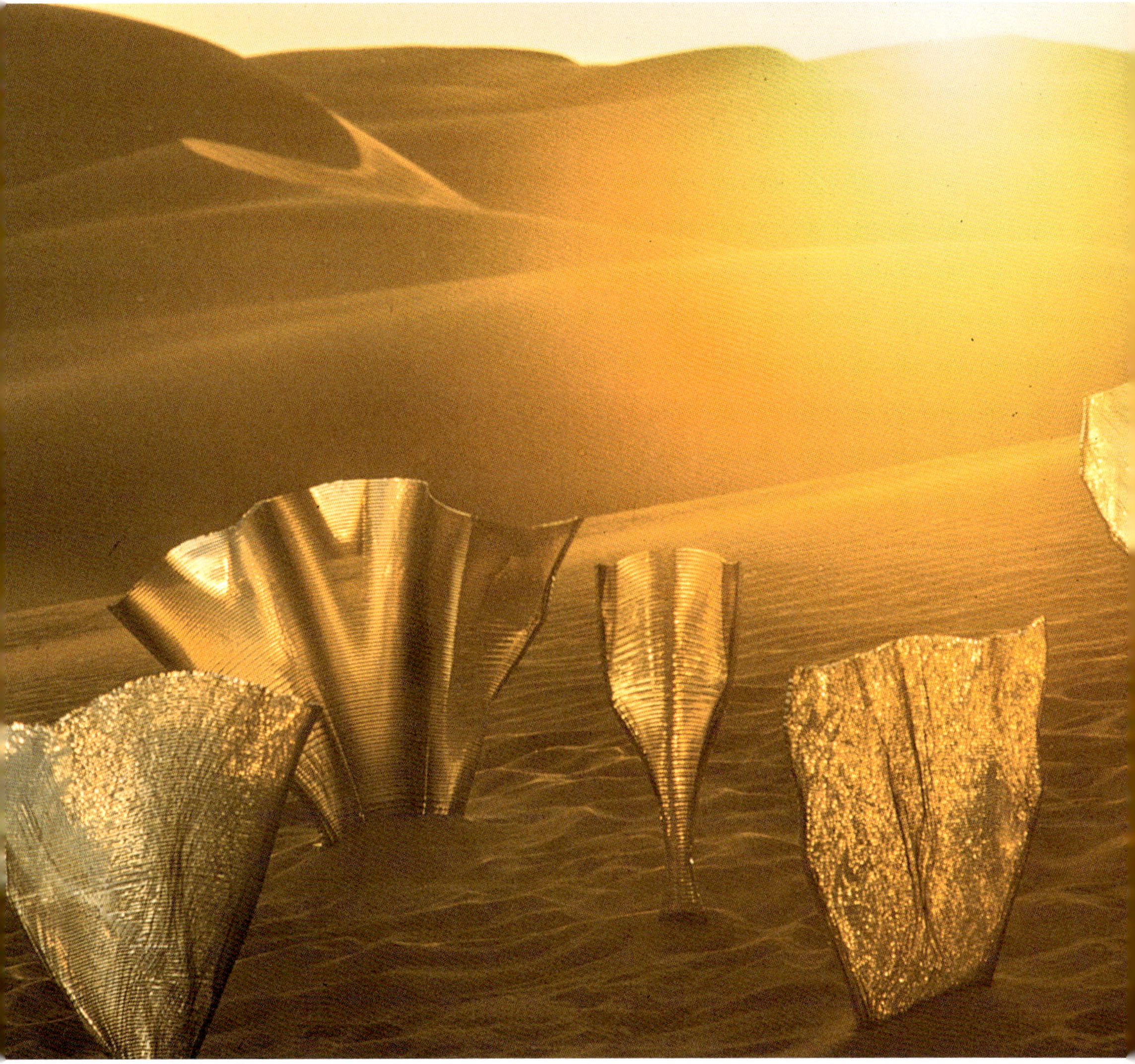

□17
Light Fans in the Grand Erg Oriental
Tunisia, 1968

(*FAZ*) reported that Mack's 'light adventures' would 'soon be flickering on German television screens'.[177] On 2 May 1969, *Tele-Mack* was shown on WDR's evening programme in the primetime slot at half-past seven. Yvonne Friedrichs had announced the 'eagerly awaited colour film' a day earlier in the *Rheinische Post*: 'Here, through the medium of colour film, op art is taken to the extreme limit of its potential impact, which is based on the harmony of light, colour, and movement.'[178] The art critic Georg Jappe noted in the *FAZ* that the 'famous "Sahara Project"' could be realised 'through the medium of colour television'. 'When the blond Mack strides and falls through the desert with a huge fluttering aluminium sail, one thinks of Icarus,' Jappe wrote. For the art critic, Mack was as good here as he could have ever been. 'The [camera] lens allows the structures of the colour reflexes to be maxed out in microcosmic and macrocosmic effects.'[179] The weekly magazine *Der Spiegel* reviewed the film in an extensive article: 'Almost simultaneously with American "Land Art" activists, Mack also went to the desert last November,' it stated. 'Near the Tunisian oasis of Kebili, he spent five days fiddling with half-technical, half-fantastic art formations in the sunlight – for television.' For the magazine *Der Spiegel*, the trip to Tunisia had been worthwhile; Mack had 'succeeded in creating unprecedented artistic effects in the wasteland'. On a natural stage without fingerprints, the 'interplay of light on static reflectors and rotating reliefs' was far more intense and purer than 'in the hullabaloo of art exhibitions. ... For Mack's artistic career, "Telemack" [*sic!*] represents a high point, perhaps even a turning point.'[180]

The film indeed represents a high point in Mack's biography: For the first time after the dissolution of ZERO in 1966, Mack received the public attention that he had previously been given only to a limited extent as an independent artist. The film was invited to the *Television* festival in London in 1969 and the Venice Film Festival in 1971, where it received an honourable mention. In 1970, *Tele-Mack* was awarded the Grimme Prize.[181] Moreover, the film also marked a turning point: Through the medium of film, the *Sahara Project* had found a form of expression with which ephemeral art events in the desert could endure beyond the moment and be widely disseminated. *Tele-Mack* is a 'new kind of art exhibition', Mack said in an interview: 'For the first time in the history of art exhibitions, this unconventional film will take on the role and function of an exhibition, namely the mediating role between art and the public.' According to Mack, many of the works photographed in the film have been destroyed, so that they do not even exist outside the film. 'The film is thus neither a reportage nor a document of an art exhibition; rather, it is itself an exhibition. The premiere and the duration of the exhibition are identical.'[182]

'REPRODUCTION THROUGH THE MASS MEDIUM OF TELEVISION' THE FILM AS AN EXHIBITION

Against the backdrop of artistic trends emerging at the time, such as Conceptual and Process art, Land Art, and Arte Povera, which sought to overcome traditional genre boundaries, the medium of television offered itself as a mediator.[183] Gerry Schum and Ursula Wevers thus also developed the *Fernsehgalerie* (Television Gallery), an 'exhibition venue for filmic art' in which 'art as an event, art as an action, but not art as an end product' was to be presented.[184] In January 1969, the couple began shooting the film *Land Art*, consisting of eight sequences, each featuring one artist. The film documented actions by Richard Long in England, Barry Flanagan and Jan Dibbets in the Netherlands, and Marinus Boezem in the Camargue region of Southern France. In the United States, Schum and Wevers filmed Dennis Oppenheim during an action on the Canadian border, Robert Smithson in a quarry in New York State, Walter De Maria in the Mojave Desert, and Michael Heizer's 'desert painting' at Coyote Dry Lake in California, although the latter ultimately withdrew his contribution to the film. *Land Art* was broadcast in Germany on ARD on 15 April 1969, a few weeks before the premiere of *Tele-Mack*.[185] Prior to this, Schum had already made other art films, also in collaboration with Mack. In the film *Konsumkunst – Kunstkonsum* (Consumption Art – Art Consumption, 1968), which questions the impact of new industrial production conditions on the concept of art, Mack introduces the idea of *Tele-Mack*. He explains that he was planning a special form of multiplication of art objects: 'reproduction through the mass medium of television'. 'It is my plan to make an exhibition that no longer takes place in a museum, that does not take place in a gallery, but that appears exclusively and only once on television,' Mack states in the film. 'All the objects that I will show in this exhibition can only be made known to the public through television and will also be destroyed by me in the end.'[186] The mediation of art through the medium of television had a social dimension for both Mack and Schum. 'I did not merely formulate once that art is made for everyone,' Mack emphasised. The presentation of art on television could reach more people than the social elite who were the primary visitors to exhibitions.[187]

Although a collaboration between Schum and Mack on the *Land Art* project would have been only logical after *Konsumkunst – Kunstkonsum*, it did not come about. Mack regrets this: 'His idea of creating a "television gallery" was bold and promising, even visionary, because he conceived of a virtual, global networking through art films. This fascinated me, because I, too, had been wondering for some time whether the medium of television would not be suitable for broadcasting virtual instead of real art exhibitions. ... In retrospect, I very much regret that the collaboration I had striven for between us did not come about.'[188] Like he himself, Schum did not have sufficient financial means to adequately realise his bold ideas, Mack explains.[189] As Ursula Wevers reported, some of Schum's plans failed not least of all because of financial difficulties. In 1973, he took his own life.[190]

In contrast, protagonists of American Land Art were often able to realise their projects thanks to generous sponsors. One important supporter was Virginia Dwan, who presented the first exhibition of the art movement under the title *Earth Art* in her gallery in New York in October 1968.[191] She also financed the *Spiral Jetty* in Utah. Robert Smithson documented the construction of his sculpture in April 1970 in a colour film roughly half an hour long that shows his *Spiral Jetty* from an aerial view and places it in a geological context by superimposing cartographic material and shots from the American Museum of Natural History in New York.[192] The material and financial conditions under which Smithson worked could hardly have been more different from those of Mack. When Mack later learned that artists like Smithson had been able to realise their projects with the help of sponsors who supported their bold ideas that defied all conventions, it was not difficult for him to continue to admire these works. He recognised their theoretical affinity with the *Sahara Project*, but would not relate them to it, since the project had been created completely autonomously and under different circumstances.[193]

Smithson had already contemplated a connection between art and television in the magazine *Artforum* in 1967. Remote places like the pine forests of New Jersey and the frozen wastelands of the North and South Poles could be 'coordinated' through art forms that would use the actual land as a medium, Smithson stated. 'Television could transmit such activity all over the world.'[194] Other artists associated with Land Art were more sceptical about the photographic or filmic reproduction of their work. Walter De Maria and Michael Heizer, for example, generally refused to show documentation such as photographs or films of their works. Long walks along and through their works, they felt, were the only way to appreciate their significance, as Virginia Dwan summarised: 'The photograph is not the work.'[195] Nevertheless, the artists created works that are almost only received through photographs due to their remote, hard-to-reach locations. In 1977, Walter De Maria installed four hundred steel rods in a desert landscape near Quemado in New Mexico. This *Lightning Field* is still financed by the Dia Art Foundation, founded in 1974, which strictly regulates visits to the work. A maximum of six people, who are accommodated for a day in a log cabin near the *Lightning Field*, are allowed to experience the work at the same time. Photography of the work is prohibited. Although some non-official photos can nevertheless be found on the Internet, control over the public image of the work has remained with the artist's testamentary executor and the foundation since his death in 2013. Following De Maria's intention to delve deeper into the sublime in nature, the installation of stainless-steel rods is designed to attract lightning. Most of the official photos of the *Lightning Field* therefore show violent flashes of lightning. The probability of experiencing the work during a lightning storm is relatively low, however: According to Dia, violent lightning storms usually only occur from mid-July to August in the region around Quemado.[196] Nevertheless, the lightning works as a kind of branding of the installation, as Wolfgang Ullrichs stated in 2009. He noted that, although one of the official photographs taken by the photographer John Cliett depicts a stormy atmosphere, the lightning did not strike one of the poles, but rather discharged at a greater distance. The fact that the artist only circulated images authorised by him betrays his intention to imprint the *Lightning Field* in the visual memory of the art public as authoritatively as if it were a painting, says Ullrich. 'If there were many – competing – photographs, it would be clear that they each offered only one perspective on the original, thus always referring to it; in contrast, a few photographs of the *Lightning Field* that have become icons take the place of the original.'[197]

If one compares images of the *Lightning Field* with the *Light Steles* Mack positioned in the Tunisian desert in 1968 during the shooting of the film *Tele-Mack*, ↘□18 the similarity between the two works becomes evident. As Uwe Rüth has already noted, Mack's metal *Light*

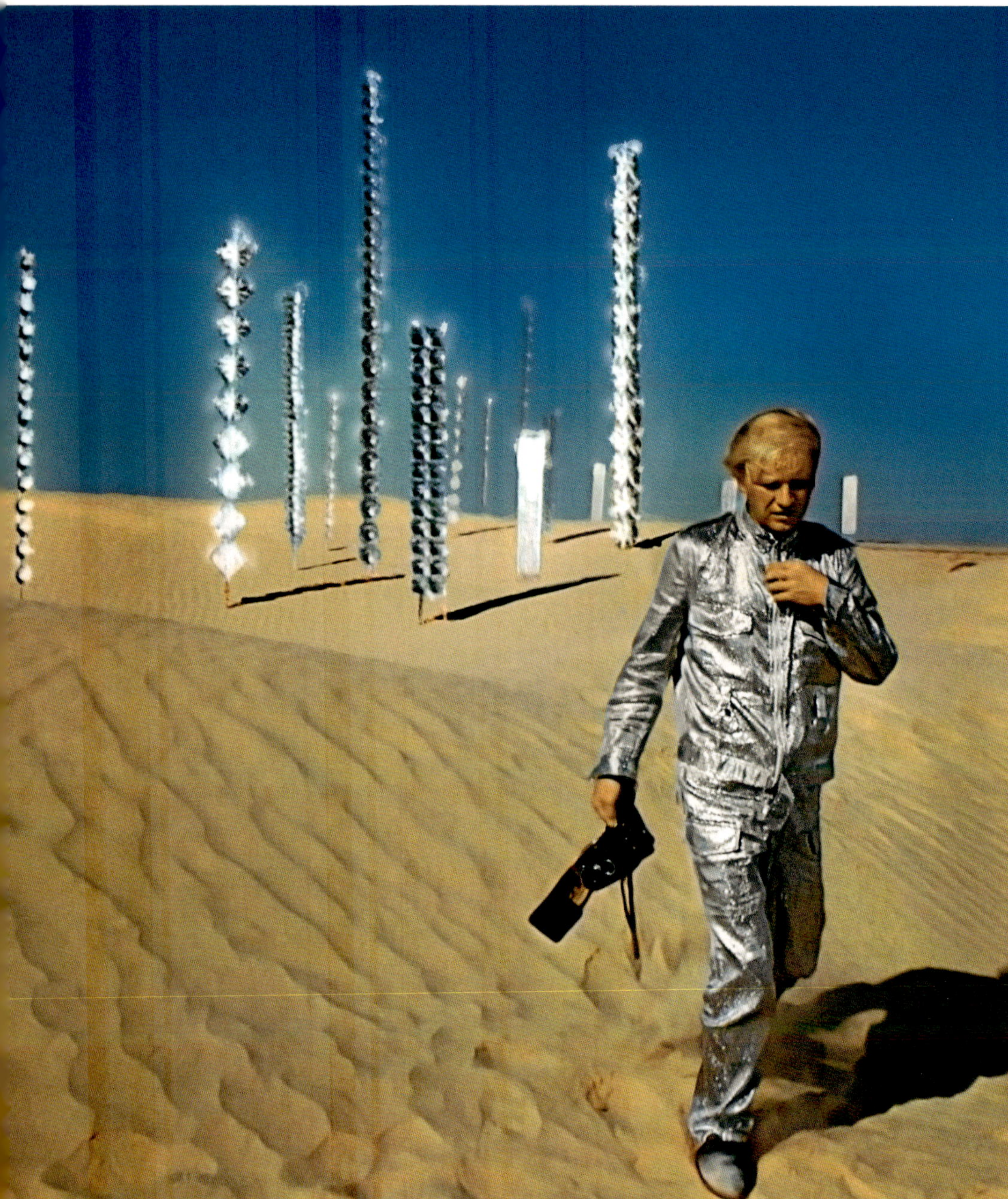

□ 18
Heinz Mack during the shoot of the film *Tele-Mack*
Tunisia, 1968

Steles and their 'direct reference to the natural phenomenon of light in this particular landscape' can be compared to the connection of De Maria's *Lightning Field* to the electrical forces of lightning storms in New Mexico.[198] It is worthy to note that Mack realised the ensemble of *Light Steles* in the desert in 1968, nine years before the installation of *Lightning Field.* Moreover, he realised the first station of his *Sahara Project* without any financial support from a sponsor, which, as he sees it, testifies to the artist's unconditional will to realise his ideas in the desert.

EXPEDITION INTO ARTIFICIAL GARDENS

1976

□ 19
Light Prisms in the Arctic (Model for a Floating Research Station)
Greenland, 1976

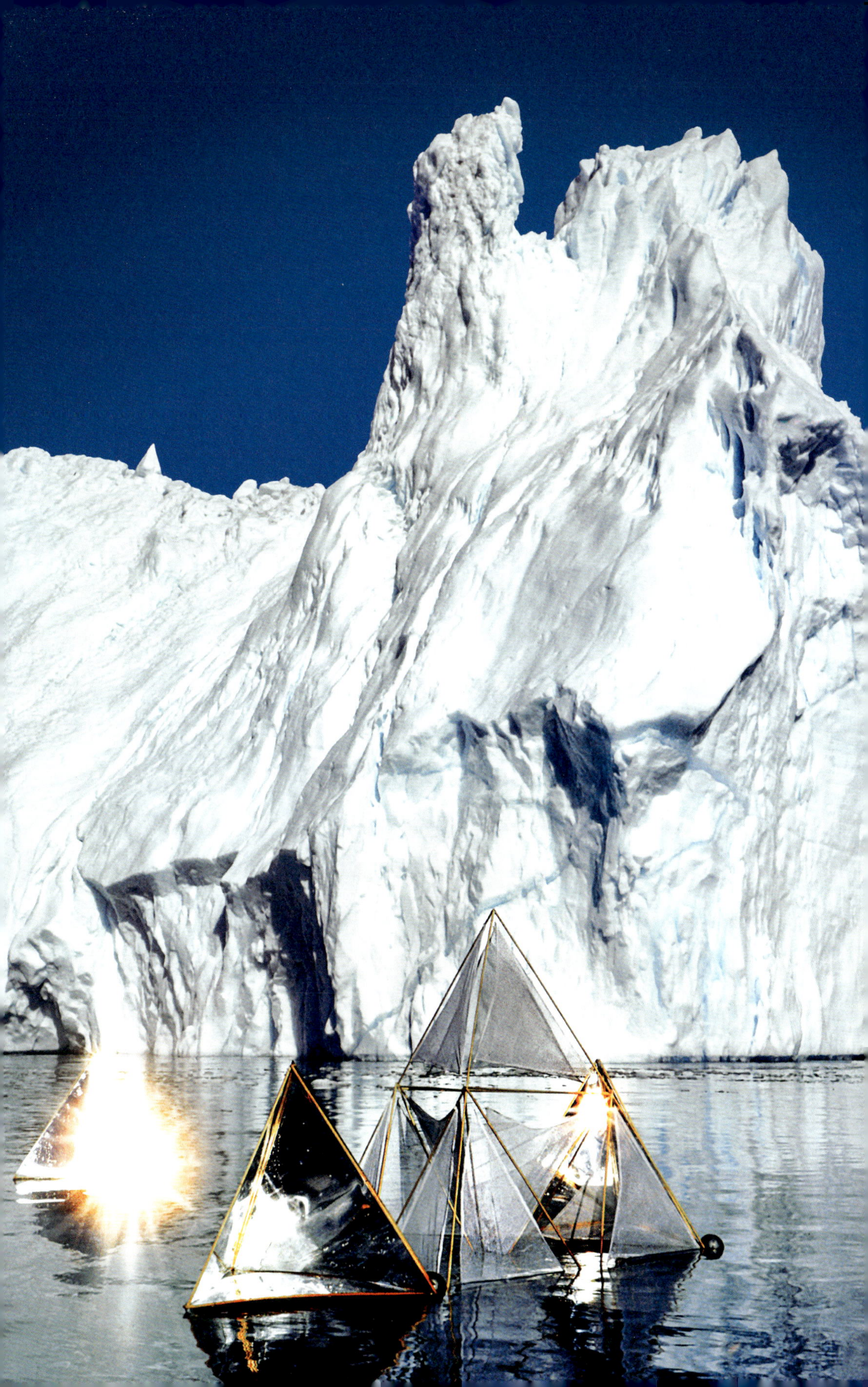

Those who enter the desert and perceive only their own heartbeat also hear its silence. Whoever sees the pure light in the polar circle and stands in this light is filled with light and becomes an object of light. Whoever stands in the emptiness and boundlessness of such landscapes understands their own physicality. Those who encounter themselves in the sand and ice deserts cannot flee from themselves.[199]

HEINZ MACK, 1976

On 10 March 1976, Heinz Mack noted in his calendar: 'Sahara expedition prepared by midnight. Material loaded onto the Hanomag.'[200] In addition to tents and tools, this included mirrors, foils, metal screens, and steles made of highly polished aluminium, as well as filigree honeycomb webs – unformed material from which a *Jardin artificiel* was to be created in the desert. The destination of the trip was the Western Grand Erg in Algeria – the second largest sand sea in the Sahara, also called the Grand Erg Occidental. In contrast to the trip to Tunisia in 1968, which had been rather spontaneous, this expedition was precisely planned. Henri Nannen, the publisher of *Stern* magazine, had heard about Mack's *Sahara Project.* He discussed this with Axel Hecht, then *Stern's* editor-in-chief for culture, and *Stern* photographer Thomas Höpker.[201] Together, Hecht, Höpker, and Mack then planned 'the hitherto most elaborate production of the cultural department – an art safari', which *Stern* wanted to document with a richly illustrated report by Axel Hecht.[202]

ALGERIA

A few days later, on 19 March, Mack and his travel companions set off for Algeria; the group also included Mack's friends Fritz Bagel, Michael Bienert, and Knut Schönburg. They travelled for three days in a heavy Hanomag truck which had been converted for the desert tour from the studio in Mönchengladbach to Marseille and then by ferry across the Mediterranean to Algiers. As Axel Hecht reported, there were difficulties at the border there: 'How do you explain an art safari to a customs officer? Photos from previous trips help, curiosity dispels initial mistrust.' They then travelled inland for days on an asphalt road. After Ghardaïa, the last town before the pure desert region, they reached the oasis of El Goléa (today El Menia). '14,000 inhabitants, 100,000 palm trees. We decide to stay. For Mack, the "expedition of my expectations" begins, for us it is the start of optical sensations.' The next morning, after sixty kilometres of driving, they arrived at the edge of the Grand Erg Occidental. A few minutes after leaving the asphalt, the full desert surrounded them. 'Not a stone, not a shrub, rarely a tuft of grass. We soon give up counting the dunes. Fifty, a hundred, five hundred? A sea of valleys and hills, the crests drawn as if with a razor.'[203]

At first, the group had to get used to this seemingly inhuman space. The sun scorched their skin, the wind whirled the sand, which was everywhere. It burned their eyes, blocked the motors and shutters of the cameras, and allowed them to walk only in slow motion. Every morning, the expedition began with a drive to the dunes of El Menia or Timimoun, the second stop. In addition to the Hanomag, the group had hired a small Fiat, which got stuck in the sand a total of nineteen times. 'The tyres spin senselessly in the sand, buzzing like angry insects,' Hecht describes. 'Get out, shovel it free, push on – and each time, the wheels hurl a sharp jet of sand into your burning face. Twenty metres further on, the oil pan slams into a boulder hidden by the shifting sand. We're stuck again.' They often got lost, caught time and again in the labyrinth of gravel valleys. When the storm blew away the wheel tracks and the walkie-talkies they carried failed, they had trouble finding their way back. 'Climbing laboriously from dune to dune, Heinz Mack and I navigate Thomas Höpker in the Fiat out of the labyrinth,' Hecht reports. 'And yet the exertions hardly last the day. The optical sensations that Mack staged remain in our memory.'[204] ↘□ 24

Heinz Mack had prepared intensively for this expedition. His 1976 calendar, which he also used as a sketchbook, contains numerous

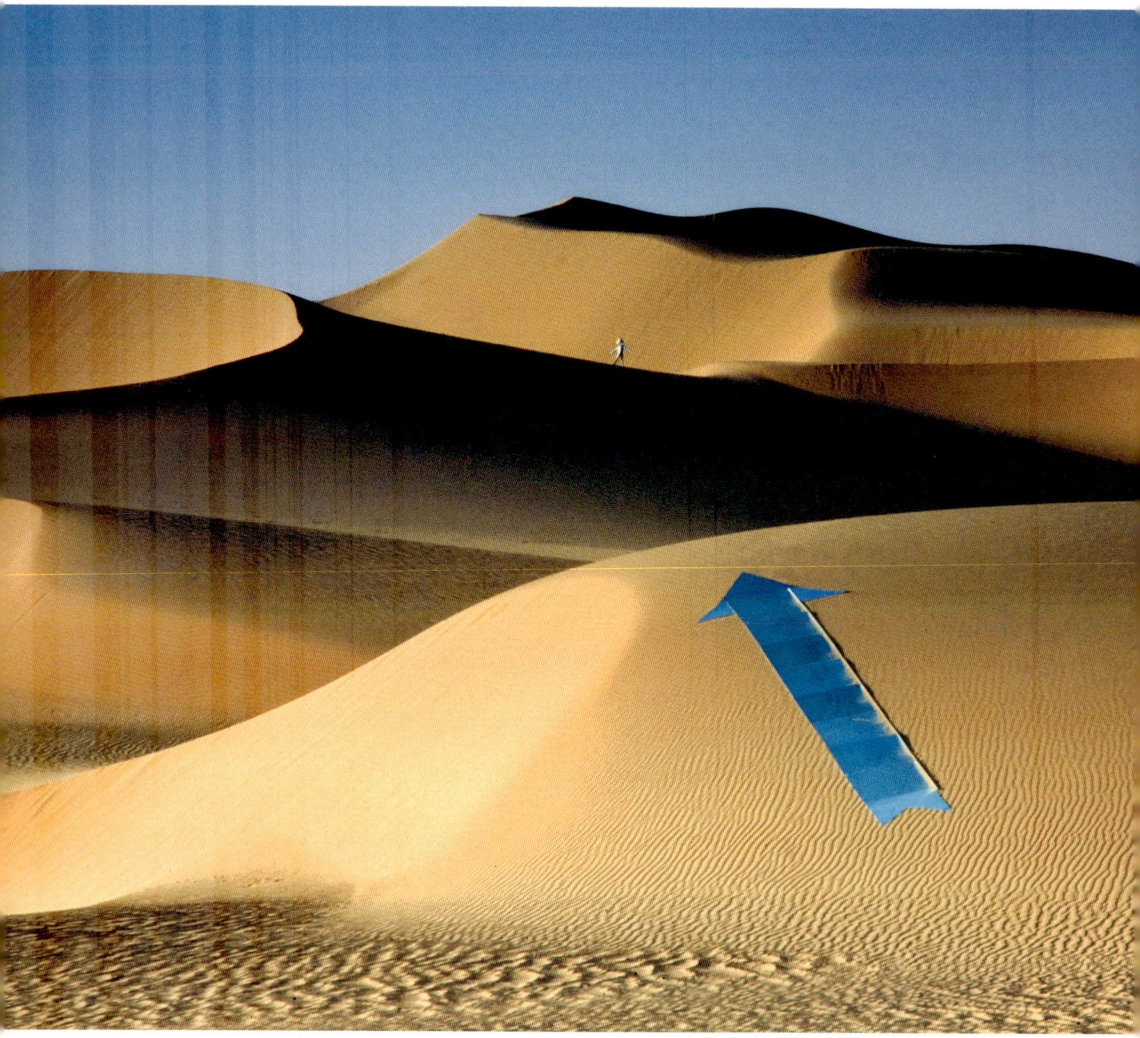

□20
Large Space Arrow in the Grand Erg Occidental
Algeria, 1976

drawings and notes in preparation for the desert tour. One sketch depicts a figure with arms outstretched, its head and hands forming arrow-like triangular shapes. To this, Mack noted: 'Me in the middle: a) silver costume, b) arrows on head and hands.'[205] He also wore his silver suit (cf. fig. 2) in Algeria, since the glowing Sahara sun is reflected by the shiny aluminium fabric. This protected him from the heat and made him visible from afar in the open space of the desert. 'Mack, followed by Höpker in the viewfinder, often runs out into the desert sea for kilometres in his silver suit, climbing laboriously over dune tops, sinking into valleys before our eyes,' Hecht describes. 'Then suddenly he reappears, hardly recognisable as a figure anymore, more like a flashing signal, a walking signpost in a space without paths.'[206]

Mack fitted his head and hands with aluminium reflectors and, in this guise, stood with his legs wide apart and his arms outstretched in the sea of sand – a variation of the Victory pose that he had already adopted on his first visit to the Sahara in 1955. cf. ↖□01 Now the silver artist has become a light catcher, a hunter and adventurer who traps the fleeting light with the help of technical instruments. An eight-metre-long arrow made of stainless-steel sheets, positioned in the endlessness of the sand dunes, points to the silver figure, whose geometric headdress is reminiscent of the figures in Oskar Schlemmer's *Triadic Ballet* (1922).[207] With the *Large Space Arrow*, Mack strove to make the directionlessness of the desert visible, which for him is a space without concrete places or boundaries: 'This creates a topographical fixation and the compass for our imagination – free from the control of the mind.'[208] ←□20

When Mack placed stainless-steel sheets in the sand, he brought the blue of the sky onto the surface of the sand, while the wind moved the sand in abstract shapes on it. The mirrors in the sand were reminiscent of maps on which imaginative seas and continents were drawn. In front of the ruins of an ancient *ksar* (fortified village), Mack laid out a garden of textured aluminium sheets that stood like a futuristic silver architecture in front of the earth-brown remains of the structure. Not far from this former fortress, he installed gleaming aluminium pillars in a jagged structure on the desert floor – a serpent of light reminiscent of a fairy-tale in which the dragon blocks the way to the castle.[209] The ruins of this fortified settlement served as a backdrop for an arrangement of mirrors that broke down the traditional North African architecture into a Cubist fragmentation reminiscent of Pablo Picasso's *Houses on the Hill* (1909).[210] Colours and shapes on the canvas were now replaced by the lights and shadows of nature, directed by Mack to form colours and shapes of light. Light forests and mirror plantations emerged in the sand and gravel deserts, integrating found architecture, rocks, and stones into the *Jardin artificiel.* Rocks and sand belong inseparably together in the Sahara, since the sand is a product of the weathering rock.[211] The artist and his helpers wrapped a huge boulder in shiny aluminium foil, which made the glistening light of the sun visible. This created light compositions and landscapes of fascinating artificiality – they articulated the space of the desert. The artist Mack and the photographer Höpker were equal partners here, planning the 'optical sensations' together.[212] →□22

Among the sketches in Mack's 1976 calendar that were realised in the Algerian Sahara is the *Caravan of Colours,* a thirty-six-metre-long structure made of acrylic glass, the title of which refers to the traditional travelling communities in the desert. The *Caravan of Colours* consists of white, red, yellow, and pink acrylic glass discs, the upper edges of which have a jagged 'saw structure', as Mack noted on the accompanying sketch. The artist planned to place the transparent colour structure 'one behind the other, somewhat uphill' on the dune – 'or to erect a long chain of colours on a flat plane in front of a dune', as this was eventually realised.[213] ↘□23 Film footage taken by Mack's friend Fritz Bagel during the expedition shows the sculpture being installed in the sand.[214] In the case of the *Caravan of Colours,* this results in the unusual situation for the *Sahara Project* that the creation of a work can be traced from the sketch and the 'making-of' to its execution in the desert, documented in the photos by Thomas Höpker. The film footage also shows Mack removing all traces in the sand with a broom before the photo was taken. For Mack's sculptures to look like artefacts in untouched nature, all imprints of their construction had to be obliterated. 'Erase footprints by shallow furrows in the sand!', Mack noted in the sketchbook.[215] In the Western Great Erg, the artist united technology and nature; the art object made of acrylic glass in the desert sand, presented without traces of human intervention, illustrates this dialectic, which is characteristic of Mack's work. Margit Staber remarked that the inspiration for aesthetic objects derived from this tension is 'completely anti-naturalistic and yet a concrete expression of reality'.[216] Thus, the artificial material of the *Caravan* nevertheless blended into the crests of the dune like an organic structure.

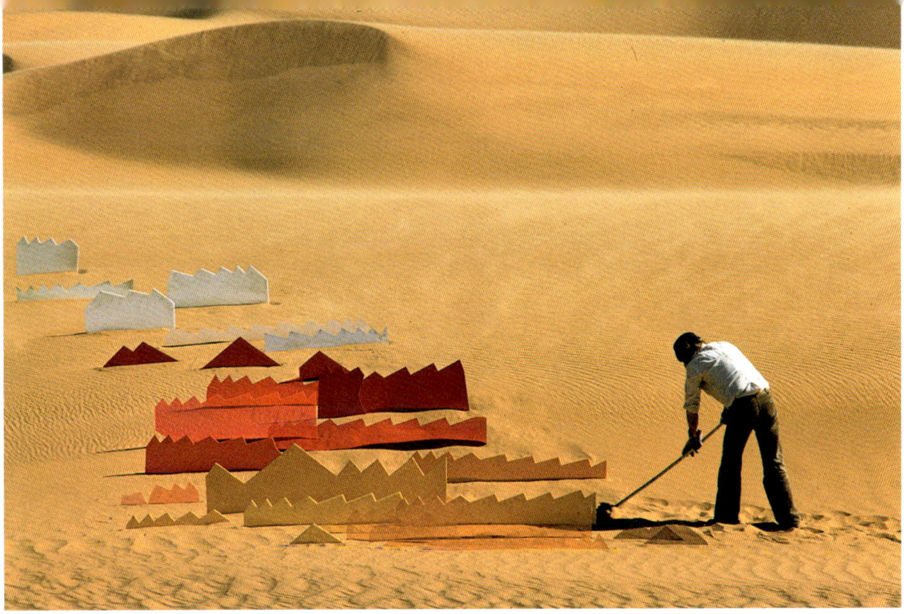

□21
Mack arranges the *Caravan of Colours* in the Grand Erg Occidental
Algeria, 1976

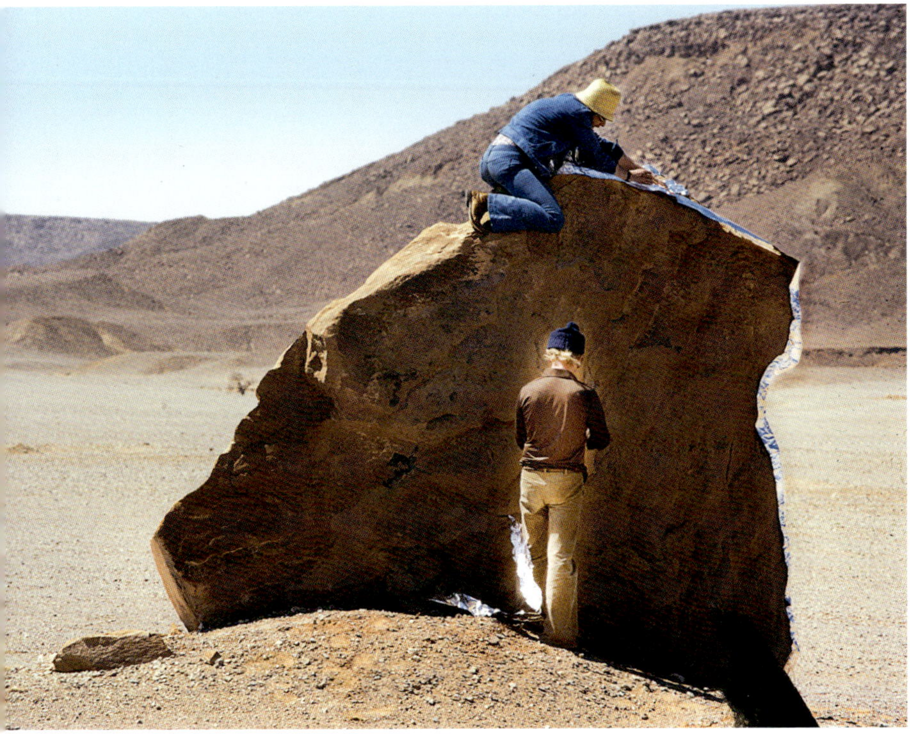

□22
Covering a rock with reflective foil
Algeria, 1976

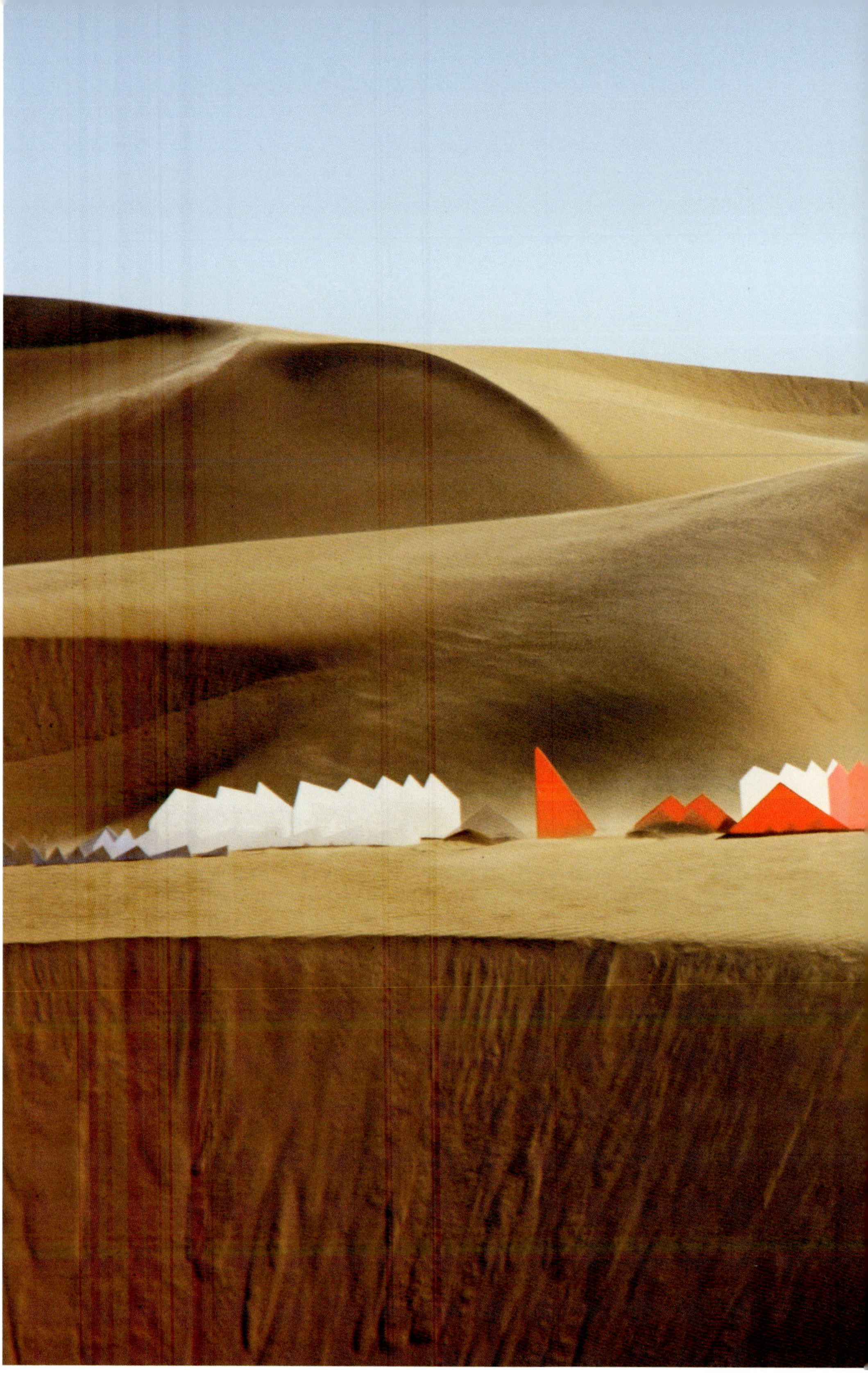

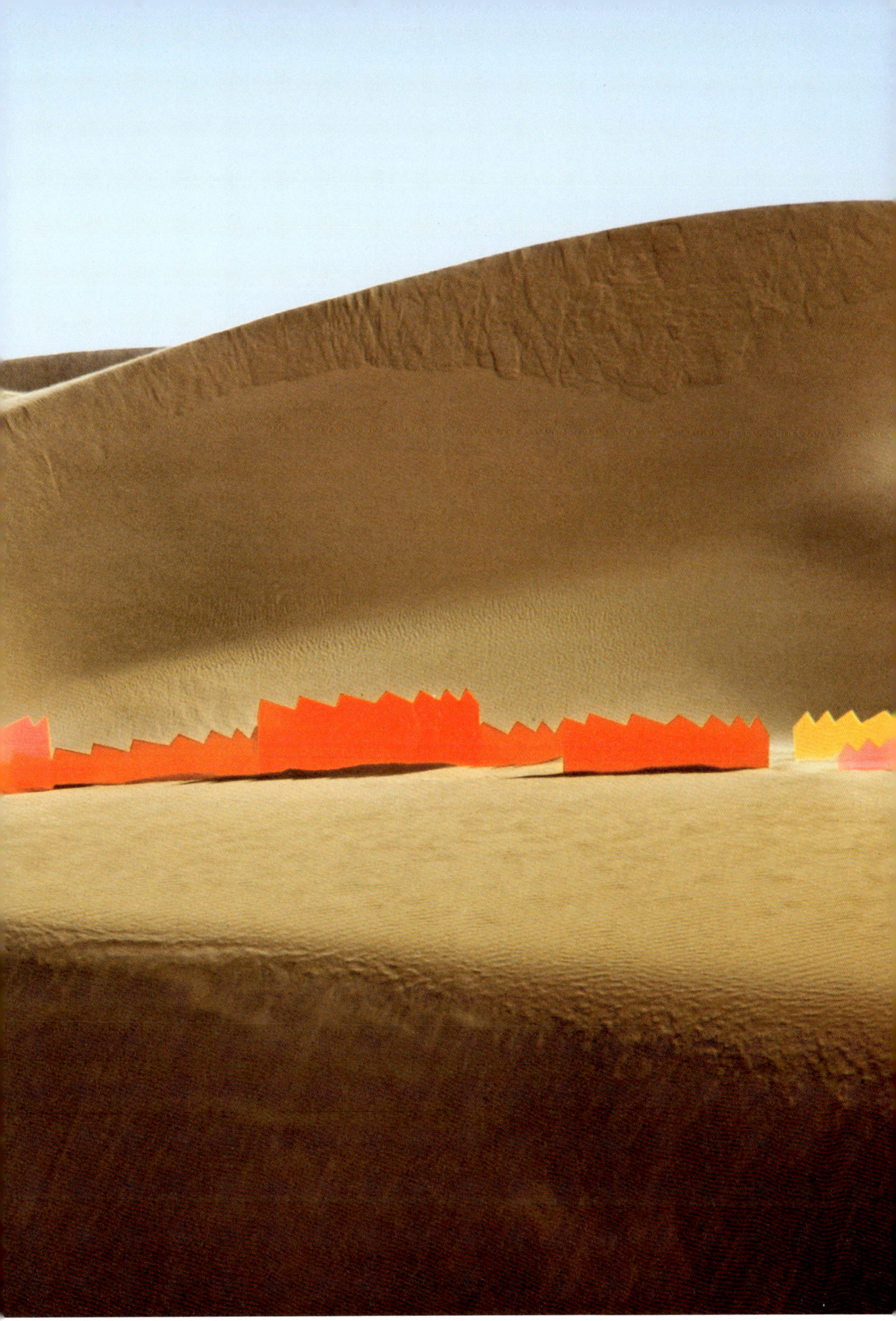

□23
Caravan of Colours
Algeria, 1976

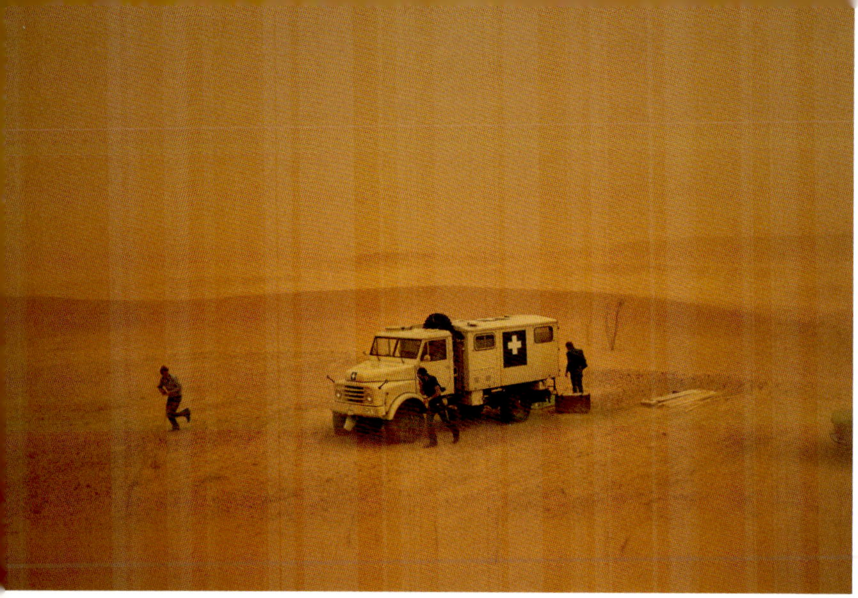

□24
A sandstorm takes the expedition by surprise
Algeria, 1976

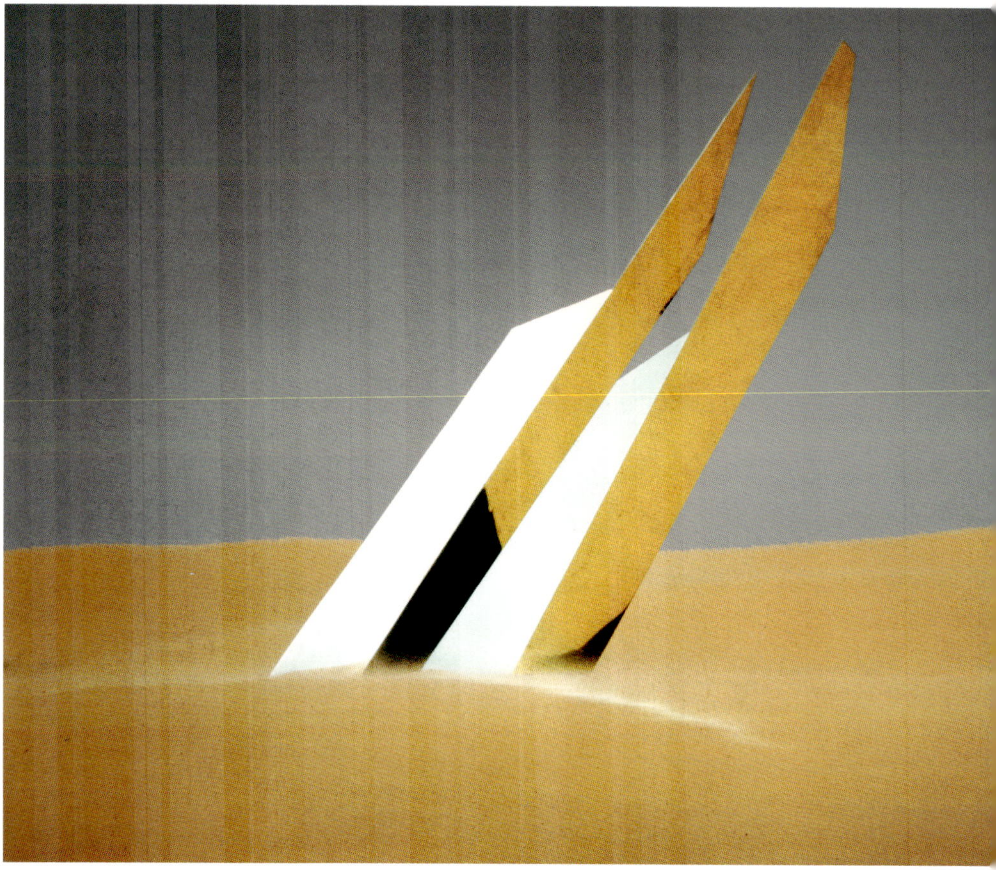

□25
The Saint-Exupéry Crash – Model of a Monument in the Algerian Desert
1976

Fritz Bagel's video also shows the construction of a sculpture made of stainless-steel sheets, the polished surfaces of which caught and amplified the Sahara sun. The metal sheets rose out of the desert sand like the wings of a silver aeroplane. In homage to the French pilot and author whose plane crashed in the Sahara, the sculpture was titled *The Crash of Saint-Exupéry* (1976):[217] 'Finally, a pair of light wings shoots diagonally into the horizon of sand and sky: double wings of a crashed plane? Rocket dynamics? Meteor impact?,' Mack wrote. 'The reality: mirror-polished sheets of stainless steel in the glaring light of the Grand Erg Occidental.'[218] In his book *Terres des hommes* (Wind, Sand, and Stars, 1939), Antoine de Saint-Exupéry describes his flights over the desert, which included a long-distance flight in 1935. Due to a lack of orientation, the pilot was unable to fly to the place planned as a stopover and crashed in the Sahara at night, roughly two hundred kilometres west of Cairo. He survived, but almost died of thirst on the subsequent trek through the desert, until he was saved by Bedouins.[219] As Bagel's film footage shows, a dust storm arose during the construction of the sculpture *The Crash of Saint-Exupéry*, which is why the sculpture had to be quickly dismantled. The view was obscured by flying grains of sand, and the previously blue sky turned brown. During a dust storm, the wind in the Sahara sucks up enormous amounts of dust until the air is so filled with it that the once bright white sun can only be seen as a dull yellow disc. The Sahara researcher Uwe George called these dust storms the 'most breath-taking and at the same time most frightening phenomena in nature': 'Often when the sky is completely clear, they move up the horizon as impenetrable, up to 3,000-metre-high rollers – comparable to clouds at sea. Travellers who experience such a storm for the first time often panic.'[220] ←□24

Mack also remembered the unpleasant experience of 'completely losing one's bearings in the desert'.[221] On numerous desert expeditions, however, he had the opportunity to become accustomed to the rough conditions. Together with Fritz Bagel, Mack undertook numerous tours, including one of the first crossings of the Ténéré desert in the winter of 1974/75. This sandy desert in the southern Sahara, also called the 'desert of deserts', is located in the north of Niger and was crossed by the expedition by car. Twelve participants drove a 1,200-kilometre route from N'Guigmi to Bilma in two special Unimog trucks, each with one-metre ground clearance.[222] 'We had a caravan guide with us who knew the desert,' Bagel recalled. 'Luckily, because GPS didn't exist back then.'[223] For days, they subsisted on dry food and chlorinated water in the hostile Ténéré, where even in the winter temperatures can reach forty degrees during the day, dropping by as much as twenty degrees at night. In the Erg du Ténéré, the participants, many of them scientists, discovered fossils of petrified fish.[224] They date back to the Cretaceous period seventy million years ago, when large areas of North Africa were covered by the Cretaceous Sea. Large parts of the Sahara's stony surface are actually marine deposits from various periods of the Earth's history. Due to the harsh climate of the desert, the sedimentary rocks are eroded, the end product being dust and sand carried away by the wind. This erosion and rearrangement lead to the uncovering of ever deeper, older layers of the Earth's crust and thus also traces of former living beings.[225] When in 1976 the members of the expedition wanted to leave Algeria, which had only gained independence from France in 1962 and subsequently developed into a dictatorship, Mack and Höpker got into trouble. In communist-influenced Algiers, they were taken to prison on suspicion of having planted hostile information in the border area with Tunisia with their mirror experiments. 'I had to very devoutly excuse my emotional protests so that all our footage would not be destroyed,' Mack recalled.[226]

GREENLAND

Fortunately, the film material was preserved and Höpker brought his photos to the editorial office of *Stern*. Back in Hamburg after the Sahara expedition, he showed a selection of his colour slides to the editor-in-chief, Henri Nannen, and the picture editor, Rolf Gillhausen, who was also called the 'head eye of *Stern*'. 'Gillhausen had been a photographer himself and he was very critical,' says Höpker. 'When the lights came back on after the projection, Gillhausen said: "Well, it's quite interesting, but the pictures are all red and brown." Then I had a bright idea and said: "Unfortunately, that's how it is in the desert, but how about we do another trip, for example to the Arctic or the Antarctic; there's a lot of ice and snow, and it's mostly white or blue." "Why not? Then do that," Gillhausen said.'[227] The plan for a second expedition was thus born, this time to Greenland.

Mack had harboured the desire to also realise his *Sahara Project* in the icy wilderness since 1959, when he wrote that 'the preserves of art' would 'rest like artificial islands' even in regions like Antarctica.[228] The opportunity now arose to travel to Greenland to install objects

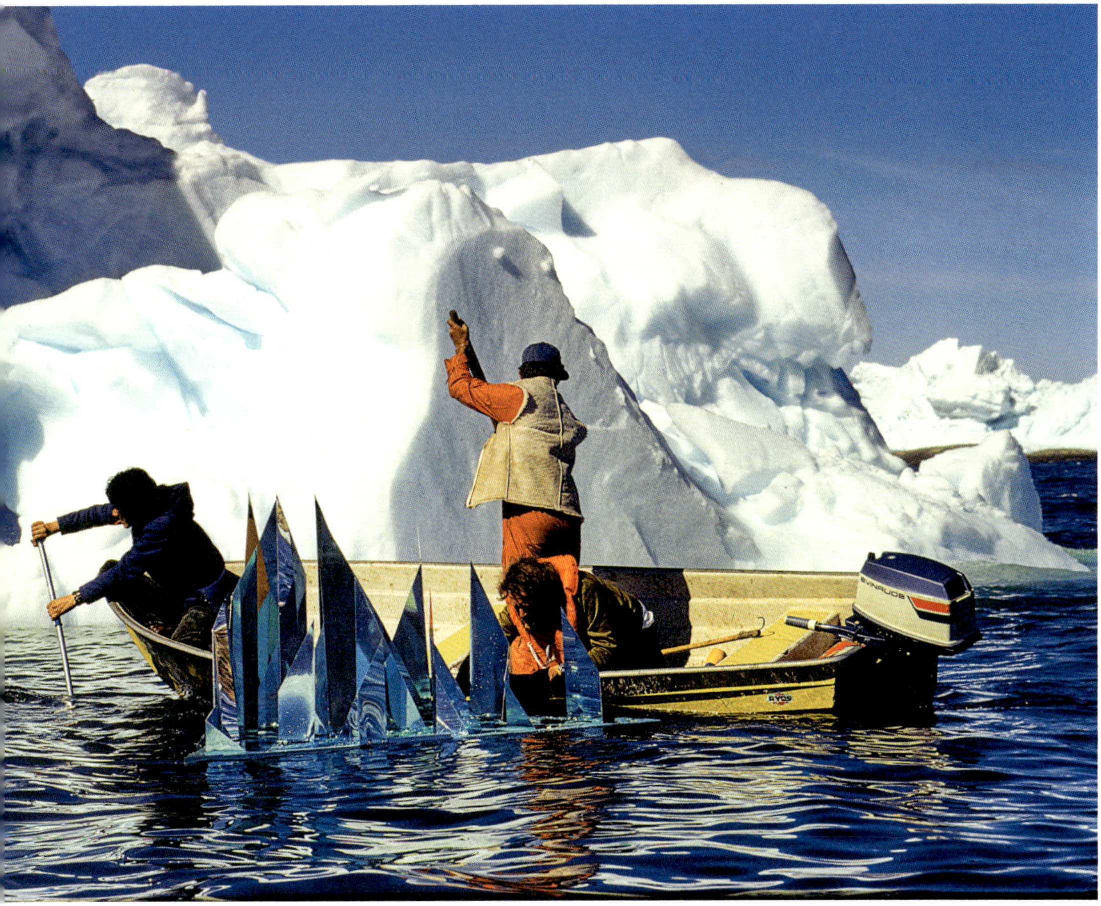

□26
A *Light Sculpture* is lowered into the sea from a fishing boat
Greenland, 1976

from the *Jardin artificiel* in the Arctic Circle. On 25 June 1976, Mack, Höpker, Hecht, and their helpers travelled from Hamburg to Copenhagen, from which they flew to the Greenland base of Kangerlussuaq (Danish: Søndre Strømfjord). There, they took the ship 'Disco', which took two days to reach Ilulissat (Danish: Jakobshavn) on Disko Bay in southwest Greenland. The crates with material had been shipped weeks earlier from Ålborg in Denmark on another freighter.[229]

Greenland is topped by a shield of ice that covers 81 per cent of the total land mass with an average of 2,000 metres of thick inland ice. After Antarctica, it is the most sparsely populated region on Earth.[230] While the differences between polar summer and winter are considerable in the Arctic, daily temperature fluctuations remain minimal. Extreme light conditions are the reason for this: Depending on latitude, the polar day or night lasts for days, weeks, or even months. In the Arctic summer, however, it takes a very long time for the snow to melt, and temperatures only rise significantly for a very short time.[231]

'Artists are border crossers between dream and reality,' says Mack. 'When the artist leaves his safe studio and goes to the Arctic Circle, for example, he enters the reality of a deadly coldness.'[232] Spending time in the icy deserts, as in any desert, is life-threatening for humans, but Mack experienced their unique colourfulness here, which he found to be an inaccessible and melancholic beauty. In this largely achromatic world, the artist noted, the snowy white dominated with its glassy, crystalline, and transparent surface. The sea was almost black but showed an intense turquoise of great luminosity near the ice.[233] 'Day and night are interchangeable here; so, with your eyes open, you dream these wide-awake, melancholy dreams.'[234] In Greenland in the summer of 1976, Mack experienced the Arctic midnight sun for the first time. 'Whether it's an icy wilderness or a sea of dunes, the purity and boundlessness of space is identical,' he told Hecht. 'But the light is melancholic – unlike that of the desert.' The rest of the team thus also initially found the light at the 69th parallel north to be 'mostly dull, cold, and grey'. In the second week of the expedition, the sun finally appeared and bathed the eternal ice in a 'dream light', Hecht recalled.[235] The latter is particularly intense in the Arctic because the ice has a high albedo, i.e. reflectivity, and hardly absorbs any solar radiation.[236]

In Greenland, a fishing boat and crew were hired daily so that the expedition could sail into the Arctic Ocean, but the work was even more arduous than in the Sahara. When the sun finally came out, the team took the boat to the icebergs. During the first experiments, there was the 'dream light' but also strong swell. The boat suddenly had engine trouble, and the participants had to turn back paddling and without having taken any photos. They found a fisherman who took them out again, only to find that clouds were gathering, and they were again unable to photograph. 'Mack is distraught, the others are disappointed,' Hecht reported. It took a while before they could realise their first projects.[237] ↖□23

'Although the conditions are even more difficult, and the frozen environment often threatens to paralyse us, it sets in again – that sensory intoxication to which we have become as addicted as Mack in the meantime,' Hecht recalled. 'When the brightly shimmering solar sails float over the turquoise ice water, when the transparent cubes give structure to the amorphous landscape, then enthusiasm sets in again.'[238] According to Mack, what connects the sandy desert and the icy wilderness is the monochrome colour of their landscape: 'The deserts of sand and ice are the only monochrome landscapes in the world.'[239] Mack had prepared excellently for the white ice of the glaciers, as Thomas Höpker recalled: He had packed 'floating timbers, sails, balloons, and glasses, which he assembled on site and lowered into the cold water.'[240] Mack entrusted surreal-looking structures to the Arctic Ocean, such as a construction of triangular white nylon sheets that floated on the icy water like the sails of a lightship. Pyramid-shaped prisms of brightly polished stainless steel reflected the blue of the sky against the white eternal ice, while the Arctic sun vibrated on their surface, outshining their materiality with glistening light. In Greenland, Mack finally succeeded in articulating the light and space of the Arctic by having his works interact with the elements of Arctic nature – the ice, the water, and the cold blue light. cf. ↖□19

A sculpture comprised of acrylic glass tubes with open tops was placed under the overhang of an iceberg that was melting in the sunshine. With his camera, Höpker documented the fine drops of water falling from the ice mass and into tubes filled with a blue liquid, imitating the colour of the natural environment. ↘□28 All the while, the members of the expedition forgot how dangerous their work was. 'Michael Bienert and Knut Schönburg, who are travelling with us, work with the dinghy under the overhang of a jagged iceberg,' Hecht reported. 'Minutes after they row out of its shadow, the cone, which weighs tons, breaks off and slaps vertically into the water. The sudden waves almost capsize the fishing boat.'[241] Sketches in Mack's calendar depict a cross-shaped sculpture, not unlike the aforementioned cross in the Sahara, consisting of 'empty troughs on the back, the bowls filled with blue water ... supported only by the Styrofoam'.[242] Mack let the *Northern Cross* (1976) float on the dark water as a blue marker.[243] For him, the cross is a sign that the artist has to set in order to bear witness to his sojourn in landscapes that are inhospitable to humans, such as the seas of sand and ice – comparable, for example, to the flags that an explorer such as Roald Amundsen had set when he reached the South Pole. In 1970, Mack had already planned a monument for Robert Falcon Scott, who had tried in vain to be the first to reach the South Pole; this was finally realised in Greenland six years later in 1976. By means of a glass prism, the light of the midnight sun during the Arctic summer was broken up into its spectrum and projected onto the ice, where millions of ice crystals reflected it.[244]

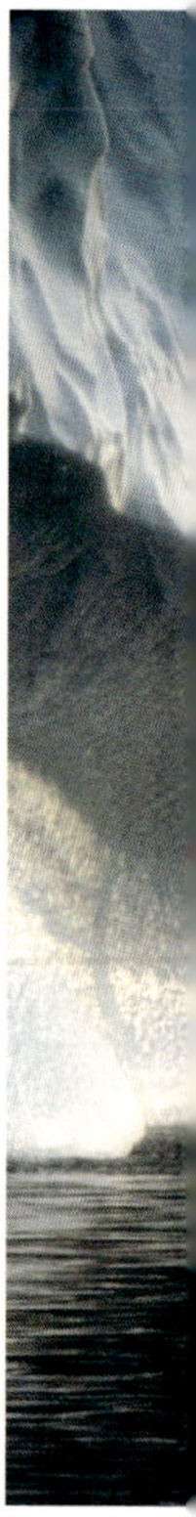

Not only the Arctic Ocean, but also the sky above the icebergs became the setting for the icy *Jardin artificiel*. In reference to the thirteenth station of the *Sahara Project, The Apparitions in the Sky*, Mack released white and red balloons into the sky, carrying coloured and silver nets. →□27 On the one hand, the balloons that were sent into the sky from the boat reflected light but did not produce the expected radiance, because the intensity of sunlight is greatly reduced in Greenland. On the other hand, Mack, who dressed in a red costume on the expedition to be visible from a distance, noticed how strongly the colour red worked in the white landscape. According to Mack, 'the red balloons stood out in the sky like the dots of colour in a painting by Joan Miró.'[245] ↖□09 Mack was also fascinated by the light of the Arctic, which he experienced in the Arctic summer as a 'crossover between day and night'.[246] Here, he wondered when the light would become dark and when it would become bright, how dim it could be without going out completely. Höpker, Mack recalled, was also so fascinated by this light that – tied to the mast of the swaying boat – he was still taking photographs when the last light of dawn had long since called the light sensitivity of the film material into question.[247] In the dusky violet light, Höpker succeeded in taking an impressive photo of the *Fire Raft*, which carried numerous torches across the sea in a grid pattern, their flames corresponding with the twilight of the sky. ↘□30 In its melancholy beauty, this photograph is reminiscent of Gerhard Richter's *Iceberg* from 1982, a photorealistic oil painting depicting the Arctic Ocean in

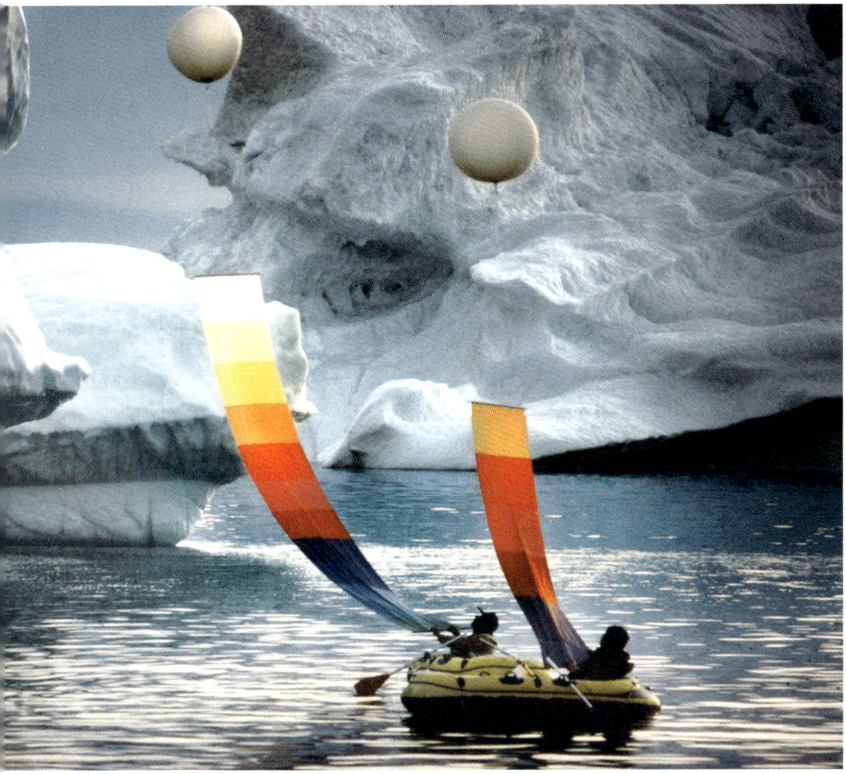

□27
Balloons are released into the sky from a boat
Greenland, 1976

□28
Mack lowers a *Water Sculpture* into the water
Greenland, 1976

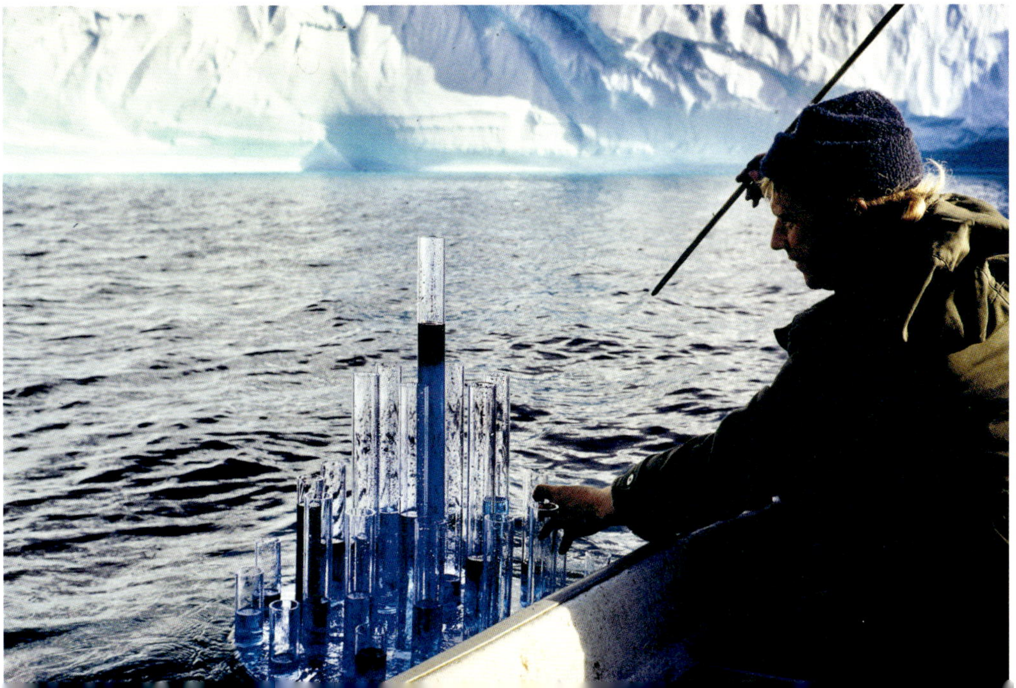

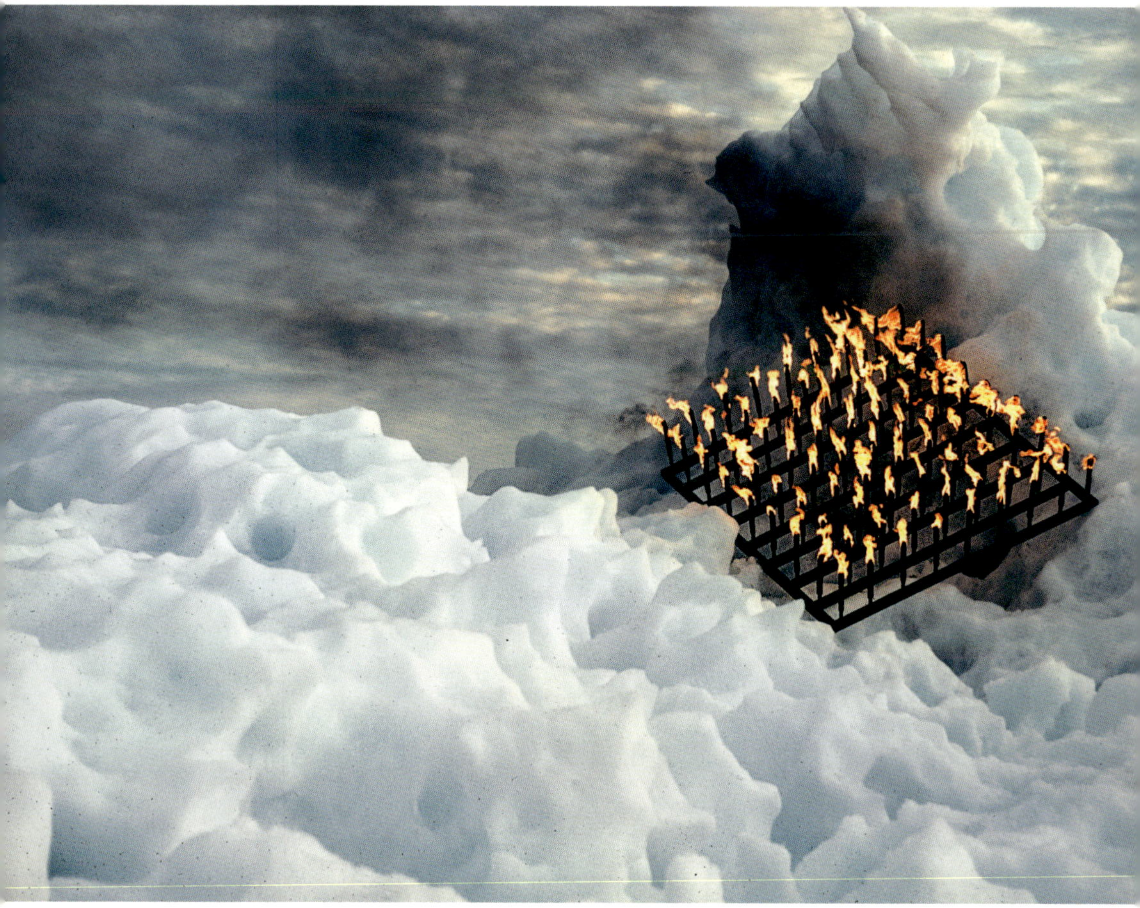

□29
The *Fire Raft* on the iceberg
Greenland, 1976

reddish twilight, the sky reflecting on a smooth surface, with a jagged white-blue iceberg. Photos from a trip to Greenland in 1972 inspired Richter to paint the scenery.[248]

But Mack also installed his *Fire Raft* in a different way. A previously unpublished photo by Höpker depicts the rectangular fire construction placed almost vertically on an iceberg, the soaring flames producing black clouds of smoke. The experiment to create contrasts with fire, however, caused the smoke to virtually pollute the crystal-clear atmosphere. 'That's why we did the fire experiments at night, which in summer only shows a state of twilight,' Mack recalls.[249] ←□29 Here, the artist contrasted the elemental forces of fire and water or ice – while the fire is able to melt the ice, it could, as it were, be extinguished by the water of the sea of ice. The photograph illustrates the destructive forces of the frozen sea in a manner similar to Caspar David Friedrich's painting *The Sea of Ice* from 1823/24, in which a battered ship is wedged between burst masses of ice, its debris protruding between the edges of the ice.[250]

The depiction of the masses of ice as both sublime and inaccessible connects Friedrich with the artists associated with Land Art, who had taken up the abovementioned sublime aspect of the forces of nature presented by German Romantic painters and their American variant, the Hudson River School.[251] Mack's 'Expedition into Artificial Gardens', which celebrated the light, colour, and forms of nature in the organic structures of the *Jardin artificiel*, can also be seen in this tradition. To this, the artist added the aspect of technology, which manifested itself in the material of his artefacts, which consisted of industry-related products such as aluminium, stainless steel, and acrylic glass. A combination of natural elements – sand, wind, fire, ice, snow, and water – as well as physical or optical phenomena – light, shadow, luminous colours – and industrially manufactured materials in art characterises the 'Expedition into Artificial Gardens'.

For their departure, those involved in the expedition took the last possible flight by helicopter from Disko Bay to Greenland's only airport shortly before it was closed for climatic reasons. Mack recalled that there was some panic on board the helicopter because visibility was lost in a violent ice storm, bizarre mountain rocks appeared in front of the glass canopy in a matter of seconds and disappeared again, and the pilot was sweating profusely, while his flight map could no longer help him. Fortunately, the team reached its destination unscathed.[252]

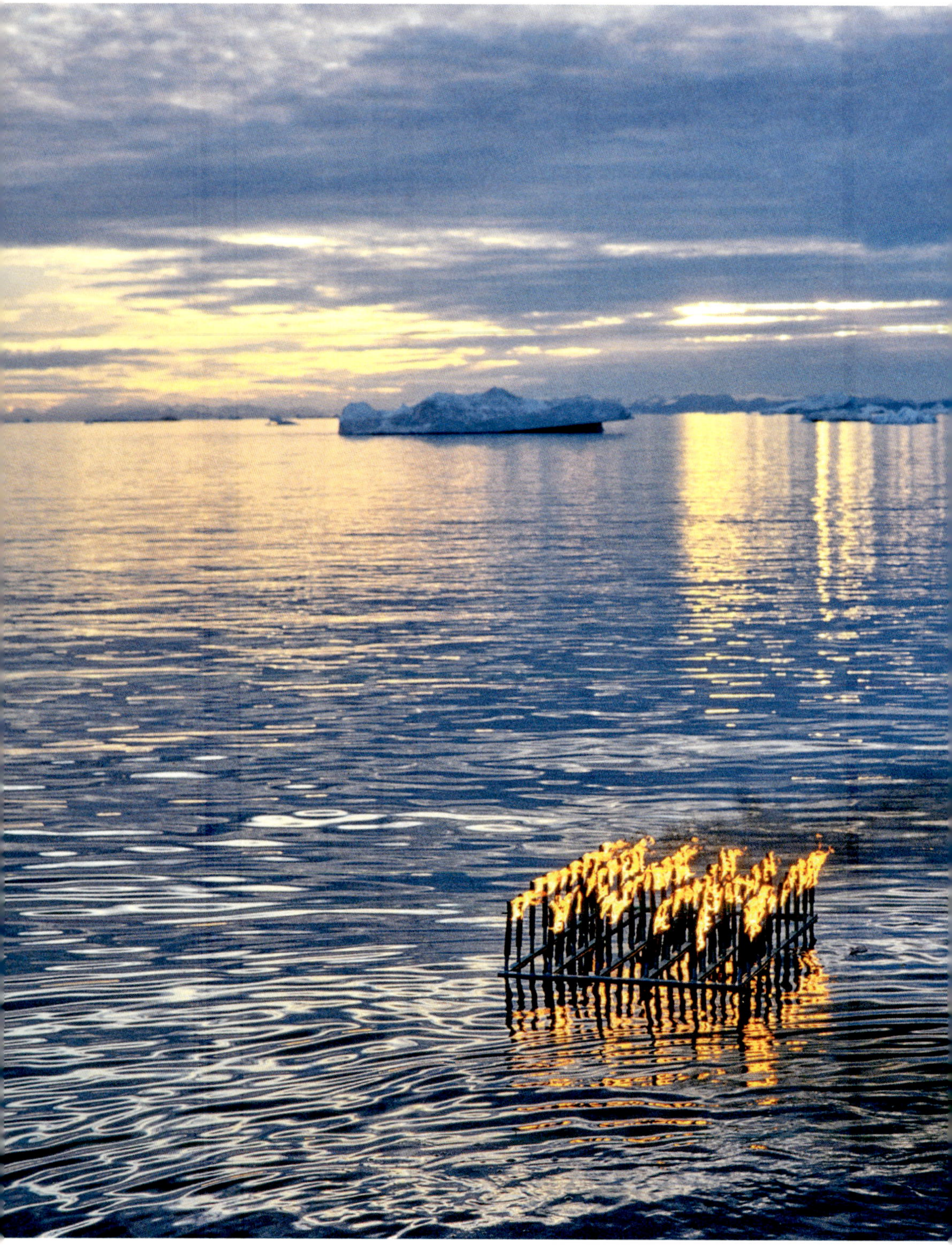

□30
The *Fire Raft* in the Arctic Sea
Greenland, 1976

'The 1976 excursion to the Sahara, as well as to the Arctic, broadened my experience with the material "light",' Mack summed up.[253] Since he was fortunate enough to be accompanied by the photographer Thomas Höpker, there was now – as an unexpected and at once desired result – photographic material from which a book was produced in 1977: *Mack. Expedition in künstliche Gärten. Fotografiert von Thomas Höpker*, edited by Henri Nannen, was published in 1977 by Gruner + Jahr. The large-format, illustrated book contains 148 pages of colour illustrations as well as numerous texts, including Hecht's report from *Stern* and a conversation between Heinz Mack and Dieter Honisch.[254] 'The book, which reports on an unparalleled journey, provides insight into how human activity can hold its own in what is actually an overpowering natural environment,' wrote the newspaper *Hamburger Abendblatt*.[255]

The book was launched at an exhibition at Galerie Brockstedt in Hamburg in April 1977, which featured seventy-two photographs by Höpker, together with *Light Sculptures* by Mack. Hans Theodor Flemming praised the works 'in their bizarre beauty': 'In all the works on view, Mack demonstrates how light and space in both the desert and the Arctic Ocean are so strong that they absorb the technical objects and the art and make them parts of the infinite vastness of nature.'[256] That same year, the exhibition of photographs and *Light Sculptures* was also shown at the Kunsthalle in Darmstadt and the Fotomuseum in the Munich Stadtmuseum. On the occasion of the presentation in Munich, the newspaper *Oberbayerisches Volksblatt* reported that Thomas Höpker had been awarded the 'Golden Eye', as well as Second Prize, for his photographs of the Mack works at the international World Press Photo Contest.[257] In November 1977, the exhibition *Expedition in künstliche Gärten* (Expedition into Artifical Gardens) was presented at the Kunsthalle Düsseldorf, where Mack showed the *Water Cross in the Sand*,[258] as well as *Light Steles* and light-kinetic sculptures. In addition, a photo edition with twenty original, dye-transfer photographs was published, edited by Galerie Photo Selection. It was first exhibited in Düsseldorf and later the Rizzoli Gallery in New York and the Unac gallery in Tokyo. In the fall of 1977, the book was published in an English translation under the title *Sculpture Safaris: Photographic Interpretations of Artifacts in Nature* by Rizzoli International Publications in New York.[259]

THE WAHIBA DESERT

1997

□ 31
Large Stele in the Wahiba desert
Oman, 1997

*Who knows himself and others,
will recognise:
Orient and Occident
Can no longer be separated.*[260]

JOHANN WOLFGANG VON GOETHE, 1819

During the 1970s and 1980s, Heinz Mack travelled extensively in Africa, Asia, and America, mostly in connection with exhibitions and project work. But he also wanted to set out on adventures; he thus visited countries such as Nepal, Sikkim, and Bhutan at a time when tourism was still largely unknown there. In Bhutan, he stayed in the King's guest house in 1979, as there was not yet a single hotel. Over time, the desire also arose to visit the deserts of the Arabian Peninsula to conduct further experiments on the *Jardin artificiel*. The artist dreamed of visiting the Rub' al Khali, the world's largest sand desert, the majority of which belongs to Saudi Arabia. But the country did not allow foreign scientists or tourists to enter the desert – which is by nature extremely dangerous and therefore already impassable for humans. Far less than fifty millimetres of precipitation per year are recorded in the region, which is characterised by a typical dry and hot desert climate. Its dunes reach heights of more than two hundred metres. The foothills of this 780,000-square-kilometre, practically lifeless, pure sand desert, however, reach as far as neighbouring Oman.[261]

Having long harboured the desire to visit the particularly beautiful sand dunes, Mack corresponded in 1997 with the German Embassy in Muscat, the capital of the Sultanate of Oman. The embassy agreed to support the artist by having him send his material in large boxes to its address. In addition, the embassy was able to arrange for a travel companion who had desert experience and language skills – i.e. both English and sufficient Arabic – but was actually Norwegian. Not only financial circumstances prevented Mack from hiring other assistants – his experience in the deserts of Africa had taught him that only the most economical, trusting concentration on a few people enables efficient work under difficult external conditions. 'In short, the more people are involved, the faster misunderstandings and difficulties arise in such special situations,' says Mack. Fortunately, the expedition companion was a strong young man who was able to help him set up his sculptural constructions. A suitable vehicle was also rented.[262]

Mack travelled to Oman in the spring of 1997 and visited the Wahiba desert, the high sand dunes of which extend in a north-south direction over an area of approximately 10,000 square kilometres. Compared to the deserts in Africa, the colours of the sand in the Wahiba Sands (now known as the Sharqiya Sands) are more varied and often form contrasts. In particular, Mack noticed that dark dunes showed the colour of copper or ducat gold, while other dunes radiated light in bright golden tones. He quickly realised that the sand has an extremely small grain size, creating problems for vehicles and making even walking extremely strenuous. The Wahiba Sands are not easy terrain, and even finding one's bearings proves difficult – especially in the south of the desert, where the dunes drift up to ten metres a year. The largely untouched desert, Mack knew, is best approached when all forces and the available working time follow the given climatic conditions both economically and efficiently. And so he set to work again in this terrain that was still unknown to him. Despite the overall extremely low amount of rainfall it had rained heavily beforehand due to the season,

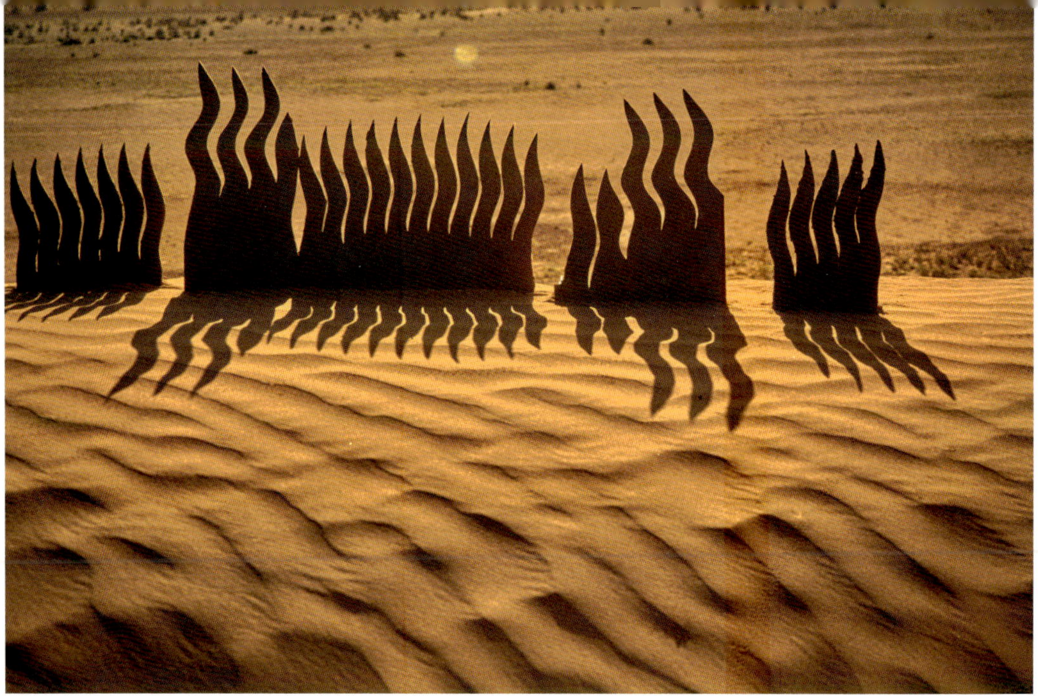

□ 32
Shadow Calligraphy
Wahiba desert, Oman, 1997

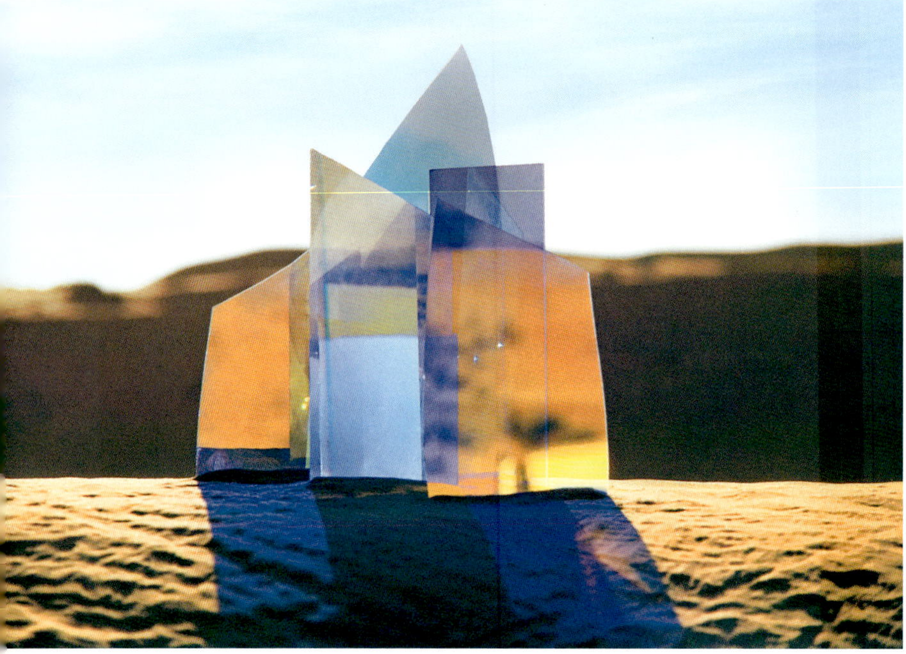

□ 33
Design for a Glass Architectural Structure
Wahiba desert, Oman, 1997

and thin grasses could be seen at the edges of the extensive sand dunes. The proximity of the Wahiba desert to the sea creates increased humidity, and in winter the desert greens up in places. On its edges grow forests of ghaf trees with deep roots, which are frequented by nomads in summer because of their cool shade.[263]

This time, Mack followed the artistic intention of also 'implanting' objects reminiscent of vegetation in the desert. In poetic correspondence to the 'artificial garden', he made linear structures out of wood that rose like grasses from the golden-brown sand. With their slender dynamics, the curved blades of grass suggested movement similar to swaying in the wind. Particularly appealing here was the unexpected effect that the shadows of this structure showed almost the same colour presence as the object itself, creating a certain sense of immateriality. ←□32 The grass structure had been created after a drawing by Mack, who during his studies at the Düsseldorf Academy of Art had made morphological pencil drawings based on nature, which he later developed into abstract, floral-looking ink drawings.[264]

With his travel companion, Mack drove many kilometres into the desert, where the last traces of vegetation disappeared. Mack recalled that it was quite strenuous – both for the vehicle and the driver – to finally reach the desert, which is completely lifeless and consists only of sand. During their expedition, they encountered no more than a dozen nomads. Their children, they could observe, were collected by state-funded vehicles to be educated in the next village, which could be up to a hundred kilometres away. Mack took photos, including one of an old, already fragile pickup truck pulling a young camel behind it on a leash. He wondered where the vehicle came from and where it was going. 'This *coming from nowhere* and *going to an unknown destination* is very puzzling in such situations,' Mack said.[265]

Panes of dichroic glass, concave, mirrored glass plates, lens glass, and structured glass had been shipped to Oman by crate. They were used to create an artificial garden in the Wahiba desert in shapes and colours that had previously been unknown in the desert. The photographs of this expedition, this time taken by the artist himself, depict abstract structures of the highest artificiality made of dichroic glass that changes colour depending on the incidence of light and the viewer's point of view, which is why it is also called 'colour effect glass'. In the approximately one-metre-high *Design for a Glass Architectural Structure* (1968-1997), we find the colours of the desert: the blue of the sky and the gold of the sand, as well as nuances of green and orange light colours, which the glass structure reflects back into the space. ↖□33 Since 1991, Mack had returned to pure colour in his painting as well. He understands 'colour as light and light as colour', which he tries to capture and shape in his *Chromatic Constellations.* ↘□44 For him, colour intensity also always correlates with light intensity, which spreads out as a colour spectrum. 'Colours are energy fields, levels of vibrancy, irrational pictorial space,' Mack explains.[266] It was in this sense that, in 1997, he brought the colours of the light spectrum into the desert in the form of glass architectural structures.

'We built the large light stele ourselves – similar to the construction in the Sahara,' Mack recalled.[267] The *Large Stele* in the Wahiba desert consisted of twenty-one aluminium reflectors and, at fourteen metres, was even higher than the stele in the Sahara in 1968. ↖□31 It was braced and held in place by thin nylon ropes – fortunately, the artist and his assistant were able to work during a calm. They positioned the stele on the crest of a high sand dune and waited for dusk to take the perfect photograph. During the sunset, which lasts only a few minutes in the desert, Mack was able to photographically capture a completely distinctive, uniquely beautiful light phenomenon. The setting sun was found again in each of the twenty-one reflectors, multiplied many times as a red ball of light as the sky and sand turned red. 'The light column growing towards the sky, illuminated by the glistening sun of the desert, leading upwards as a flickering, vibrating, and dematerialised vertical movement in a flowing rhythm, is truly a worthy continuation of Brâncuși's idea of the *Endless Column,*' Uwe Rüth judged. Rarely has a photograph been able to reproduce a work as convincingly as the photograph of the *Large Stele* from 1997 standing in the red evening light of the Wahiba desert. 'Only those who have seen this light for themselves have an idea of the uniqueness, the fascination of the sensual experience of having seen this work there.'[268]

TRANSIT BETWEEN OCCIDENT AND ORIENT ONE ASPECT OF THE ARTIST'S WORK

The vegetation of the *Jardin artificiel* in the Wahiba desert included a pyramid-shaped structure of golden squares positioned on the slope of a sand dune, where it shone in the sunlight to such an extent that parts of its surface appeared completely dematerialised. ↘□34 The golden ornamentation that comprised the triangular construction revealed a structural principle that is not to be confused with decoration. Because of this association, the ornamental is often misunderstood in the new Western art tradition and plays a rather controversial role. However, understood as a structural pictorial device, the ornament pervades numerous phases and aspects of Mack's oeuvre. At the same time, it represents an inner connection to artistic traditions of the Orient, which here refers primarily the Middle East. Mack admires the ornaments of Islamic art and consciously uses them in his work as a concept of order, the free application of which transforms static patterns into virtual movement.[269] Mack applied this principle in his sculpture in the desert as well as in the *Chromatic Constellations*. Museum exhibitions in Tehran, Berlin, Istanbul, and Dakar have already addressed Mack's inner relationship to Islamic art by demonstrating the connection between Orient and Occident in his work.[270]

The dialogue between Oriental and Occidental art traditions is an explicit concern of the artist, resulting among other things from his intensive engagement with Johann Wolfgang von Goethe. Goethe's *West-östlicher Divan* (West–Eastern Diwan), a homage to the fourteenth-century Persian poet Hafez published in 1819, inspired Mack to pursue a special project:[271] In 1999, on the occasion of Goethe's 250th birthday, a special bibliophile edition of the *West-östlicher Divan* was published, in which Mack approached the pictorial traditions of the Middle East with his colourful pastels and ink drawings. The works on paper are not to be understood as illustrations to the *Divan*, but rather as an artist's 'declaration of love' to Goethe's poetry.[272]

'For half a century, I have repeatedly encountered oriental culture, the influence of which I could not and did not want to escape,' Mack recalled. In addition to this creative transfer of ideas, however, elective and visual affinities also arose that surprised him – that is to say, they appeared as if by chance. 'It's precisely this that fascinates me,' says Mack.[273] A pastel from 1998 depicts an ornamental structure of geometric pictorial elements that enters into a clear relationship with the ornaments of Islamic art. ↘□35 Here, as in the golden pyramid with the ornamental grid structure that Mack positioned two years later in the sands of the Wahiba desert, this coincidental visual affinity reveals itself.

After the expedition was completed, the artist's materials that had been shipped to Oman were disposed of there. Mack, however, took a souvenir from his trip of a different kind when he filled a bucket with

□34
Golden Pyramid in the Desert Sand
Oman, 1997

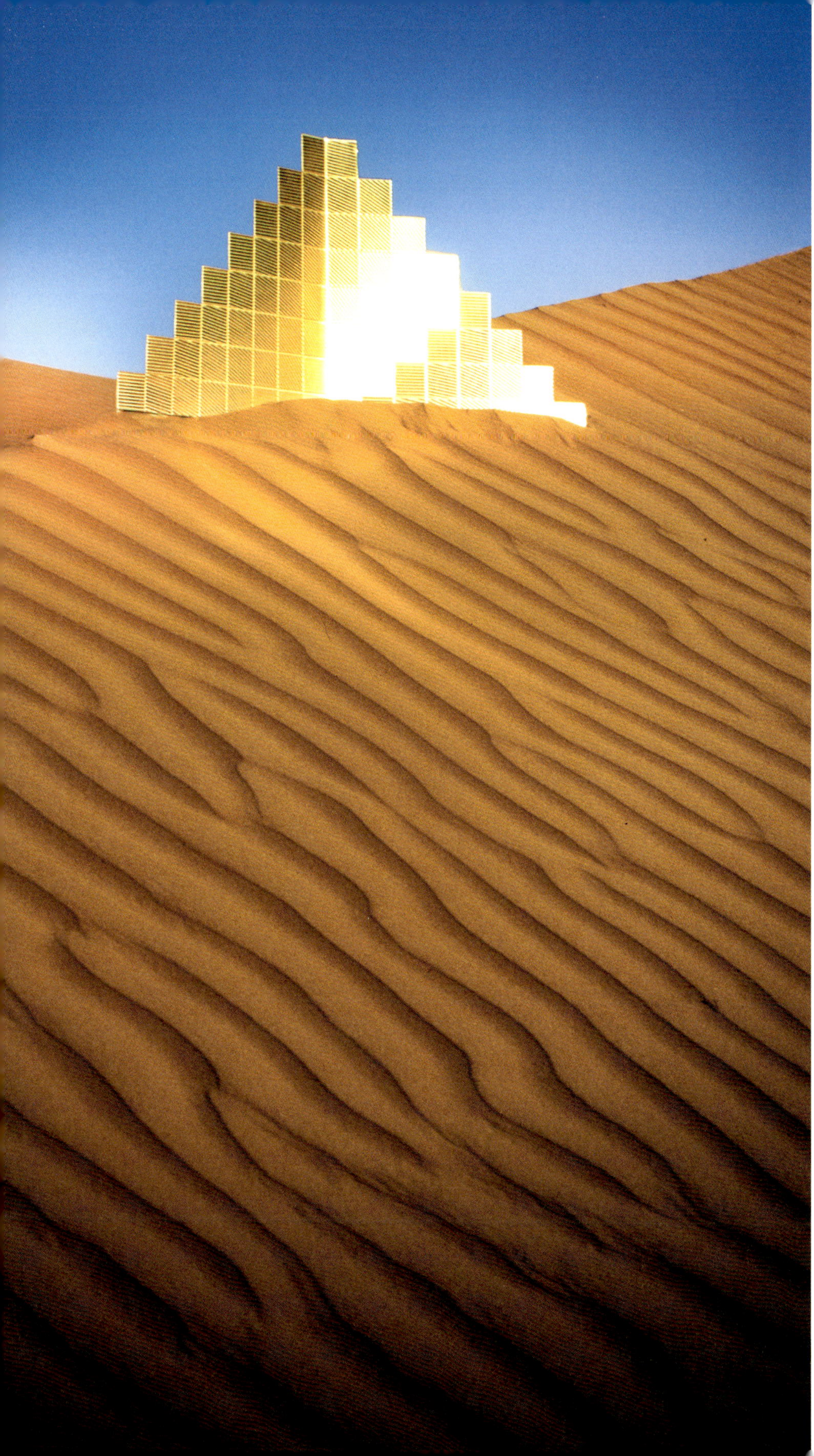

desert sand and had it sent to Germany. 'I don't think anyone in the world has ever done that except me,' says the artist.[274] He later used this material to make his *Sand Reliefs*, which clearly show how fine-grained the sand is, similar to the material in an hourglass.[275] This was the end of Heinz Mack's hitherto last artistic expedition to the desert. He had also visited many other deserts in his life, for example the Namib in Southwest Africa and the Gobi in Mongolia. In the process, he developed further ideas that he fears he will probably no longer be able to realise due to his advanced age.[276]

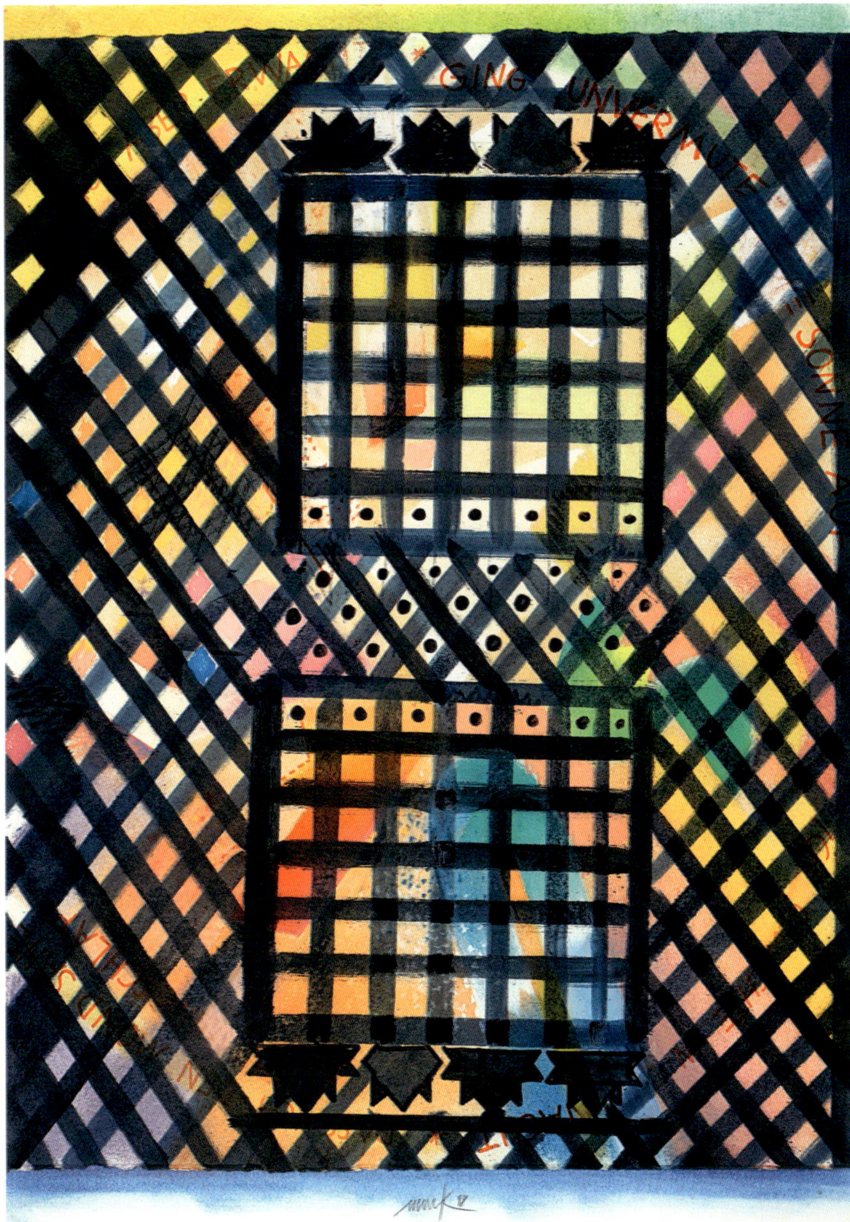

□35
Untitled (from the suite of pictures to the *West-Eastern Divan* by Johann Wolfgang v. Goethe)
1998

THE ELEMENTS IN THE JARDIN ARTIFICIEL – ASPECTS OF (IM-) MATERIALITY

□ 36
2nd Hommage à Georges de La Tour
Galerie Schmela, Düsseldorf, 1965

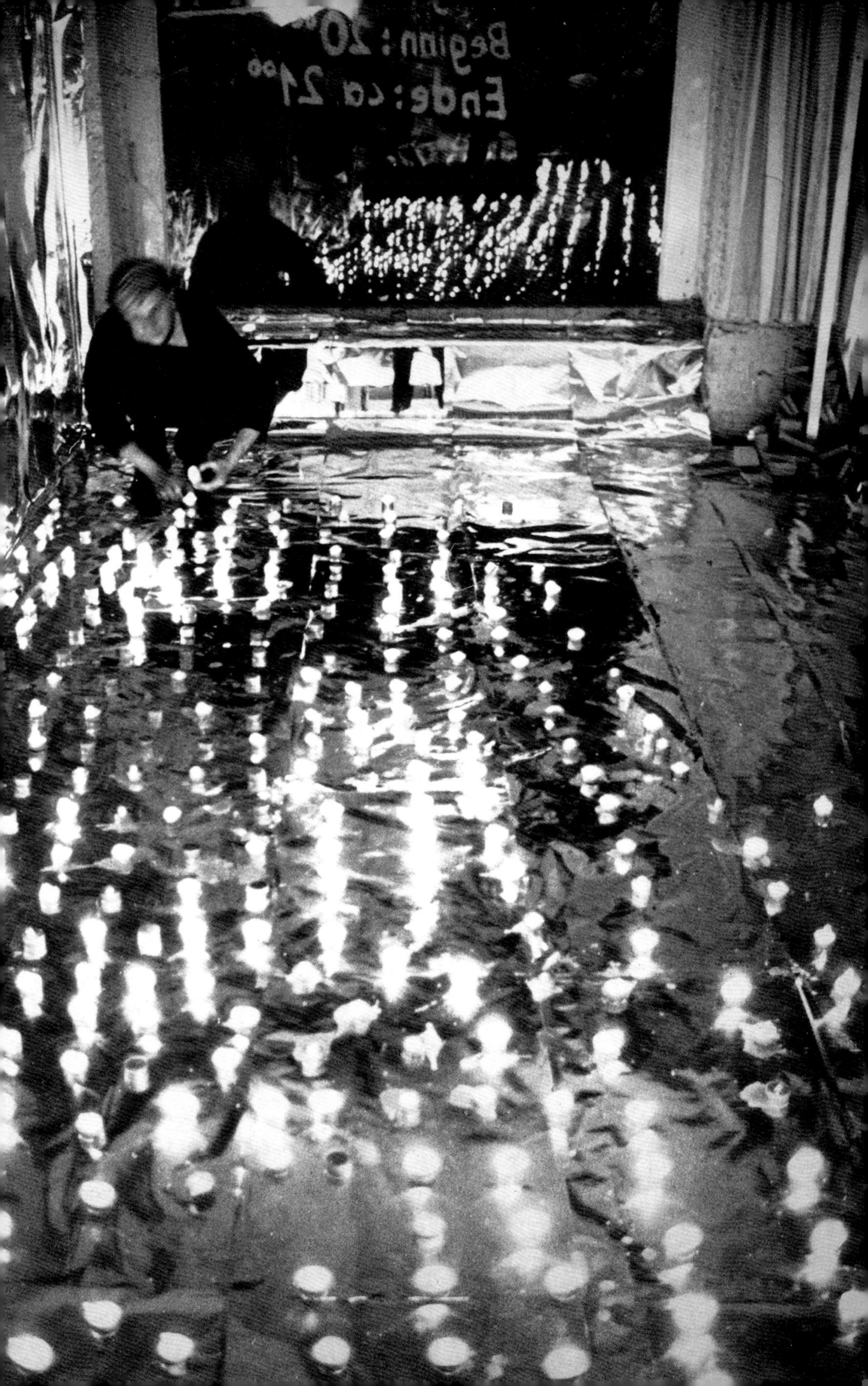
Beginn: 20
Ende: ca. 21^{00}

Although it may seem that I have devoted my work exclusively to light, I must explain that my sole intention has always been, and still is, to make objects, the mode of appearance of which is immaterial; for this I use – above all others – light and movement.[277]

Heinz Mack, 1966

The ZERO artists came to the fore through their use of 'innovative, non-art materials', such as polished metal foil, aluminium nets, mirrors, optical lenses, and acrylic glass.[278] By using these reflective, distorting, or transparent materials, Mack strives for a dematerialisation of his works. On the surfaces of reliefs, rotors, and steles, light gathers and exponentiates itself and is reflected back into the space with increased intensity. In this context, Ulrike Schmitt emphasises the interaction between the work and the viewer and characterises immateriality as 'an aesthetic sensation that arises at the moment of viewing ... which emerges from a conflation of the gaze and the surface of the work and demonstrates to the viewer that his or her perception becomes the determining factor in the creation of the image'.[279]

Furthermore, Mack and his contemporaries used unstable and volatile substances and phenomena such as fire, smoke, ice, water, mist, wind, and light, which equally contributed to the dematerialisation of the works.[280] In their efforts to harmonise the relationship between humans and nature, the ZERO artists declared the four elements to be the tools of their art.[281] They illustrated this intention in volume 3 of the publication *ZERO*, the first pages of which depict images of the stars in the nocturnal sky, the sun behind a veil of clouds, the surface of the sea with reflections of sunlight, a closed blanket of snow, and sand dunes in the desert.[282] Mack, Piene, Uecker, and their artist friends sought to touch on the entire cosmos, as their works, texts, and projects clearly demonstrate.

However, as with the topos of the desert, the reference to the four elements is also part of a long tradition. After semi-mythological beginnings, the classical elements were scientised in Greek antiquity and remained a foundation of philosophical-scientific thought for roughly two thousand years. The transition from myth to science was initiated in the fifth century BCE by Empedocles with his two-part doctrinal poem *On Nature*. Here, the four-part matrix of the elements was established, with Empedocles associating them with the gods Zeus (fire), Hera (earth), Aidoneus (air), and Nestis (water). He did not yet use the term 'elements' but instead called them 'root forces' (*rhizōmata*).[283] In the fifth and fourth centuries BCE, the four elements were scientised by Plato and Aristotle. In the dialogue *Timaeus* (c. 360 BCE), Plato introduced the concept of the elements and assigned them to the geometric 'primordial bodies'.[284] In his treatises *De caelo* (On the Heavens, c. 350 BCE) and *De generatione et corruptione* (On Generation and Perishing, c. 350 BCE), Aristotle dealt with the physics of the elements and combined these with the specific qualities of warm/cold and moist/dry.[285] In addition, he introduced 'aether' as a fifth element, also known as 'divine matter'. He described this *quinta essentia* as the eternal sphere of the cosmos, which could also be light or a light-bearer. In *De anima* (On the Soul, c. 350 BCE), he described light as translucent *energeia*, characterising it as immaterial substance. In his *Metamorphoses* (first century CE), Ovid also described aether as a layer of pure immateriality that encompassed the Earth.[286] Since light plays a key role in Heinz Mack's *Sahara Project*, it is also treated here as the 'fifth element'. As already described, the *Sahara Project* contains many proposals for the integration of the elements. They are closely related to the elemental (im)materiality of the ZERO period and beyond.[287] Other related works and projects are now presented in relation to the four or rather five elements.

In Christian iconography, the Earth is symbolised as a nurturing mother, often affirmed in her representation with a lactating breast. As an allegory of the *natura lactans*, the Earth stands for fertility, which is why fruits and grain are among its attributes.[288] However, numerous artists of the twentieth century consciously distanced themselves from traditional pictorial traditions when they discovered soil or sand as artistic materials. Instead of depicting the elements, they were now used as a material for artistic design. The first work in which Heinz Mack integrated the element earth was *Marking of the Earth* (1960), the abovementioned relief of soil and lime on a ploughed field. cf. ↖□10 But even earlier than soil, he had integrated sand into his artworks. Since his first journeys to Africa, he had produced *Sand Reliefs* as sculptural works of art in his studio, some of them from real Sahara sand that he had brought back with him from his expeditions. One of the earliest *Sand Reliefs* was thus created in 1956/57 after the artist had returned from his first trip to North Africa. →□37 In this case, the Sahara sand was applied with gold-bronze onto cardboard, formed into 'square enclosures that appear to wind down into unfathomable depths'.[289] In its labyrinthine structure, the work anticipates the fourth station of the *Sahara Project*, in which the *Sand Reliefs* are described as 'labyrinths of wind carrying sand through the air'.[290] Mack's oeuvre contains numerous reliefs made of sand with a serially structured surface, the sand-coloured, at times golden monochrome surface of which is only interrupted by the grid structure of the pictorial ground.

Other *Sand Reliefs* by Mack are combined with objects, such as the *Sahara Relief with Mirror* from 1959 and *The Temperature of Sand* from 1964, which also includes a thermometer made of acrylic glass.[291] Here, one finds cross-connections to the technique of assemblage propagated by Jean Dubuffet, which – building on the technique of collage deployed by the Cubists – was picked up on by Pop artists in the 1950s and further developed since 1960 by representatives of Nouveau réalisme. The exhibition *The Art of Assemblage*, curated by William C. Seitz, took place at The Museum of Modern Art in New York in 1961, and included artists associated with ZERO, such as Arman and Daniel Spoerri.[292] Robert Rauschenberg presented his *Combine Paintings* from the late 1950s here. At the beginning of the decade, he had already produced *Growing Paintings*, which not only consisted of soil and dirt, but were in a state of constant change or 'vegetation'.[293]

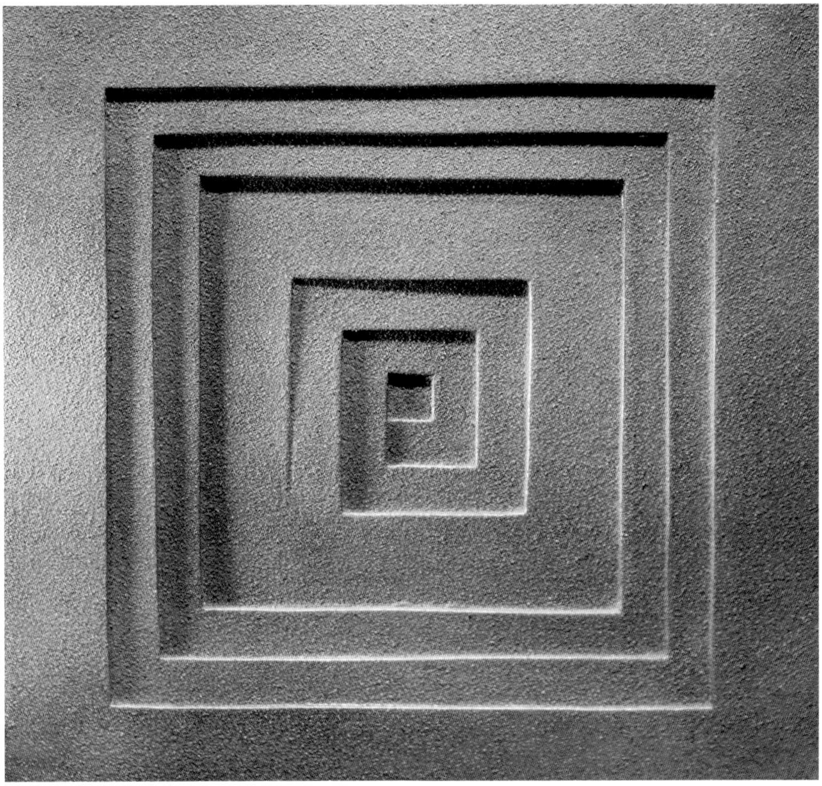

□37
Sand Relief
1956/57

□38
Model for a Sand Wedge in the Desert
1970

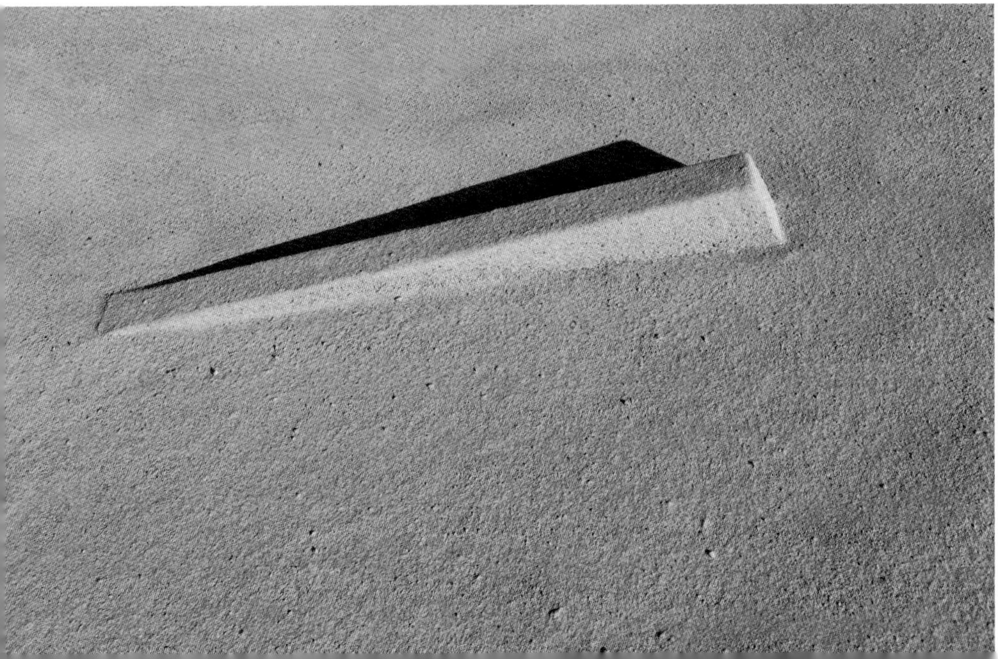

Mack used sand as a material in paintings, prints, reliefs, and sculptures. The *Model for a Sand Wedge in the Desert* from 1970 represents a proposal for a monumental project. ↖□38 The artist planned to place a sculptural wedge-shape made of a durable material in the desert so that the sand moved by the wind would find resistance and form an artificial dune. The model resembles Isamu Noguchi's *Memorial to Man – Sculpture to Be Seen from Mars* (1947), which is considered one of the earliest drafts for a landscape sculpture in the desert. The nose of the 'primitive' face of sand, reminiscent of Mack's *Sand Wedge* (1970) in its elongated wedge shape, was to be one mile long. Noguchi, who is considered a pioneer of Land Art, had already drawn up plans for a monumental pyramid in the desert as early as 1930.[294]

Whereas Mack's *Sahara Project* is largely tied to the African continent, his American colleagues saw their work as part of a different tradition. As early as the 1940s, Abstract Expressionist painters had become enthusiastic about indigenous cultures and myths of North America. The exhibition *Indian Art of the United States*, which took place at The Museum of Modern Art in 1941, inspired many artists in the United States, including Jackson Pollock. The term 'action painting', coined by the New York-based art critic Harold Rosenberg, is associated with the painter and his specific technique of dripping.[295] Pollock thus worked in dynamic movements from all sides on canvases laid out on the floor, on which he dripped and splashed paint. The artist himself described his painting method as 'akin to the method of the Indian sand painters of the West'.[296] The Navajo also painted their sand pictures from many sides and designed these for a frontal rather than a horizontal view. With this reference, Pollock set himself apart from the European art tradition.[297]

In the 1960s, the prehistoric Nazca Lines, which Maria Reiche had surveyed and studied in the Nazca region in Peru, became popular in the United States. These 'geoglyphs', which stretch across an extensive desert area, depict – viewed from a bird's eye perspective – large-scale representations of animals and geometric structures. They were only (re)discovered in 1939, after aircraft first crossed the area in the Pampa San José northwest of Nazca. Although the prehistoric earth lines had been explored since the 1940s, it was not until the 1960s that a wider public, including Mack, began to take an interest in them.[298] It is against this backdrop that the term 'earthworks' emerged in the context of American Land Art or Earth Art as a designation for works made of

Earth-bound materials such as soil, sand, stones, turf, or wood.[299] In 1966, Robert Smithson created his first earthwork titled *Tar Pool and Gravel Pit*, which was intended to evoke the 'primal ooze'.[300] The artist poured tar into a square basin surrounded by another square basin of coarse gravel. The molten substance cooled and flattened into a sticky, flat deposit. Smithson said of the work that this 'carbonaceous sediment' reminded him of 'a tertiary world of petroleum, asphalts, ozokerite, and bituminous agglomerations'.[301] In her detailed chronology *Six Years: The Dematerialization of the Art Object from 1966 to 1972*, Lucy Lippard describes the 'dematerialisation' of art from 1966 onwards using the example of numerous artworks, projects, and texts from the fields of Minimal and Earth Art, Process and Conceptual Art. In her concentration on artists from the English-speaking world, however, she overlooked most of the protagonists of the ZERO movement, whose work had already pursued the quest for a dematerialisation of art before 1966.[302]

A groundbreaking exhibition for Land Art took place at Cornell University in Ithaca, New York, in early 1969. Titled *Earth Art*, the exhibition presented works by American and European artists in the galleries of the Andrew Dickson White Museum of Art, as well as on the university campus. The curator, Willoughby Sharp, purported 'that each artist in the show had to touch dirt' – that is to say, that each work exhibited stood in relation to soil or 'dirt'.[303] In the accompanying catalogue, he wrote about sources of origin and inspiration for earthworks, citing, among others, the works by Pollock mentioned above. It is worthy to note that Sharp also referred to Mack's *Sahara Project* as a pioneering work of Earth Art. He described it as an 'art reserve' aimed at sculpturally activating an extensive land mass. Despite the extremely diverse origins of Earth Art, various sculptural concerns are largely common among the 'earth artists', Sharp wrote, including the complete absence of anthropomorphism and a pervasive notion of the natural order of reality – a feature, incidentally, also inherent in the stations of the *Sahara Project*. A further common aspect, Sharp pointed out, is that all the works are without pedestals, grounded in their surroundings, be these indoors or outdoors.[304]

Günther Uecker was the only ZERO artist invited to participate in the *Earth Art* exhibition. In Ithaca, he presented a variation of his *Sand Mill*. In a smaller gallery, he installed a construction with two steel wings on a constantly rotating axle. Roughly 1,300 kilograms of white sand were poured over it and spread out throughout the space.

Whereas the sand hid the axle and its drive unit, the pointed ends of the steel wings remained visible. They rotated in the centre of the mound of sand, which was thus in a state of constant motion.[305] Sharp recalled that some of the American artists had initially been against Uecker's participation. Smithson, De Maria, and Heizer, for example, had pressured him at the beginning of the exhibition not to invite European artists: 'They wanted "Earth Art" to be an American thing ... *their* thing.' But Sharp did not heed their pleas and showed Uecker's work.[306]

The American 'Earth artists' were keen to declare Earth or Land Art as their own invention. Later, they often realised their projects in the deserts of North America, for example Smithson in Utah (*Spiral Jetty*, 1970) and De Maria in New Mexico (*Lightning Field*, 1977). Such interventions in the landscape were thus in the geographical and historical context of, for example, Navajo sand painting and the prehistoric Nazca Lines in Peru. In contrast, the desert projects by European artists after World War II[307] arose from the desire, especially in Mack's case, to break out of the densely populated cities destroyed by the war and find an emptiness and vastness of immense proportions in the Sahara.

FIRE, SMOKE, DESTRUCTION

In addition to earth and sand, fire is another element that was important for both the *Sahara Project* and the art of the 1960s and 1970s. The artists integrated fire into their works in its positive and negative dimensions: warmth and light, as well as smoke and destruction. On the one hand, fire is associated with the destructive power of wildfires and volcanic eruptions and, in a religious sense, with purgatory and the embers of Hell. On the other hand, the element stands for the light of the sun as the 'lamp of life', as well as for the warming hearth and forge fire.[308]

In the *Sahara Project*, there are numerous proposals for integrating fire into the *Jardin artificiel*: 'grids of rising columns of smoke and fire', 'catapults of light', and artificial suns.[309] Fire is so important within Mack's oeuvre that it claims its own chapter in the first catalogue raisonné of sculptures. Dieter Honisch emphasises here that Mack combined the element into large light ensembles in fireworks, fire ships, and light spirals.[310] As early as 1958, the artist used fire for the work *Black Light in Relief*. Here, the black colour of a charred piece of corrugated cardboard stands in the centre of a panel of black chipboard. The 'black light' in this relief is fire as an ambiguous source of both light and destruction.[311] From 1959 onwards, Otto Piene also created his *Smoke Drawings*, for which he 'sieved' the smoke from a candle or paraffin lamp onto the paper through grids. The smoke smouldering through the holes left a dot-like structure on the surface.[312] Furthermore, Piene also developed a technique of gelling the paint on the canvas with the help of fire. His *Fire Paintings* show the crusts and bubbles that the heat left on the canvas.[313] And Yves Klein had already been producing his *Peintures de feu* since 1957. In 1961, the museum Haus Lange in Krefeld hosted the exhibition *Yves Klein: Monochromes and Fire*, where a *Fire Wall* with one hundred flames and *Fire Fountains* were presented in the villa's garden.[314]

In 1960, Heinz Mack organised an *Hommage à Georges de La Tour* at Galerie Diogenes in West Berlin. An image of the Baroque artist, in whose painting candlelight is omnipresent, was projected onto a wall.[315] The homage included two hundred burning candles placed in strict serial order on a two-square-metre mirror in the gallery's basement. 'On the evening of the opening, about as many people filled the basement rooms and a great warmth soon developed,' Mack recalled. With a white tablecloth, which two young women first dipped into a bowl of water, the 'fire board', which resembled that of a *fakir*, was extinguished as the two stretched the cloth over the billowing, vibrating surface of the fire, only to drop it the moment Mack called out 'ZERO' during the countdown. 'In the darkness that came so abruptly, our inner eye projected an unreal afterimage.'[316] Mack repeated the candle installation in modified form at Galerie Schmela in Düsseldorf in 1965. ↖□36

Around 1960, several Parisian artists around the critic Pierre Restany formed the group of *Nouveaux réalistes*. Some of the members, such as Arman and Niki de Saint Phalle, used fire and destruction as strategies of artistic creation.[317] The Swiss artist Daniel Spoerri, also a 'New Realist' in the circle of the ZERO movement, contributed a *Pyromaniac Guide* to volume 3 of the magazine *ZERO*. On the last page of the publication, the reader was invited to burn the magazine with an enclosed match. After explaining in detail how to light a match, it stated: 'Subject the present magazine Zero 3 to the same process by taking advantage of the heat present. To do this, hold the flat stick close enough to the brochure, which has been deliberately produced from a material that undergoes the same transformation process.' A

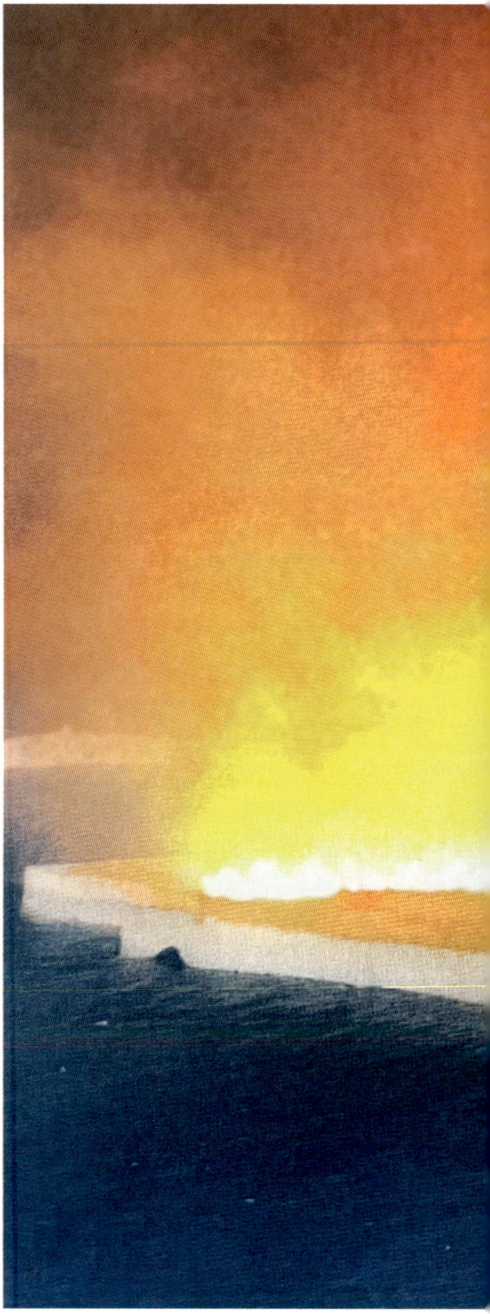

□39
***Fire Ridge* project**
1975, photo-collage

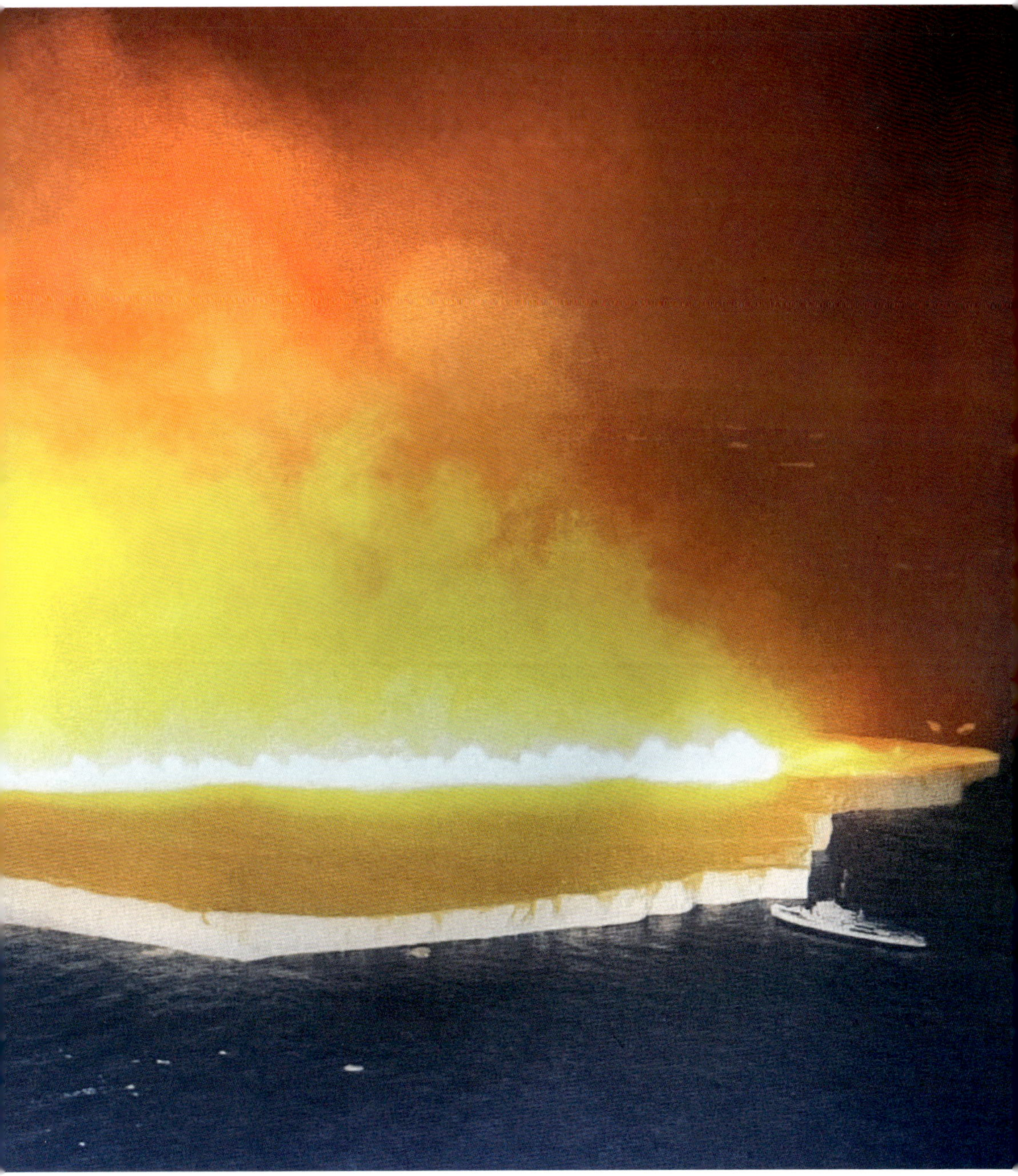

sunflower seed was pasted over it with the note: 'Jean Tinguely recommends that you plant this sunflower seed in good soil before following these instructions.'[318]

Jean Tinguely's self-destructing installations addressed destruction by fire in art. In 1960, he staged the sensational *Hommage à New York* in the garden of The Museum of Modern Art, in which a monumental kinetic sculpture destroyed itself in an automated process.[319] After the success in New York, Tinguely came to the attention of American television, which produced a film about his *Study for an End of the World, No. 2* (1962) in the Nevada desert. Together with Niki de Saint Phalle, the artist gathered debris, scrap metal, bulky waste, fireworks, and dynamite on Jean Dry Lake in Nevada. The construction of the sculpture and its spectacular explosion were recorded by NBC.[320] In 1968, Michael Heizer, Robert Smithson, and Nancy Holt also travelled to Jean Dry Lake, unaware that the European artist couple had already been to the site six years earlier. The three protagonists of Land Art travelled there to install *Rift*, the first of Heizer's *Nine Nevada Depressions*. They dug out a zigzag channel of roughly fifteen metres in length from the ground with shovels and pickaxes, moving a ton and a half of earth in the process.[321] Suzaan Boettger has pointed out the destructive connotation of *Rift*, which stems from the title and its proximity to the nuclear test site: The naming of the work, Boettger suggests, could refer to the United States Atomic Research and Test Center not far away, where experimental explosions had split the earth into a twelve-mile-long chasm near Las Vegas.[322]

In addition to the *Fire Ship* (1968, cf. ↸□13) and the *Fire Raft* (1976, cf. ↸□29&30), which have already been mentioned here, Mack designed another work in which fire played a role. The *Fire Ridge* project (1975) envisaged drawing an approximately three-hundred-metre-long furrow on a large, floating slab of ice in the Arctic with the help of a rotary snowplough. This was to be filled from a helicopter with paraffin and petrol, a mixture that was to be electrically ignited at dusk. ↸□39 The realisation of the idea failed due to the objection of the Danish Ministry of Defence, but – if executed – would have shown a certain similarity to the 'rift' that Michael Heizer had drawn in the salt lake in Nevada.[323]

The tendency of American artists to deal with explosions, blasts, and destructive activities can be traced back to the tradition of the sublime already touched upon, which also included the destructive forces of nature. However, when Mack and other ZERO artists integrated fire into their works, it was less about demonstrating the sublime forces of nature than about the optical phenomenon of light and the dematerialisation of art. The fire and light experiments Mack carried out produced ephemeral phenomena that existed only for the moment and were documented with the help of film and photography.

AIR

Air stands, on the one hand, for breath, especially the 'breath of life'; on the other, winds can act as stormy, destructive forces. Since time immemorial, the element has also been associated with the dream of flying, from the mythological figure of Icarus to the first hot-air balloon of the Montgolfier brothers in the eighteenth century.[324] Around 1960, this aspect of the air element was taken up again by artists as a connection between art and technology.

The first work by Heinz Mack to focus on the element of air confronts the viewer with a paradox. The *Air Saw* from 1955 is a saw blade with sharp-edged prongs mounted on a roughly one-metre-high stand. How could air – the invisible element – be sawed? Matthieu Poirier called the work a 'ready-made *arrangé*' because Mack had converted a tool, the saw blade, into an artwork.[325] Marcel Duchamp had used actual air as a material in one of his own readymades: For *Air de Paris (50 cc of Paris Air)* (1919), fifty cubic centimetres of air were enclosed in a small glass ampoule.[326] The Land Art protagonist Robert Morris created a direct reference to this work by Duchamp in 1963 with *Twelve Bottles of Fresh Air*.[327]

ZERO artists had integrated the element of air into their artworks early on. Yves Klein's revolutionary exhibition *Le Vide* (The Void) at Galerie Iris Clert in Paris in 1958 featured an empty gallery space, which was thus filled with nothing but air. In 1961, Klein, together with the architect Werner Ruhnau, conceived the *Project for an Aerial Architecture* in which air and heavy gases were to be used as architectural elements. In his manifesto *Le Dépassement de la problématique de l'art* (Overcoming the Problematics of Art, 1959), Klein had divided the Earth and its atmosphere into four zones.[328] A further ZERO artist who also worked with air was Piero Manzoni, whose edition of spherical bodies filled with (breathing) air was shown at Galleria Azimut in Milan in 1960.[329] At the event *ZERO Edition, Exposition, Demonstration* at Galerie Schmela in Düsseldorf in 1961, a balloon filled with

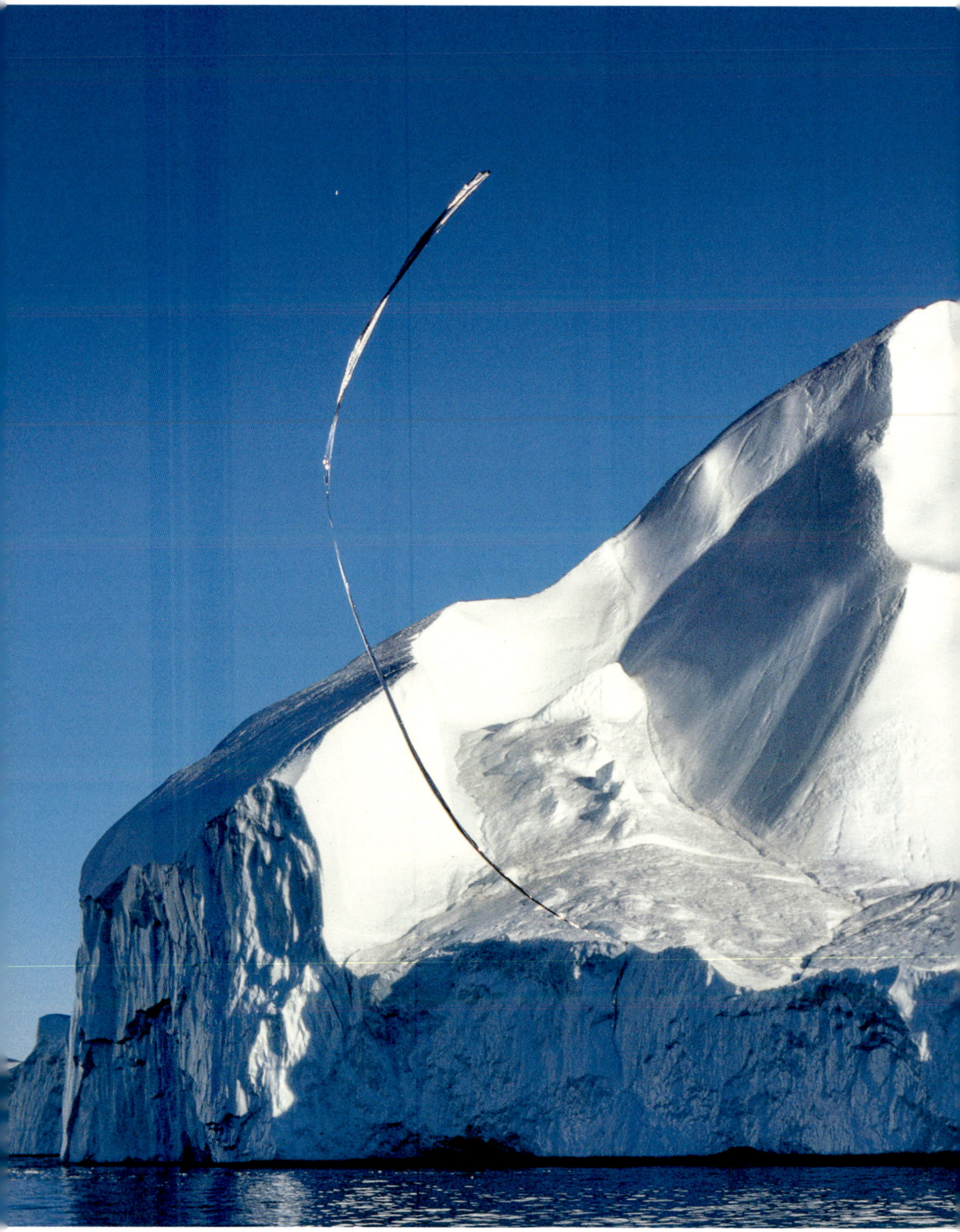

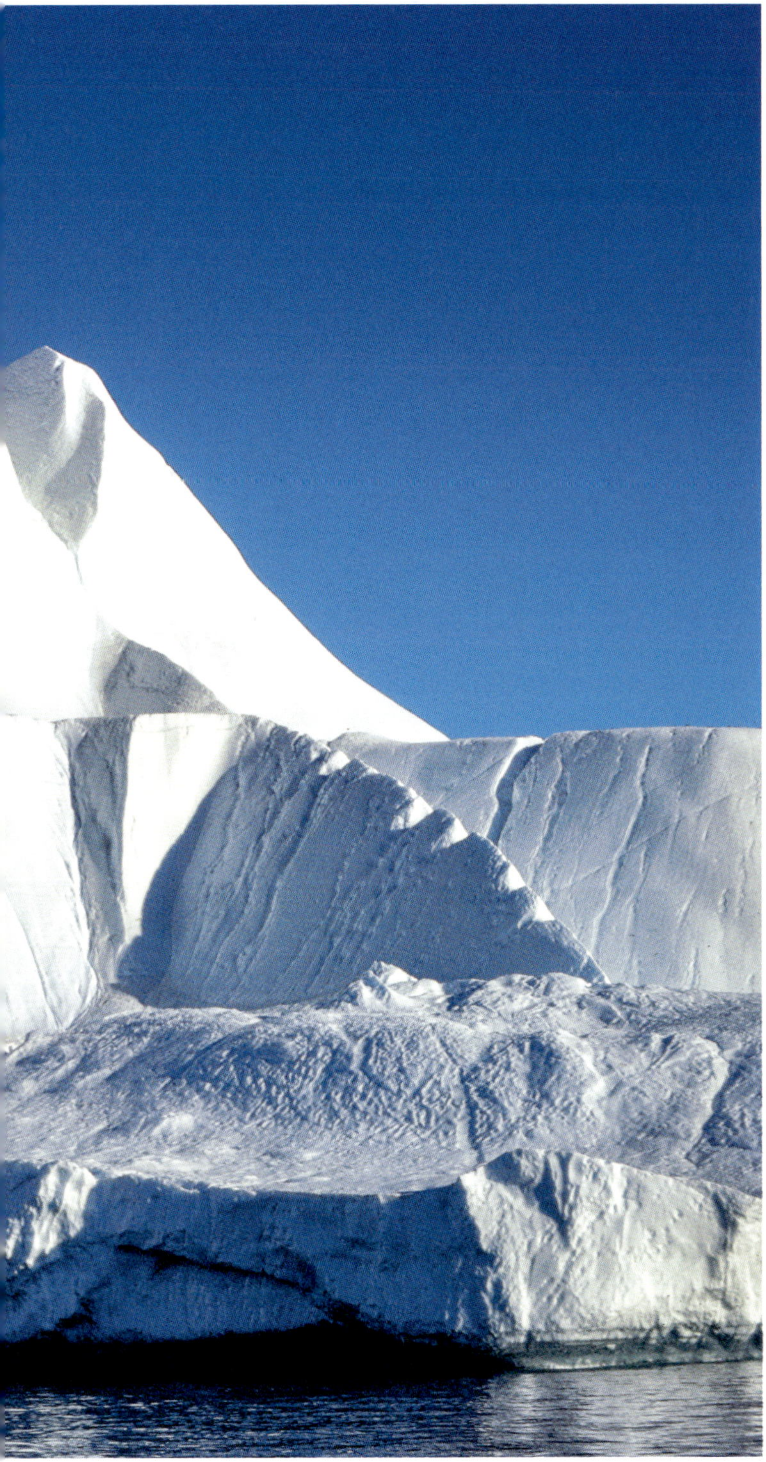

□40
Dream of the Navigator
Greenland, 1976

hot air rose into the sky. According to Jack Burnham, the ZERO balloons signalled a transfer of the material art form into a new field of action. He described them as an artistic departure into new spheres, followed by Andy Warhol's *Silver Clouds* (1966).[330] After Otto Piene moved to the United States in 1968, he developed his *Sky Art* and *Inflatable Sculpture* at the Center for Advanced Visual Studies of the Massachusetts Institute of Techonology (MIT). His so-called *Sky Events* consisted of polyethylene tubes filled with helium and stretched into arches in the sky, which were first presented at the *Line Light Event* in Boston in 1968.[331]

'In order to make air tangible at all, it must be made visible, for example through smoke, through a flag, a sail,' write Gernot and Hartmut Böhme in their *Kulturgeschichte der Elemente* (A Cultural History of the Elements, 1996).[332] This was also the concern of Mack, who in several works made air visible through technical means. One of these works is titled *Do You See the Wind? Greetings to Tinguely* (1962).[333] Silvery strips of aluminium foil are attached to a two-metre-high fan. The aerodynamic process caused by the rotation of the fan is made visible by the strips of foil fluttering in the wind. Here, Mack added a visual experience to a sensory one, which was further enhanced by the aluminium strips reflecting the light. A similar visualisation of air is at the core of Hans Haacke's *Blue Sail* (1964/65).[334] The blue sail is attached to the side walls of a gallery, while it receives updrafts from a fan mounted on the floor and is in a state of constant motion. In 1976, based on the third station of the *Sahara Project*, Mack also stretched a silver sail across the Arctic Ocean. The silver line, roughly one hundred metres long, rose high above the iceberg in the Arctic wind and was poetically titled *Dream of the Navigator* (1976, ↖□40). 'The preserve of art exists not only on Earth,' Mack had written in the *Sahara Project*, thus also declaring the sky to be the sphere of the *Jardin artificiel*.[335]

WATER, ICE

The oceans, which cover approximately two thirds of the Earth's surface, serve as a biosphere, and rain is the 'water of life' that makes fertility possible. However with the element of water, an 'excess of forces' can never be ruled out; as a deluge, it can bring chaos and death. In the annual cycle, water is also associated with winter because of its aggregate states as ice or snow.[336] This is why works of art made of ice and snow are also presented here.

Already at the beginning of his text on the *Sahara Project*, Mack proposes the integration of water and its equivalent aggregate states. It is stated here that, in the search for a new dimension of art, the artist must seek out new spaces – not only the desert, but also the sea or Antarctica.[337] Mack also used water as a material for objects and actions. Around 1962, he produced a work that visualised the condensation of water. *Light, Rain, Shadow* consists of a glass cube, the inner sides of which are moistened with water. This was placed on an aluminium grille over an electric heating plate so that the water inside the cube condensed.[338] The condensation of water on the glass walls of a cube was also the theme of Hans Haacke's work *Condensation Cube*, which was created somewhat later than Mack's work in 1965.[339] As Karin Thomas explained, Haacke limited himself here, as in other works, to the exemplary demonstration of complex and 'self-contained systems of conditions'.[340] 'The fact that Hans Haacke shared many artistic expectations with me during the ZERO period means a lot to me and remains unforgotten,' Mack explained. 'It is remarkable how soon he liberated himself from these ZERO ideals to go his own way, for which his name now has an international standing and rank in art.'[341]

On the occasion of the *ZERO* exhibition at Galerie Diogenes in West Berlin in 1963, Mack created a *Foam Sculpture*. A photograph documents the installation of this ephemeral sculpture: Mack stands with a water hose in his hand in front of a sign reading 'ZERO' and produces a mound of white foam held together by a net-like structure. ↘□42 For the action *ZERO on Sea* (1965), which the ZERO artists planned two years later for the pier of Scheveningen, there were many suggestions concerning the element of water. In a letter to Mack, Uecker expressed the idea of colouring the sea and the beach, as well as 'pouring many tons of rhinestones or glass beads into the sea'.[342] Armando suggested amplifying the sounds of the surf on the entire pier and colouring the sea black as in his *Black Water Project* (1964). Henk Peeters suggested the *Water Ceiling* for the project, which he realised in the same year, 1965, in the Stedelijk Museum in Amsterdam.[343]

Artists associated with Land Art created many works and actions in snow and ice landscapes. In 1968, the American sculptor Dennis Oppenheim realised snow projects in northern Maine, such as the *Annual Rings* on the border between the United States and Canada. The circles drawn in the snow are separated in the middle by a river, so that one half of the sculpture is in Fort Kent, Maine (USA), and the other half in Clair, New Brunswick (Canada). They are thus also in different time zones, one hour apart.[344] Like many ephemeral sculptures of Land Art, this work also thematises time and space. Uecker's action *Walking over Snow*, which he presented at the 1969 *Earth Art* symposium at Cornell University in Ithaca, is also one of these.[345]

Mack created an important work in 1972 on the occasion of the Olympic Games in Munich. In cooperation with Siemens, he installed the monumental *Water Cloud* on the Olympic Lake, which took up a base area of 30 × 14 metres and reached a maximum height of 36 metres. →□41 The water cloud was hydraulically driven by sixteen submersible pumps, pressure distributors, and nozzle systems with a total of ninety-eight nozzles that set up to 74,000 litres of water in motion per minute. In the evening, 112 underwater floodlights created a luminous apparition of the cloud. Its movement was controlled in such a way that height changes of individual sections of the cloud were possible. It thus had a variable programme and could be increased in three phases from the horizontal position to an extraordinarily high fountain. Mack's water sculpture was the centrepiece of the opening ceremony of the Olympic Games, with Piene's helium sculpture *Olympic Rainbow* (1972) stretched over it. It was in action on the Olympic Lake for the entire duration of the Games and for many years after.[346]

'Whoever sees the pure light in the Arctic Circle and stands in this light is filled with light and becomes an object of light', is how Mack described his experiences in the icy wilderness of Greenland.[347] In 1976, he had created several sculptures there that were related to the Arctic Ocean and have already been mentioned above. A hitherto unpublished photograph depicts an *Ice Sculpture* of a special kind: ↘□43 The honeycomb aluminium web, shaped into a fan, is completely frozen within a block of ice. The light rays of the Arctic sun are reflected by the surface of both the ice and the aluminium, making this element of the *Jardin artificiel* appear highly unreal.

The works Mack created in connection with the *Sahara Project* reveal similarities with works of Land Art in that they address the dimensions of time and space. This is especially true for the works that were formed from water, ice, or snow or were created in landscapes of ice and snow. Even more so than the works made of soil or sand, they have an ephemeral character and contrast with the constants of the earthbound.

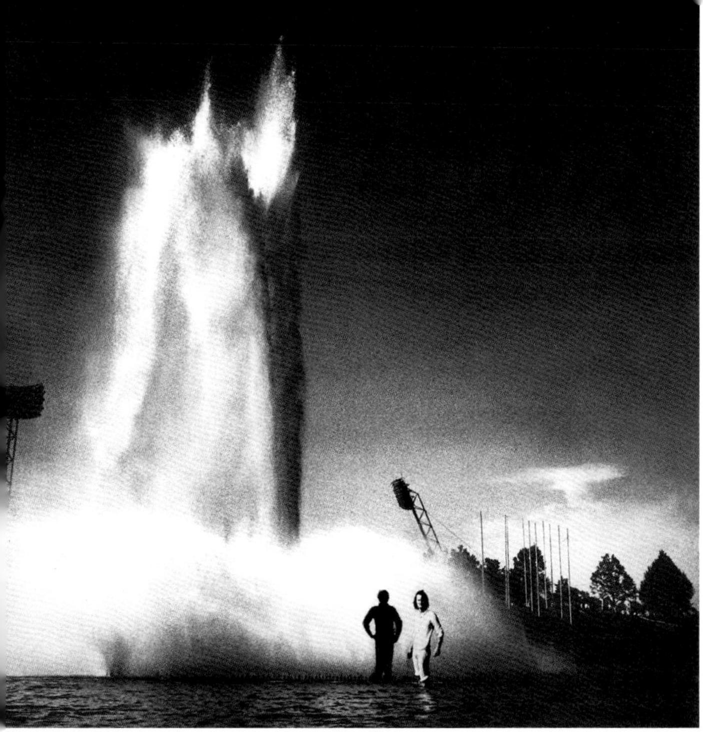

□41
Water Cloud on the Olympic Lake
Munich, 1972

□42
Foam Sculpture
Galerie Diogenes, West Berlin, 1963

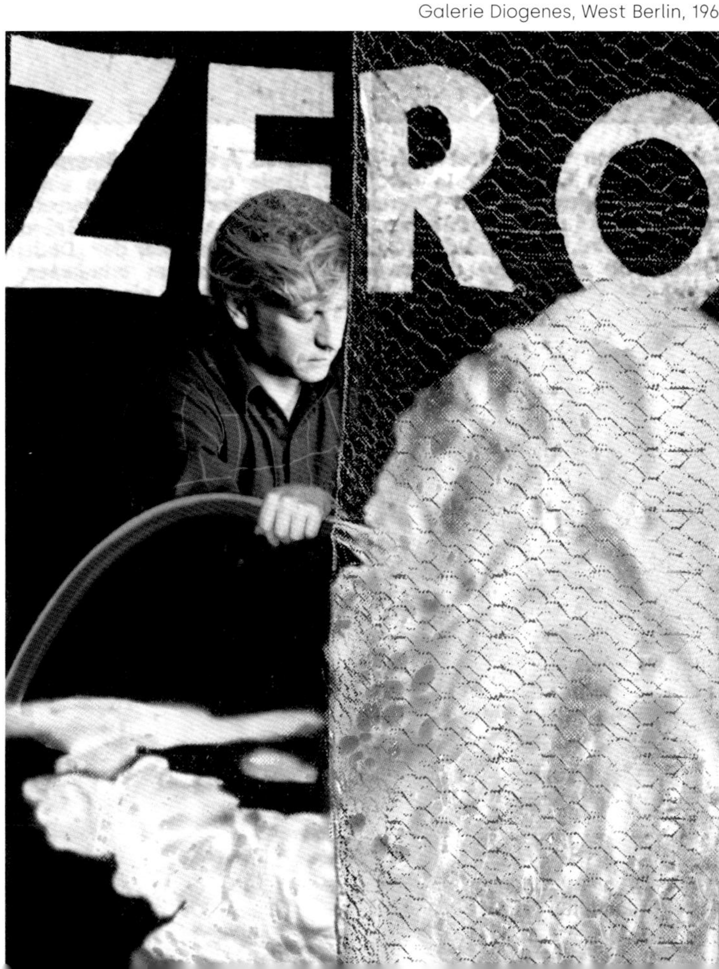

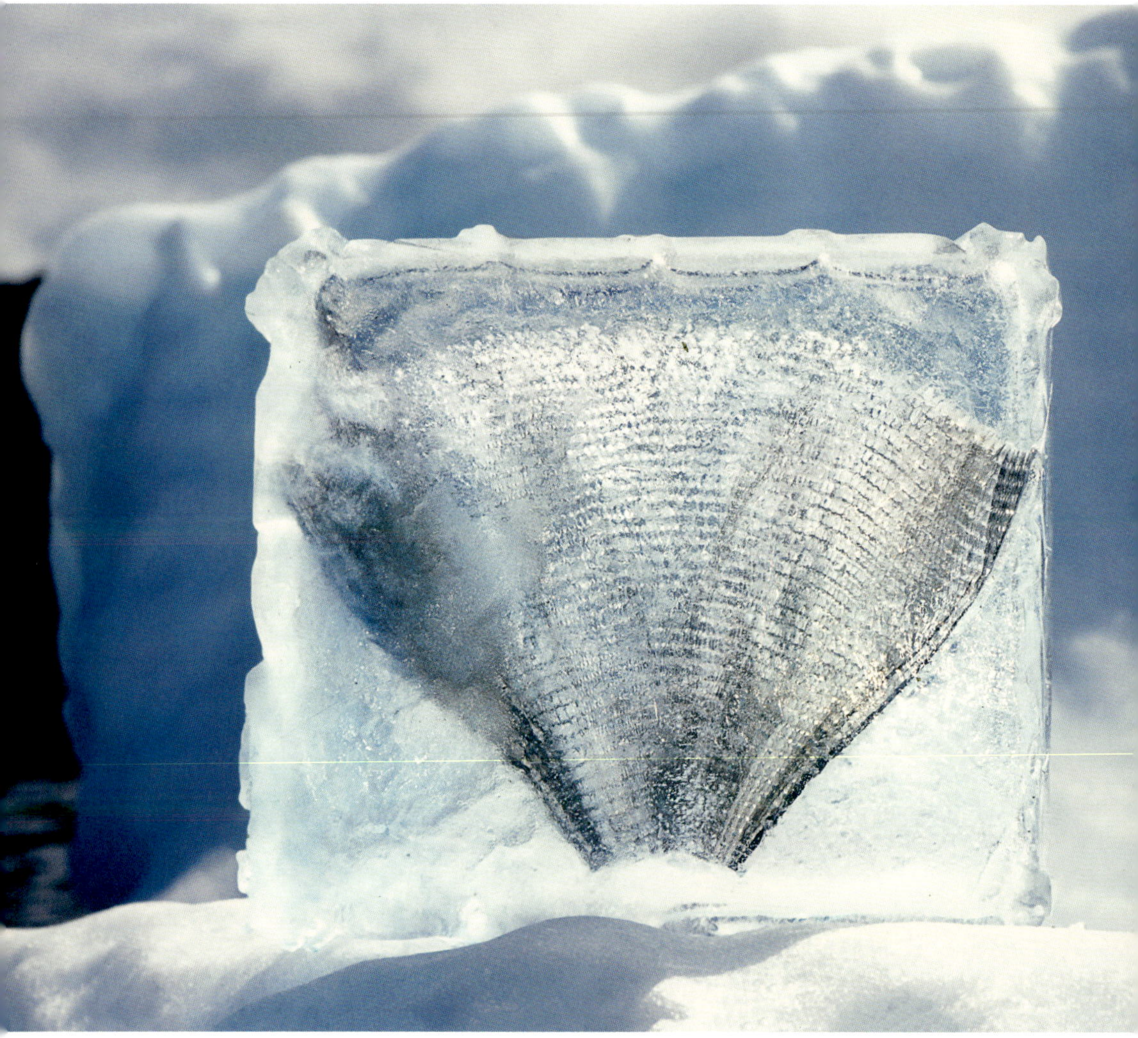

□43
Ice Sculpture
Greenland, 1976

LIGHT

As already mentioned, the doctrine of the four elements was extended for the first time by the addition of the aether in Plato's immediate circle. The quintet of Platonic bodies forced the addition of a fifth element, the 'aether', by which was meant the upper celestial sphere or a type of air.[348] Aristotle mentioned the aether as the *quinta essentia*, which could be not only the outermost eternal sphere of the cosmos, but also light or a light-bearer. In his treatise *De anima*, Aristotle established the systematic relationship between aether and light, which he described as translucent *energeia* – a specific natural phenomenon found, for example, in water and air. In Greek antiquity, the concept of the aether was associated with the divine, the soul, and light, as well as beauty.[349] Plato thus equated light-filled seeing with imaginative thinking, while Plotinus identified light with truth. In medieval metaphysics, this led to the equation of light and God, who, according to the Old Testament, with his first words, *fiat lux* (Let there be light), represented the best, most similar to his being in materiality, 'as if light were an analogue of spirit and God among the creatures'.[350] Peter Sloterdijk has emphasised that the Islamic culture of the Middle Ages also produced a wealth of treatises on the philosophy of light. For example, in his treatise *The Niche of Lights* (c. 1100), the Arab philosopher Abu Hamid Muhammad al-Ghazali identified light with the Koran: 'The symbol of the Koran is sunlight, and the symbol of reason is eyesight' (DE: *Augenlicht*, literally 'the light of the eye').[351] In an examination of al-Ghazali's mysticism of light, Heinz Mack dedicated a graphic suite to his verses titled *On Bliss and on Light* (2003).[352]

Goethe also discussed the connection between God, sunlight, and the eye in the poetic introduction to his *Theory of Colours* (1810):

> If the eye were not sunny,
> how could we perceive light?
> If God's own strength lived not in us,
> how could we delight in Divine things?[353]

Goethe began his scientific studies on colour and light shortly after his journey to Italy (1786–88), whereupon he published 'Contributions to Optics' (1790/91). In the three-volume edition of *Theory of Colours*, his most comprehensive treatise on colour, he dealt with the double phenomenon of light and colour. It was published in 1810, only a few months after Philipp Otto Runge's treatise on the *Colour Sphere*. Both authors agreed on the view that colour was not a part of light, but that light produced colour. This fundamental error contradicted Isaac Newton's thesis that white light contains the entire colour spectrum, which eventually proved to be correct.[354] In their preoccupation with light and colour, Mack and Goethe are linked by a profound inner closeness, as Volkmar Hansen has written: 'For Heinz Mack, the double phenomenon of light/colour is also central, but an impressive separation into the sculptural work, to which light is assigned, and the painterly work, in which the colour scale occupies a special place, becomes apparent.'[355] Hansen was referring here to Mack's *Light Reliefs* and *Light Steles*, which take on an immaterial appearance through light, as well as to the painted *Chromatic Constellations*, with which Mack has been exploring the spectrum of colours since 1991. ↘□44

Heinz-Norbert Jocks has emphasised that Mack's entire oeuvre 'aims especially and above all to bring the wonder of cosmic light to bear as completely and utterly as possible and to unfold it before us in an artistic manner.' Light, he said, is so essential for his art that everything else seems peripheral. Jocks noted that Mack cites poetry and philosophy as sources of his experience, as well as natural sciences and technology, in order to enrich his knowledge of light in every conceivable way. In doing so, Mack was concerned with a 'cross-media aesthetic'.[356]

Light is the central artistic theme in the work of Heinz Mack. Although the artist also produced numerous works with artificial light, like his contemporaries James Turrell and Dan Flavin, the focus here is on natural light. During a trip to Corsica in 1966, Mack contemplated the differences between natural and artificial light and came to the conclusion: 'Light is not light.' The quality of light, he said, is an aesthetic category that is not physically relevant. 'Intensity, concentration, or dispersion of the volume of light – as well as its spectral structure – are indeed physically determined, ... but the quality of light, that is to say its beauty, is essentially a pure sensory value, that is to say a creative act of freedom within the sphere of our sensibility.' The quality of light, he said, can be verified by aesthetics alone. 'Another difficulty for aesthetics is the distinction between natural and artificial light; the difference between the natural beautiful and the artificial beautiful proves particularly clear in the concept of light.' Natural light and artificial light, Mack continues, have 'entirely unequal energies': 'Thus, in nature, light always has a “correct”, that is to say best possible, relationship to space and time; it is unique and not interchangeable.'[357]

Beginning with the *Model of a Vibrating Light Stele in the Desert* (1958), all the ideas of the *Sahara Project* are related to natural light and its relationship to space and time. Ever since Mack created the first *Light Relief* in 1957, the overcoming of materiality through light has been the most important concern of his sculptural oeuvre. Mack investigated the 'purity of the light spectrum' in numerous light and photo experiments with optical lenses and prisms in both the desert and the Arctic.[358] In the artist's catalogue raisonné, a separate chapter is devoted to experiments with prisms, with Honisch noting in 1986 that they were 'among Mack's most complicated and perhaps least known works'.[359] Under the term 'prism', Mack groups together regular, symmetrical bodies of transparent material, the basic shape of which is the triangle or its spatial manifestation, the pyramid. 'When the crystalline bodies are transparent, a simple refraction of light takes place,' Mack explains. 'If all the side edges are parallel and the base is a triangle, the light can fan out into its colour spectrum.'[360] In Greenland, Mack lowered triangular constructions of white nylon sails into the water, grouped with pyramid-shaped light prisms made of fibreglass and stainless steel. The *Model for a Floating Research Station* (1976) in the Arctic, which appeared like a mirage, shone in the light of the polar midnight sun of the Arctic summer, the colour spectrum of which became manifest in a fascinating view. ↘□45

A preoccupation with the prism links Mack to Goethe, who had converted a room in his house in Weimar into a large, walk-in camera obscura. He conducted an experiment with prisms that mistakenly led to the rejection of Newton's teachings. Goethe carried out further experiments with the aid of black, white, and colourfully printed cards that could be viewed through a prism. His 'new theory of light, shadows, and colours' was published as *Erstes Stück der Beiträge zur Optik* (Part One of the Contributions to Optics, 1971) and was received rather sceptically by representatives of the natural sciences. Despite his error, Goethe's *Theory of Colours* eventually produced insights that were incorporated into the fine arts.[361] To this day, by linking aesthetics and natural science, Goethe acts as a kindred spirit to visual artists such as Mack, who combine aspects of art and the natural sciences. 'In the coloured reflection we have life', is a quote from Goethe's *Faust* (1790), to which Mack likes to refer.[362] In 2018, the Goethe Museum in Düssel-

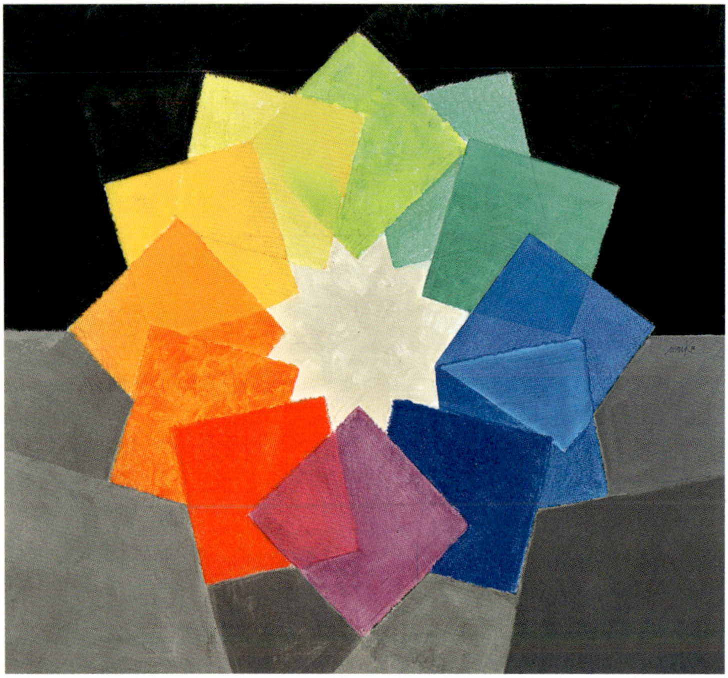

□44
Untitled (Chromatic Constellation)
2016

□45
Light Prisms in the Arctic (Model for a Floating Research Station)
Greenland, 1976

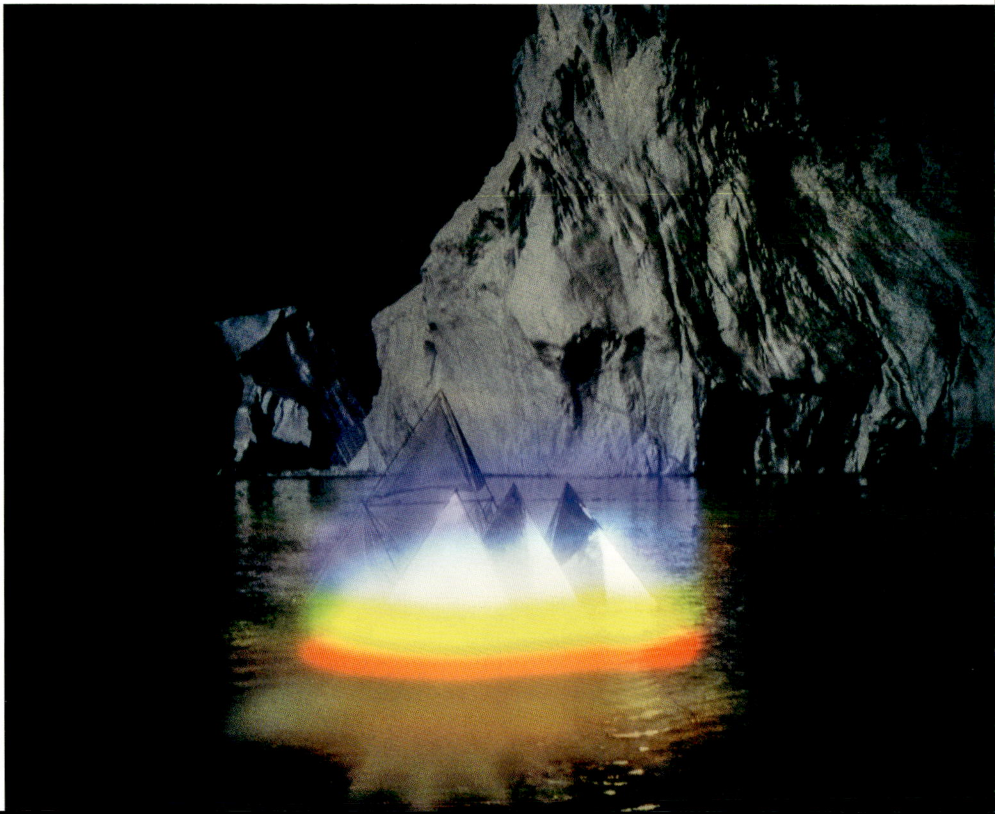

dorf dedicated a special exhibition to theme of *Taten des Lichts. Mack und Goethe* (Deeds of Light: Mack and Goethe).[363]

Like Mack, several protagonists of Land Art have dedicated some of their works to natural phenomena. For example, Robert Morris's *Observatory*, created between 1971 and 1977 in the Netherlands, is a monumental, ring-shaped structure in the landscape that displays the sunrise on specific days: at the summer and winter solstices and at the equinoxes. Seen from the centre of the *Observatory*, the sun rises exactly in one of the indentations of the rings every year around 21 March, 21 June, 21 September and 21 December.[364] Works such as the *Observatory* are in the tradition of solar observatories dating back to the site of Stonehenge, built between 2700 and 1500 BCE in what is today Wiltshire, England. Stonehenge is aligned in such a way that the rising sun shines into the centre of the site onto an altar stone at the time of the summer solstice. 'Countless testimonies in archaic cultures are related to observing the stars or incorporating (sun)light into ritual structures,' explains Patrick Werkner. Numerous artists have been inspired by these models: 'The art of the 1970s was particularly rich in expressions that took archaic or modern cosmologies as their starting point.'[365]

Nancy Holt also aligned her *Sun Tunnels* (1973–76) in the Great Basin Desert of Utah in the United States precisely to the incidence of sunlight. Four concrete tubes, six metres long and three metres in diameter, are laid out in intersecting axes determined by the summer and winter solstices. As with Morris's *Observatory*, sunrise and sunset can be observed in the tubes at these times. In addition, each of the four tubes reveals perforations that follow the patterns of four stellar constellations. The light falling through the holes projects the shapes of the constellations as spots of light inside.[366]

James Turrell has been creating so-called *Skyspaces* since the 1970s. The spaces have a large opening in the ceiling so that the sky seems to be inserted into them like a flat surface. Viewers are invited to watch the sky change colour at different times of day, such as sunrise or sunset. Turrell's largest project is located in an extinct volcano near Flagstaff, Arizona. Since the 1970s, the artist has been working on the completion of his *Roden Crater Project*, a monumental sky observatory with over twenty rooms in which the light falling from the sky and the movements of the stars can be observed.[367] Turrell's work focuses on making light visible, just like Mack's *Light Reliefs* and *Light Steles*. Both artists strive for the dematerialisation of their art through light. Like Mack, who uses prism experiments in the tradition of Goethe to fan light out into its coloured spectrum, Turrell also deals with light on a scientific level. His preoccupation with astronomy is reflected in the cosmological orientation of his works.

Since the 1950s, Mack has integrated the four elements of earth, fire, air, and water, as well as light as a 'fifth element' into his work. The *Sahara Project* in particular contains numerous suggestions for their artistic application. Not only Mack, but also many of his contemporaries used the elements and their powers. The use of the volatile substances and phenomena of air, water, light, and fire was accompanied by a dematerialisation of art. In contrast, the works with earth and sand constituted a materiality that was linked to a traditional geological connection, especially in American Land Art.

A PROJECT FOR THE TWENTY-FIRST CENTURY

Since its conception in 1959, the *Sahara Project* has had a decisive influence on Mack's sculptural oeuvre; at the same time, however, it retains its intended immanence. This includes a visionary quality which, more than sixty years after its formulation, has lost none of its topicality. Mack, who has also been called 'a twenty-first-century artist',[368] made numerous proposals in the *Sahara Project* which were clearly ahead of his time. For example, the ideas of a monumental *Light Stele* as well as a plantation of mirror reflectors in the desert have long since become reality in energy technology.[369] In the Mojave Desert in California, there are enormous light towers, the mirror reflectors of which supply expansive solar plantations with concentrated sunlight.[370] On the coasts of the world's oceans are huge parks of wind turbines for energy generation – reminiscent of Mack's enormous *Rotors*, which he conceived as 'artificial suns' with a diameter of more than fifty metres.[371] Since Mack – unlike the American protagonists of Land Art – did not receive any funding from private sponsors or public institutions for his *Sahara Project*, many of the project's ideas were only realised experimentally and rudimentarily. With the help of today's technologies, however, it would be possible not only to realise visions such as the *Mirror Wall* – an uninterrupted mirror surface more than one hundred metres long in the Sahara – but also to reconcile them with the generation of solar energy. Thus, in the face of the climate crisis, which is considered by scientists and activists to be the most pressing issue of our time, artists like Heinz Mack could also be involved in the aesthetic design of future technologies, and the ideas of the *Sahara Project* could be further considered in the twenty-first century.

But no artistic imagination will suffice … if art gives up its immanent claim to change the world – for the better.[372]

Heinz Mack, 1988

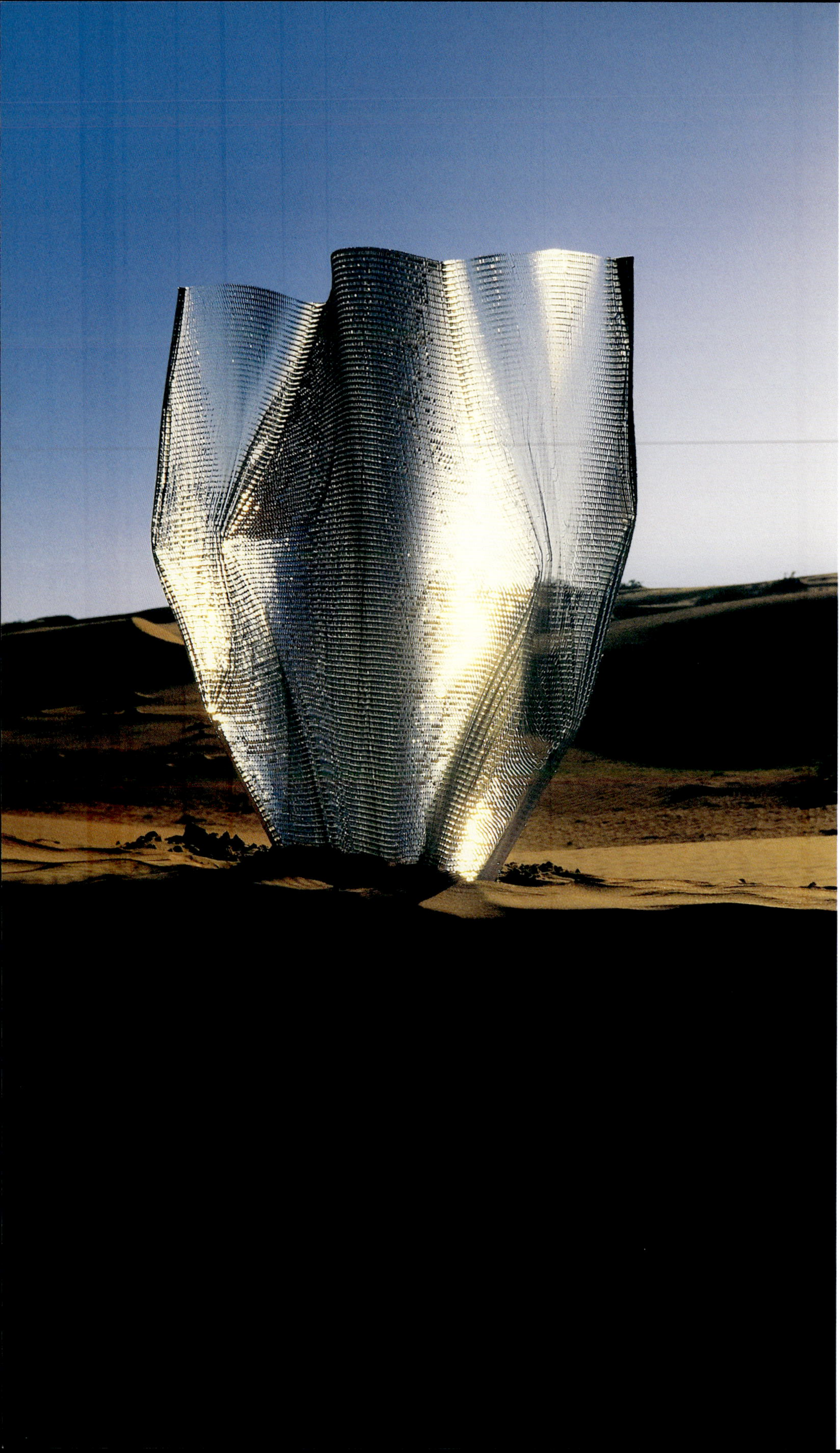

1 Cf. Mack 2018 a.
2 Latin for 'fear of empty space'.
3 Mack 1959, p. 1 [translated].
4 Kröpelin 2021, p. 85 [translated].
5 Cf. Martin 2016, p. 247.
6 Cf. George 1986, pp. 38f.
7 Cf. Rüth 2001, p. 18.
8 Heinz Mack in conversation with the author, Mönchengladbach, 24 February 2015.
9 Mack 1959, p. 1 [translated].
10 Cf. Mack 1999 a, unpaginated.
11 Mack had promised his mother that he would become a schoolteacher to support his family and thus enrolled in the painting class for art teachers. However, after Ewald Mataré recognised his talent, he encouraged Mack by accepting him as a guest student in his sculpture class; cf. ibid.
12 The painting is now in the collection of the Musée Picasso, Paris.
13 Mack, quoted in: Jocks 2009, p. 39 [translated].
14 Cf. Baldassari/Cowling/Elderfield 2002, pp. 82–89.
15 Cf. Mack/Mack 2011, p. 11.
16 Cf. ibid.
17 Mack, quoted in: Schwarzer 2005, p. 14 [translated].
18 Cf. ibid.
19 In 1965, he finally gave up this profession as his greatest wish was to be an independent artist.
20 Cf. Otten 2003, p. 9.
21 Cf. Schmitt 2013, p. 52.
22 Cf. Pörschmann 2015.
23 Today in the collection of The Museum of Modern Art, New York.
24 Cf. Meister 2006, p. 60.
25 Mack 2013, unpaginated [translated].
26 Mack 1958 a; cf. Schmitt 2013, p. 93.
27 Mack 1958 a.
28 Cf. Zell 2015, pp. 432, 459.
29 Mack 1958 b; quoted in English in: *ZERO*, exh. cat. Museum of Old and New Art, Berriedale, Tasmania, 2018/19, unpaginated.
30 Cf. Schmitt 2013, pp. 122f.
31 Cf. ibid., pp. 11f.
32 Cf. Hillings 2014, p. 21.
33 Mack/Piene 1960. Actually, the exhibition had no title, but *Vision in Motion* established itself as such since the catalogue referred to László Moholy-Nagy's eponymous book published in 1947; cf. Zell 2015, p. 436.
34 Mack 2009, unpaginated.
35 Permanently installed in Târgu Jiu, Romania.
36 Cf. Mack 2009, unpaginated.
37 Cf. Wyss 2021, p. 386.
38 Cf. Mack 2018 b, p. 17.
39 Cf. Rüth 2001, p. 20.
40 Mack 1959, p. 1 [translated].
41 Stachelhaus 1993, p. 82.
42 Mack 1959, pp. 1-2.
43 Ibid., p. 1 [translated].
44 Ibid., pp. 1–4 [translated]; cf. Fleck/Lehmann-Tolkmitt 2019, p. 57.
45 The term 'utopia' is composed of the ancient Greek *ou* (not) and *tópos* (place), literally meaning 'non-place'; cf. Schmidt 1991, p. 749.
46 Mack 1959, pp. 2f. [translated].
47 Ibid., p. 2 [translated].
48 Cf. Wyss 2021, p. 386.
49 'La symphonie immatérielle que nous présente Mack dans ses reliefs aluminium.' Iris Clert opened the exhibition *Reliefs lumineux et peintures de Mack* on 17 April 1959; cf. archive of the Galerie Iris Clert in the Bibliothèque Kandinsky, Centre Georges Pompidou, Paris, Fonds Galerie Iris Clert, GALCLER 18.
50 Mack 1966, p. 1 [translated].
51 Mack, quoted in: Honisch 1986, p. 44 [translated].
52 Cf. Beck/Eggeling 2014, p. 51.
53 Mack, quoted in: Beck/Eggeling 2014, p. 50.
54 Mack 1968, p. 94 [translated].
55 Mack 1959, p. 3 [translated].
56 Cf. Fleck/Lehmann-Tolkmitt 2019, p. 11.
57 Cf. ibid., pp. 12f.
58 Cf. Mack 2008 a, p. 110.
59 Cf. Beck/Eggeling 2014.
60 Mack 1959, p. 3 [translated].
61 Cf. Schmied 1998, p. 34.
62 Ibid., p. 35.
63 Cf. Mack 2008 a, pp. 144f., 329f.
64 Mack 1959, p. 4 [translated].
65 Mack 1961 [translated].
66 Mack, quoted in: Nannen 1977 [translated].
67 Cf. Schmied 1998, p. 32.
68 Mack, quoted in: Nannen 1977 [translated].
69 Mack 1959, p. 4 [translated].
70 For more information on these works, see Fleck/Lehmann-Tolkmitt 2019, pp. 50, 81ff.
71 Ibid., p. 81, quote p. 82f.
72 Mack 1959, p. 4 [translated].
73 For information on the collaboration of Yves Klein and Werner Ruhnau in Gelsenkirchen, see Fleck 2018, pp. 91ff.
74 Cf. Schmitt 2013, pp. 114f.
75 Mack/Piene 1961, unpaginated [translated].
76 Mack 1959, p. 4 [translated].
77 In 1960, in the garden of The Museum of Modern Art in New York, Tinguely presented a more than eight-metre-high self-destructing machine made of bicycle tyres, motors, a piano, a bathtub, and other recycled objects. During the approximately thirty-minute public demonstration, the machine produced coloured smoke, painted pictures, blew up balloons and popped them again, and threw bottles on the ground; cf. Caianiello 2018, pp. 103f.

78 Mack had conceived it for the 1963 Foire de Paris, but the performance there never came to fruition.
79 In 1968, the performance of the *Fire Ship* was recorded for the film *Tele-Mack* on a lake near Mönchengladbach; further performances took place in Duisburg and Stuttgart in 1979, as well as in Düsseldorf in 2010.
80 Mack 1959, p. 5 [translated].
81 For information regarding the cultural history of wind, see Böhme/Böhme 2014, p. 217.
82 Cf. Pola 2015, p. 86.
83 Mack 1959, p. 5 [translated].
84 Cf. Mack 2008 a, pp. 43, 321; In the meantime, the reliefs have been dismantled.
85 Cf. Fleck 2018, pp. 24-25.
86 Mack 1959, pp. 5f. [translated].
87 Emmerling 2015, p. 56 [translated].
88 Mack 1959, p. 6 [translated].
89 Ibid., p. 2 [translated].
90 This can be seen in the proofs, cf. Mack, Heinz: Druckfahnen 'Sahara Projekt', for ZERO 3, 1961, p. 4, Vorlass Heinz Mack, ZERO foundation, Düsseldorf, mkp.ZERO.1.IV. Sahara. In the German version, however, these footnotes were removed again, while they were published in the English and French translations; cf. Mack/Piene 1961.
91 Heinz Mack, 'Biographische Notiz' (undated), Vorlass (promised bequest) Heinz Mack, ZERO foundation, Düsseldorf, mkp. ZERO.1.IV. Eigene Texte.
92 Mack 1959, p. 6 [translated].
93 Cf. Honisch 1986, pp. 12–17.
94 Mack 1958 b [translated].
95 Cf. Schmitt 2015, p. 11.
96 Mack 1959, p. 7 [translated]; in later versions of the text, this station is called 'Monuments of Light'; cf. Mack/Piene 1961.
97 Honisch 1986, p. 16 [translated].
98 Cf. Özbek 2016, p. 135.
99 Mack 1959, p. 7 [translated].
100 Cf. Honisch 1986, p. 16.
101 For more information on the *Rotors*, see Fleck/Lehmann-Tolkmitt 2019, pp. 47ff.
102 Mack, quoted in: Schwarzer 2005, p. 2 [translated].
103 Mack 1959, p. 8 [translated].
104 Cf. Stachelhaus 1993, p. 183.
105 Schmied 1998, p. 184 [translated].
106 Otto Piene, 'Wege zum Paradies', in: Mack/Piene 1961, unpaginated [translated].
107 Mack 1959, p. 8 [translated].
108 Fleck/Lehmann-Tolkmitt 2019, p. 57.
109 Mack 1959, p. 9 [translated].
110 Cf. Sloterdijk 1993, p. 95.
111 Noll 2020, pp. 32f. [translated].
112 Matthew 4: 1–11; Luke 4: 1–13.
113 Cf. Bahr 2000, pp. 50–53; Enger 2000, p. 38.
114 Kuni 2000, p. 101.
115 The copperplate engraving (c. 1470) by Schongauer in, among others, the Staatliche Museen zu Berlin, Kupferstichkabinett; Bosch's triptych in the Museu Nacional de Arte Antiga, Lisbon.
116 Dalí's interpretation is connected with the competition for the film *The Private Affairs of Bel Ami* (1947), in which Max Ernst also participated; cf. Kuni 2000, pp. 101-105. Dalí's painting is now in the Musées royaux des Beaux-Arts de Belgique, Brussels, and the work by Ernst in the Wilhelm Lehmbruck Museum, Duisburg.
117 Today in the Musée Picasso, Paris; cf. Baldassari/Cowling/Elderfield 2002, pp. 82–89.
118 Cf. Flam 1984, pp. 228–233.
119 The Museum of Modern Art, New York.
120 Cf. Rubin 1984 b, pp. 9–11.
121 Mack 2018 b, p. 17 [translated].
122 Cf. ibid., pp. 31f.
123 Cf. Otterbeck 2007, pp. 147–166. The work is now in the collection of The Metropolitan Museum of Art, New York.
124 Werkner 1992, p. 13 [translated].
125 The term 'Land Art' is widespread in Germany, while in the United States 'Earth Art' is more common as a term for this art movement; cf. ibid.
126 Cf. Kaiser/Kwon 2012, p. 19.
127 Smithson 1967/96, p. 56.
128 Cf. Flemming 1998, p. 199; Kuhn 1998, p. 123.
129 Cf. Kaiser/Kwon 2012, p. 165.
130 Since no buyer was found for a permanent installation, after a short time the work had to make way for the advancing construction site; cf. Lorz 2012.
131 Cf. Kaiser/Kwon 2012, p. 160.
132 Cf. Herzog 2013.
133 Rüth 2001, p. 53 [translated].
134 An indoor earthwork could also be a 'non-site'; Smithson 1968/96.
135 Cf. Werkner 1992, pp. 86f.
136 Cf. ibid., p. 84.
137 Cf. ibid.
138 Cf. ibid., pp. 19ff.
139 Cf. Baumgärtel 2011, p. 374. The work is now in the collection of the Brooklyn Museum, New York.
140 De Maria 1963.
141 Mack 1959, pp. 5–8.
142 Ibid., p. 9 [translated].
143 Bernd Wolfgang Schmidt, 'Heinz Mack sucht neue Dimensionen der Kunst. Kinetisches Happening mit Wüstensand und Sonne', excerpt from an unknown source, 1968, Mack Archive [translated].
144 Emmerling 2015, p. 55 [translated].
145 Ibid., p. 56 [translated].
146 Cf. ibid., p. 57.
147 The commentary was spoken by the director Hans Emmerling; cf. Emmerling/Mack 1968/69 [translated].
148 Cf. Mack 2008 a, pp. 44 (*Playing Wall*), p. 140 (*Model for Montreal*).
149 Emmerling/Mack 1968/69 [translated].
150 Ibid. [translated].
151 Mack 1959, p. 3 [translated].
152 Cf. ibid.

153 Emmerling 2015, p. 60.
154 Ibid., pp. 57f. [translated].
155 In addition to Mack and Emmerling, the film team included the cameramen Edwin Braun, Leonhard Mauderer, and Klaus P. Weber; cf. Institut für moderne Kunst 1969, p. 55.
156 Emmerling 2015, p. 59 [translated].
157 Cf. Mack 1968.
158 Heinz Mack in conversation with the author, Mönchengladbach, 25 January 2021 [translated].
159 Cf. Institut für moderne Kunst 1969, p. 17.
160 Cf. ibid., p. 18.
161 Cf. ibid., pp. 28–45.
162 Mack 1968, pp. 94f. [translated].
163 Cf. ibid.
164 Cf. Institut für moderne Kunst 1969, p. 27.
165 Mack 1968, p. 94 [translated].
166 Ibid. [translated].
167 Cf. Emmerling 2015, pp. 61f.
168 Mack 2008 b [translated].
169 Ibid. [translated].
170 Cf. Fleck 2015, pp. 265ff.
171 Institut für moderne Kunst 1969, p. 50 [translated].
172 Mack 1968, p. 95 [translated].
173 Boucher 2014.
174 Emmerling 2015, p. 61 [translated].
175 Xhayet 1968 [translated].
176 Stachelhaus 1968 [translated].
177 FAZ 1969 [translated].
178 Friedrichs 1969 [translated].
179 Jappe 1969 [translated].
180 *Der Spiegel* 1969 [translated].
181 Cf. Friedrichs 1969; Emmerling 2015, p. 59.
182 Mack, quoted in: Eo Plunien, 'Silberstelen in der Sahara', in: *Die Welt*, 23 January 1969, Mack Archive [translated].
183 Cf. the foreword in: Groos et al. 2003, pp. 6f., here p. 6.
184 Wevers 2003, p. 26 [translated].
185 Cf. ibid., pp. 28–31; Groos et al. 2003, pp. 58–106.
186 Mack, quoted in: Hess 2003, p. 19 [translated].
187 Heinz Mack in conversation with the author, Mönchengladbach, 11 September 2017.
188 Heinz Mack in conversation with the author, Mönchengladbach, 11 March 2015 [translated].
189 Cf. Heinz Mack in conversation with the author, Mönchengladbach, 11 September 2017.
190 Cf. Wevers 2003, p. 45.
191 Cf. Dwan 2012.
192 The aerial view is the dominant view of the earthworks by the artists who worked in the desert. Like Antoine de Saint-Exupéry, 'one of the greatest desert poets of the twentieth century', Smithson was an avid pilot; Holert 2004.
193 Heinz Mack in conversation with the author, Mönchengladbach, 10 March 2015.
194 Smithson 1967/96, p. 56.
195 Dwan 2012, p. 93.
196 Cf. De Maria undated.
197 Ullrichs 2009, pp. 78–81, here p. 81 [translated].
198 Rüth 2001, p. 53 [translated].
199 Mack 1977 [translated].
200 Heinz Mack's calendar (1976), Mack Archive [translated].
201 Heinz Mack in conversation with the author, Mönchengladbach, 18 December 2017. Hecht later became editor-in-chief of the magazine *art*; Höpker was the first German photographer to become a full member of Magnum Photos and later president of the agency.
202 Stern, vol. 29, no. 45, 4 November 1976, p. 3; Hecht 1976 [translated].
203 Hecht 1976, pp. 53ff. [translated].
204 Ibid., p. 55 [translated].
205 Heinz Mack's calendar (1976 II), Mack Archive [translated].
206 Hecht 1976, p. 55 [translated].
207 Cf. the figurines in the Staatsgalerie Stuttgart.
208 Mack, quoted in: Nannen 1977, unpaginated [translated].
209 Cf. Nannen 1977, unpaginated.
210 Staatliche Museen zu Berlin, Nationalgalerie, Museum Berggruen.
211 Cf. Martin 2016, p. 254.
212 Hecht 1976, p. 55 [translated].
213 Heinz Mack's calendar (1976 II), Mack Archive [translated].
214 Mack Archive.
215 Ibid. [translated].
216 Staber 1968, p. 37 [translated].
217 Cf. Nannen 1977, unpaginated.
218 Mack 1977, unpaginated [translated].
219 Cf. Saint-Exupéry 1939/56, pp. 119ff.
220 George 1986, p. 45 [translated].
221 Mack/Mack 2011, p. 15 [translated].
222 Cf. Xhayet 1975.
223 Bagel 2015, p. 122 [translated].
224 Cf. Xhayet 1975.
225 Cf. George 1986, pp. 86f.
226 Mack/Mack 2011, p. 15 [translated].
227 Thomas Höpker, e-mail to the author, 11 January 2018 [translated].
228 Mack 1959, p. 2 [translated].
229 Cf. Hecht 1976, p. 55.
230 Cf. Martin 2016, p. 95.
231 Cf. ibid., pp. 28f.
232 Mack, quoted in: Nannen 1977, unpaginated [translated].
233 Heinz Mack in conversation with the author, Mönchengladbach, 19 June 2015.
234 Mack, quoted in: Nannen 1977, unpaginated [translated].
235 Hecht 1976, p. 56 [translated].
236 Cf. Martin 2016, p. 28.
237 Hecht 1976, p. 56 [translated].
238 Ibid. [translated].
239 Heinz Mack in conversation with the author, Mönchengladbach, 16 November 2015 [translated].
240 Thomas Höpker, e-mail to the author, 11 January 2018 [translated].

241 Hecht 1976, p. 56 [translated].
242 Heinz Mack's calendar (1976 II), Mack Archive [translated].
243 Cf. Schmied 1998, p. 59.
244 Cf. Honisch 1986, pp. 267f.
245 Mack, quoted in: Nannen 1977, unpaginated [translated]; cf. also Heinz Mack in conversation with the author, Mönchengladbach, 19 July 2015.
246 Mack, quoted in: Nannen 1977, unpaginated [translated].
247 Ibid.
248 Cf. Richter 2011, unpaginated.
249 Heinz Mack in conversation with the author, Mönchengladbach, 19 July 2015 [translated].
250 Cf. Schmied 1975, p. 102, Hamburger Kunsthalle.
251 Cf. Werkner 1992, pp. 19ff.
252 Cf. Mack/Mack 2011, p. 15.
253 Mack, quoted in: Nannen 1977, unpaginated [translated].
254 Nannen 1977.
255 Hoffmann 1977 [translated].
256 Flemming 1977 [translated].
257 Oberbayerisches Volksblatt 1977.
258 Cf. Honisch 1986, pp. 188, 190.
259 Cf. Mack/Höpker 1977.
260 Goethe 1819/1999, p. 521; quoted in English in: Paul Michael Lützeler, 'Goethe and Europe', in: *South Atlantic Review*, vol. 65, no. 2, 2000, pp. 95–113, here p. 99.
261 Cf. Martin 2016, p. 159.
262 Heinz Mack in conversation with the author, Mönchengladbach, 25 January 2021 [translated].
263 Cf. ibid.; Steinbauer-Grötsch 2001.
264 Cf. Steingießer 2018, p. 276.
265 Heinz Mack in conversation with the author, Mönchengladbach, 25 January 2021 [translated].
266 Mack, quoted in: Schwarzer 2005, p. 41 [translated].
267 Heinz Mack in conversation with the author, Mönchengladbach, 25 January 2021 [translated].
268 Rüth 2001, p. 34 [translated].
269 Cf. Fleck/Lehmann-Tolkmitt 2019, pp. 115–117.
270 Cf. Finkeldey 2001; Haase 2006; Özbek 2016; Geuer 2019.
271 Cf. Fleck/Lehmann-Tolkmitt 2019, p. 118.
272 Mack 1999 b [translated].
273 Mack, quoted in: Haase 2006, p. 16 [translated].
274 Heinz Mack in conversation with the author, Mönchengladbach, 25 January 2021 [translated].
275 Cf. Wyss 2021, pp. 423ff.
276 Heinz Mack in conversation with the author, Mönchengladbach, 25 January 2021.
277 Mack 1966, p. 1 [translated].
278 Schmitt 2013, p. 12.
279 Ibid., p. 255 [translated].
280 Cf. ibid., p. 12.
281 Cf. Westenholz 2015 b, p. 376.
282 Mack/Piene 1961.
283 It was not until the emergence of the modern natural sciences around 1800 that the theory of elements replaced the view of the 'cosmos as a unity' or the history of nature as a unified whole; cf. Böhme/Böhme 2014, pp. 11, 93–96.
284 Tetrahedron = fire, octahedron = air, icosahedron = water, hexahedron (or cube) = earth. The fifth Platonic primordial body is the dodecahedron, which Plato used to refer to the entire 'universe'; ibid, pp. 102–104.
285 Fire = warm/dry, earth = dry/cold, air = moist/warm, water = cold/humid; cf. ibid, p. 115.
286 Cf. ibid., pp. 111–115, 143–147.
287 Mack's works are considered here exclusively in the context of ZERO and Land Art; beyond this, it would also be possible to present interconnections to artistic movements such as Gutai, Arte Povera, and Fluxus.
288 Cf. Böhme/Böhme 2014, pp. 221–242.
289 Haase 2015, p. 57 [translated].
290 Mack 1959, p. 4 [translated].
291 Cf. Galerie am Lindenplatz 2004, unpaginated; Fleck 2015, p. 320.
292 Cf. Geiger 2008.
293 The majority of these were created around 1953. It is not possible to say exactly how many were produced, as most of them have not been preserved; cf. Healy 2015, unpaginated.
294 Cf. Kaiser/Kwon 2012, p. 222.
295 Cf. Rosenberg 1952/2005.
296 Jackson Pollock, quoted in: Ballew Neff 2006, p. 271.
297 Cf. Varnedoe 1984, p. 654.
298 Cf. Reiche 1974; Schulze/Zetzsche 2005.
299 Cf. Werkner 1992, p. 13.
300 Cf. ibid., p. 80.
301 Smithson, in: *Artforum*, September 1968; quoted in: Lippard 1973/2001, p. 13.
302 Lippard's selection does not claim to be exhaustive, as she emphasises in the preface; ibid., pp. viiff.
303 Sharp 2012, p. 39.
304 Sharp 1969, pp. 17–19.
305 Cf. ibid., pp. 50f.
306 Sharp 2012, p. 40.
307 Cf. Günther Uecker's Action: *Wiping Out Tracks (On the Trails of Lost Memory)* in Libya in 1974 (cf. Beuckers/Salwig 2004, p. 228) and the joint action *Sand Drawings* by Joseph Beuys with Charles Wilp in Kenya in 1974/75 (photographs of which are in collection of the Staatsgalerie Stuttgart).
308 Böhme/Böhme 2014, pp. 30–53, quote p. 53 [translated].
309 Mack/Piene 1961, unpaginated [translated].
310 Cf. Honisch 1986, p. 17.
311 Cf. Pörschmann/Shavemaker 2015, p. 523.
312 Cf. ibid., pp. 528f.
313 Cf. Rennert/von Wiese 1996, p. 51.
314 Cf. Kramer-Mallordy/Klein-Moquay 2017,

pp. 190–193; Fleck 2018, p. 105.
315 In fact, the painting *St. Sebastian Tended by St. Irene* (c. 1649) comes from the workshop of Georges de la Tour and is now in the collection of the Gemäldegalerie, Staatliche Museen zu Berlin.
316 Mack 1994, p. 181 [translated].
317 Arman collaged an exploded firework on paper and blew up a sports car in a spectacular action, which he then presented on the wall as a quasi-destroyed readymade (*White Orchid*, 1963); cf. Maak 2014. Niki de Saint Phalle pursued a similarly destructive-creative approach from 1960 onwards with her series of *Tirs*; cf. Restany 1961/2016, p. 64.
318 Spoerri, in: Mack/Piene 1961, unpaginated [translated].
319 Cf. Caianiello 2018, pp. 103f.
320 Cf. Scott 2012, pp. 68–69, 74–75.
321 Cf. ibid., p. 84; Werkner 1992, p. 48.
322 Cf. Boettger 2002, p. 114.
323 Cf. Schmied 1998, pp. 63f.
324 Cf. Böhme/Böhme 2014, pp. 217–225, 31.
325 Poirier 2016, p. 34, and in the same catalogue p. 43.
326 Philadelphia Museum of Art.
327 Cf. Lippard 1973/2001, pp. 27, 18.
328 Klein spoke first of *vide* (void, emptiness), which he connected with the *lumière bleue* (blue light) that envelops the Earth. He associated the stratosphere, i.e. the layer of the Earth's atmosphere at an altitude of eleven to fifty kilometres, with the word 'energy'. He assigned *air lourd* (stuffy, humid air), other heavy and dense gases, as well as the elements fire and water, to the *atmosphere*. Light, magnetism, sound, and scents were also tabulated under the term atmosphère. He designated *terre* (earth) as the last layer with mortar, concrete, rock, clay, and iron. The opening of the exhibition *Le Vide* was also associated with blue light; here, the outer wall of the gallery was illuminated in blue, and blue cocktails were served. In addition, Yves Klein had intended to illuminate the obelisk on the Place de la Concorde in blue on the occasion of the opening, but this could not be realized; cf. Kellein 1989, pp. 20–23.
329 Cf. Pola 2015, p. 86.
330 Cf. Burnham 1968, p. 47.
331 Cf. Rennert/von Wiese 1996, p. 127.
332 Böhme/Böhme 2014, p. 291 [translated].
333 ZERO foundation, Düsseldorf.
334 Museum für Gegenwartskunst, Siegen.
335 Mack 1959, p. 8 [translated].
336 Böhme/Böhme 2014, pp. 25–53, quote p. 53 [translated].
337 Cf. Mack 1959, p. 2.
338 Cf. Honisch 1986, p. 158.
339 Museu d'Art Contemporani de Barcelona.
340 Thomas 1972, p. 74 [translated].
341 Heinz Mack, 'Hans Haacke und Heinz Mack' (April 2011), Mack Archive [translated].
342 Letter from Günther Uecker to Heinz Mack (1965), Vorlass (promised bequest) Heinz Mack, ZERO foundation, Düsseldorf, mkp. ZERO.1.I.823 [translated].
343 Cf. Westenholz 2015 a, pp. 25f.
344 Cf. Schneckenburger 2010, p. 548.
345 Cf. Tolnay 2006, p. 181.
346 Cf. Stachelhaus 1993, pp. 105f., 181.
347 Mack 1977 [translated].
348 The aether is described as the upper celestial sphere in the dialogue Phaedrus, and as a type of air in the Timaeus; cf. Böhme/Böhme 2014, pp. 143f.
349 Cf. ibid., pp. 143–149.
350 Sloterdijk 2014, p. 88 [translated].
351 Ibid., p. 90 [translated].
352 *Über die Glückseligkeit und über das Licht. Graphische Suite nach den Versen von al-Ghazali mit Bildern von Heinz Mack* (2003); cf. Geuer/Breckner 2011, pp. 60ff.
353 Johann Wolfgang von Goethe, 'Introduction' in: idem, Goethe's *Theory of Colours*, trans. Charles Lock Eastlake (London: John Murray, 1840), pp. xxxvii– xlviii, here p. xxxix.
354 Isaac Newton's *Opticks: or, A Treatise of the Reflexions, Refractions, Inflexions and Colours of Light*, was first published in 1704.
355 Hansen 2001, unpaginated [translated].
356 Jocks 2017, p. 21 [translated].
357 Mack 1966, p. 1 [translated].
358 Schmied 1998, p. 106.
359 Honisch 1986, pp. 16–17.
360 Mack, quoted in: Kunstverein Ahlen 1994, p. 17 [translated].
361 Cf. Krätz 1998, pp. 168–170, quote p. 169 [translated].
362 Johann Wolfgang von Goethe, Goethe's *Faust*, Part II, trans. Leopold J. Bernays (London: Sampson Low and Karlsruhe: A. Bielefeld, 1839), Act 1, Scene 1, p. 4; quoted in German in: Kunstverein Ahlen 1994, p. 134; Hansen 2001.
363 Cf. Steingießer 2018.
364 The work was first installed in Santpoort/Velsen in 1971 as part of the *Sonsbeek '71* exhibition and then dismantled until it was re-installed as a permanent site in Oostelijk, Flevoland, in 1977 on the initiative of the Stedelijk Museum, Amsterdam; cf. Werkner 1992, p. 114.
365 Ibid., p. 113 [translated].
366 Cf. ibid., p. 115.
367 Andrews 2015, p. 20.
368 Fleck/Lehmann-Tolkmitt 2019.
369 In 2016, Norman Rosenthal was the first to draw attention to this specific connection between Mack's *Sahara Project* and modern technologies based on renewable energy sources; Rosenthal 2016.
370 The Ivanphar Solar Electric Plant was completed in 2014.
371 Mack 1959, p. 7.
372 Mack, quoted in: Schmied 1998, p. 9 [translated].

SOURCES AND LITERATURE

All of the author's conversations with Heinz Mack and other contemporary witnesses are documented in the library of the ZERO foundation, Düsseldorf, sig. 1550/W177.

Andrews 2015
Richard Andrews, 'Das Licht fassen', in Astrid Kühl-Ulrich et al. (eds.), *James Turrell: Extraordinary Ideas – Realized* (Dornbirn, 2015), pp. 19–21.

Bagel 2015
Fritz Bagel in conversation with Annette Bosetti, in Jürgen Wilhelm (ed.), *Mack im Gespräch* (Munich, 2015), pp. 119–124.

Bahr 2000
Petra Bahr, 'Wüste Orte, wüste Lektüren. Zum Wüstenmotiv im Neuen Testament', in Uwe Lindemann and Monika Schmitz-Emans (eds.), *Was ist eine Wüste? Interdisziplinäre Annäherungen an einen interkulturellen Topos* (Würzburg, 2000), pp. 45–57.

Baldassari/Cowling/Elderfield 2002
Anne Baldassari, Elizabeth Cowling and John Elderfield, *Matisse Picasso*, exh. cat. Tate Modern, London; Galeries nationales du Grand Palais, Paris; The Museum of Modern Art, New York (London, 2002), pp. 82–89.

Ballew Neff 2006
Emily Ballew Neff (ed.), *The Modern West: American Landscapes, 1890–1950*, exh. cat. The Museum of Fine Arts, Houston; Los Angeles County Museum of Art (Houston, 2006).

Baumgärtel 2011
Bettina Baumgärtel, 'Chronik der Düsseldorfer Malerschule 1815–2011', in idem (ed.), *Die Düsseldorfer Malerschule und ihre internationale Ausstrahlung, 1819–1918*, vol. 1: *Essays* (Petersberg, 2011), pp. 353–376.

Beck/Eggeling 2014
Michael Beck and Ute Eggeling (eds.), *MACK. The Sky Over Nine Columns* (Düsseldorf, 2014).

Beuckers/Salwig 2004
Klaus Gereon Beuckers and Katrin Salwig, 'Verzeichnis der Aktionen von Günther Uecker, 1958–1975', in Klaus Gereon Beuckers (ed.), *Günther Uecker. Die Aktionen* (Petersberg, 2004), pp. 219–228.

Boettger 2002
Suzaan Boettger, *Earthworks: Art and the Landscape of the Sixties* (Berkeley et al., 2002).

Böhme/Böhme 2014
Gernot Böhme and Hartmut Böhme, *Feuer, Wasser, Erde, Luft. Eine Kulturgeschichte der Elemente* (Munich, 2014).

Boucher 2014
Brian Boucher, 'The Man Who Fell to Earth – by Heinz Mack, as told to Brian Boucher', *Art in America*, November 2014, p. 61.

Burnham 1968
Jack Burnham, *Beyond Modern Sculpture* (New York, 1968).

Caianiello 2018
Tiziana Caianiello, 'Between Media: Connections between Performance and Installation Art, and Their Implications for Conservation', *Beiträge zu Kunst und Kulturgut*, 1/2018, pp. 102–110.

Caianiello/Visser 2015
Tiziana Caianiello and Mattijs Visser (eds.), *The Artist as Curator: Collaborative Initiatives in the International ZERO Movement, 1957–1967* (Ghent, 2015).

De Maria 1963
Walter De Maria, 'On the Importance of Natural Disasters', in La Monte Young (ed.), *An Anthology of chance operations, concept art, anti art, indeterminacy, plans of action, diagrams, music, dance constructions, improvisation, meaningless work, natural disasters, compositions, mathematics, essays, poetry* (n.p. [New York], 1963), p. 28.

De Maria n.d.
Dia Art Foundation, Walter De Maria, *The Lightning Field*, n.d., online: diaart.org (last accessed on 26 November 2021).

Der Spiegel 1969
Anonymous, 'Mack. Zittern am Waschbrett', *Der Spiegel*, vol. 23, no. 44, 27 October 1969, pp. 207–209.

Dwan 2012
Virgina Dwan, 'Changing Boundaries', in Kaiser/Kwon 2012, pp. 93–95.

Emmerling 2015
Hans Emmerling in conversation with Annette Bosetti, in Jürgen Wilhelm (ed.), *Mack im Gespräch* (Munich, 2015), pp. 55–62.

Emmerling/Mack 1968/69
Hans Emmerling and Heinz Mack, *Tele-Mack*, 16mm colour film, sound, 45:40 min., Institut für moderne Kunst, Nuremberg, produced by Telefilm Saar GmbH on behalf of Saarländischer Rundfunk and WDR Fernsehen, 1968/69.

Enger 2000
Philipp Enger, 'Eine Wüstenwanderung mit Israel', in Uwe Lindemann and Monika Schmitz-Emans (eds.), *Was ist eine Wüste? Interdisziplinäre Annäherungen an einen interkulturellen Topos* (Würzburg, 2000), pp. 29–43.

FAZ 1969
Anonymous, ['Die Welt jenseits der Zivilisation (...)'], *Frankfurter Allgemeine Zeitung*, 10 March 1969.

Finkeldey 2001
Bernd Finkeldey (ed.), *Heinz Mack. Wahlverwandtschaften*, exh. cat. Tehran Museum of Contemporary Art; Wilhelm-Hack-Museum, Ludwigshafen (Tehran, 2001).

Flam 1984
Jack D. Flam, 'Matisse und die Fauvisten', in Rubin 1984 a, pp. 219–247.

Fleck 2015
Robert Fleck (ed.), *Mack: Reliefs* (Munich, 2015)

Fleck 2018
Robert Fleck, *Yves Klein: L'Aventure allemande* (Paris, 2018).

Fleck/Lehmann-Tolkmitt 2019
Robert Fleck and Antonia Lehmann-Tolkmitt, *Heinz Mack: A Twenty-First Century Artist*, trans. Gérard A. Goodrow (Munich, 2019).

Flemming 1977
Hans Theodor Flemming, 'Auf der Suche nach neuen Dimensionen ...', *Die Welt*, 18 April 1977.

Flemming 1998
Klaus Flemming, 'Mit Kunst bezeichnet. Ein sprachlicher Annäherungsversuch an ein Environment von Heinz Mack', in Schmied 1998, pp. 197–202.

Friedrichs 1969
Yvonne Friedrichs, 'Macks Garten in der Wüste. Morgen wird das "Sahara-Projekt" im Fernsehen gezeigt', *Mönchengladbacher Stadtpost/Rheinische Post*, 1 May 1969.

Galerie am Lindenplatz 2004
Heinz Mack. ZERO, exh. cat. Galerie am Lindenplatz, Vaduz, 2004.

Geiger 2008
Stephan Geiger, *The Art of Assemblage. The Museum of Modern Art, 1961: Die neue Realität der Kunst in den frühen sechziger Jahren* (Munich, 2008).

George 1986
Uwe George, *Die Wüste. Vorstoß zu den Grenzen des Lebens* (Hamburg, 1986).

Geuer 2019
Dirk Geuer (ed.), *Heinz Mack. Mouvement et lumière / Movement and Light*, exh. cat. Musée Théodore-Monod d'art africain, Dakar, 2019.

Geuer/Breckner 2011
Geuer & Breckner Galerie (ed.), *Mack. Druckgraphik, 2001–2011* (Düsseldorf, 2011).

Goethe 1819/1999
Johann Wolfgang Goethe, *West-östlicher Divan* [1819], *Studienausgabe*, ed. Michael Knaupp (Stuttgart 1999).

Goethe 1839
Johann Wolfgang Goethe, *Goethe's Faust, Part II*, trans. Leopold J. Bernays (London and Karlsruhe, 1839).

Groos et al. 2003
Ulrike Groos, Barbara Hess and Ursula Wevers (eds.), *Ready to Shoot. Fernsehgalerie Gerry Schum*, exh. cat. Kunsthalle Düsseldorf et al. (Cologne, 2003).

Haase 2006
Haase, Claus-Peter (ed.), *Heinz Mack. Transit zwischen Okzident und Orient. Faszination und Inspiration der islamischen Kultur im Werk des Künstlers – ein Werkaspekt 1950–2006*, exh. cat. Staatliche Museen zu Berlin, Museum für Islamische Kunst (Cologne, 2006).

Haase 2015
Haase, Claus-Peter, 'Heinz Mack und der Orient. Die Auseinandersetzung mit dem Licht und seiner Brechung', in Robert Fleck (ed.), *Mack. Reliefs* (Munich, 2015), pp. 50–67.

Hansen 2001
Volkmar Hansen, 'Die Chromatik Goethes', in Finkeldey 2001, unpaginated.

Healy 2015
Charlotte Healy, 'A Radical Disregard for the Preservation of Art: Robert Rauschenberg's Elemental Paintings', *Interventions-journal*, vol. 4, no. 1: *Object Lesson. Texts*, 23 January 2015, online: https://www.academia.edu/13279289 (last accessed on 26 November 2021).

Hecht 1976
Axel Hecht, 'Heinz Mack/Thomas Höpker. Expedition in künstliche Gärten', *Stern*, vol. 29, no. 45, 4 November 1976, pp. 36–56.

Herzog 2013
Günter Herzog, 'Galerie Heiner Friedrich. Munich, Cologne, New York, 1963–1980', in Zentralarchiv des Internationalen Kunsthandels (ed.), *Galerie Heiner Friedrich. Munich, Cologne, New York, 1963–1980* [*Sediment*, nos. 21/22] (Nuremberg, 2013), pp. 9–21.

Hess 2003
Barbara Hess, 'Abendschau. Drei Filme über Kunst', in Groos et al. 2003, pp. 9–21.

Hillings 2014
Valerie L. Hillings, 'Countdown to a New Beginning: The Multinational ZERO Network, 1950s–60s', in The Solomon R. Guggenheim Foundation (ed.), *ZERO: Countdown to Tomorrow, 1950s–60s*, exh. cat. Solomon R. Guggenheim Museum, New York, 2014, pp. 16–43.

Hoffmann 1977
Paul Theodor Hoffmann, 'Expedition in künstliche Gärten', *Hamburger Abendblatt*, 22 April 1977.

Holert 2004
Tom Holert, 'Strudel und Wüsten des Politischen. Michelangelo Antonioni, Robert Smithson und Michael Snow' [2004], online: medienkunstnetz.de (last accessed on 26 November 2021).

Honisch 1986
Dieter Honisch, *Mack. Skulpturen, 1953–1986* (Düsseldorf and Vienna, 1986).

Institut für moderne Kunst 1969
Institut für moderne Kunst, Nuremberg (ed.), *Mack. Kunst in der Wüste. Bilder zum Sahara-Projekt* (Starnberg, 1969).

Jappe 1969
Georg Jappe, 'Ikarus in der Wüste. "Telemack" im WDR', *Frankfurter Allgemeine Zeitung*, 8 May 1969.

Jocks 2009
Heinz-Norbert Jocks, 'Interview mit Heinz Mack', in Anneliese Lenz and Ulrike Bleicker-Honisch (eds.), *Das Ohr am Tatort* (Ostfildern, 2009), pp. 35–69.

Jocks 2017
Heinz-Norbert Jocks, 'Die Fata Morgana des Lichts', in Helmut Friedel (ed.), *Mack. Licht / Light / Lumière* (Munich, 2017), pp. 20–27.

Kaiser/Kwon 2012
Philipp Kaiser and Miwon Kwon (eds.), *Ends of the Earth: Land Art to 1974*, exh. cat. The Museum of Contemporary Art, Los Angeles; Haus der Kunst, Munich (Munich, London, and New York, 2012).

Kellein 1989
Thomas Kellein, *Sputnik-Schock und Mondlandung. Künstlerische Großprojekte von Yves Klein zu Christo* (Stuttgart, 1989).

Kramer-Mallordy/Klein-Moquay 2017
Antja Kramer-Mallordy and Rotraut Klein-Moquay, *Yves Klein – Germany* (Paris, 2017).

Krätz 1998
Otto Krätz, *Goethe und die Naturwissenschaften* (Munich, 1998).

Kröpelin 2021
Stefan Kröpelin, 'Kunstraum Wüste', in Heike van den Valentyn (ed.), *Heinz Mack*, exh. cat. Museum Kunstpalast, Düsseldorf (Cologne, 2021), pp. 84–87.

Kuhn 1998
Anette Kuhn, 'Reservate der Kunst. Zu den Projekten der Zero-Zeit', in Schmied 1998, pp. 119–125.

Kuni 2000
Verena Kuni, 'Die Wüste als Ort der Kunst', in Uwe Lindemann and Monika Schmitz-Emans (eds.), *Was ist eine Wüste? Interdisziplinäre Annäherungen an einen interkulturellen Topos* (Würzburg, 2000), pp. 101–114.

Kunstverein Ahlen 1994
Kunstverein Ahlen e. V. (ed.), *MACK. lichtkunst*, exh. cat. Kunst-Museum Ahlen (Cologne, 1994).

Lippard 1973/2001
Lucy Lippard, *Six Years: The Dematerialization of the Art Object from 1966 to 1972* (Berkeley and Los Angeles, 1973/2001).

Lorz 2012
Julienne Lorz, 'The Case of Munich, 1968–1972', in Kaiser/Kwon 2012, pp. 161–171.

Lützeler 2000
Paul Michael Lützeler, 'Goethe and Europe', *South Atlantic Review*, vol. 65, no. 2, 2000, pp. 95–113.

Maak 2014
Niklas Maak, 'Das Geheimnis der weißen Orchidee', *Monopol. Magazin für Kunst und Leben*, September 2014, pp. 74–82.

Mack 1958 a
Heinz Mack, 'Die neue dynamische Struktur', in idem and Otto Piene (eds.), *ZERO*, vol. 1 (Düsseldorf, 1958), unpaginated, Vorlass (living bequest) Heinz Mack, ZERO foundation, Düsseldorf, mkp.ZERO.1.VII.137; reprinted in Pörschmann/Visser 2012, unpaginated.

Mack 1958 b
Heinz Mack, 'Die Ruhe der Unruhe', in idem and Otto Piene (eds.), *ZERO*, vol. 2 (Düsseldorf, 1958), unpaginated, Vorlass (living bequest) Heinz Mack, ZERO foundation, Düsseldorf, mkp.ZERO.1.VII.139; reprinted in Pörschmann/Visser 2012, unpaginated.

Mack 1959
Heinz Mack, 'Das Sahara-Projekt', 1959, original typescript, Mack Archive; first published in Mack/Piene 1961, unpaginated.

Mack 1961
Heinz Mack, 'visuell tractat. über die wüste', 1961, Vorlass (living bequest) Heinz Mack, ZERO foundation, Düsseldorf, mkp. ZERO.1.IV.26

Mack 1966
Heinz Mack, 'Licht ist nicht Licht', 1966, Mack Archive.

Mack 1968
Heinz Mack, 'Sahara – 1968', in Staber 1968, pp. 94–95.

Mack 1977
Heinz Mack, 'Wer die Wüste betritt ...' [1976], in Nannen 1977, unpaginated.

Mack 1994
Heinz Mack, 'Kommentar zur "1. Hommage à Georges de la Tour" in der Galerie Diogenes, Berlin 1960', in Kunstverein Ahlen 1994, pp. 180–181.

Mack 1999 a
Heinz Mack, 'Hellgrau im Dunkelgrau – Kindheit und Jugend', 1999, Mack Archive.

Mack 1999 b
Heinz Mack, *Mack. Ein Buch der Bilder zum West-östlichen Divan von Johann Wolfgang v. Goethe* (Mönchengladbach, 1999); reprint (Düsseldorf, 2015).

Mack 2008 a
Heinz Mack, (ed.), *Ars Urbana. Kunst für die Stadt, 1952–2008* (Munich, 2008).

Mack 2008 b
Heinz Mack, 'Kälte', 2008, Mack Archive.

Mack 2009
Heinz Mack, 'Meine Beziehung zu Brancusi (Skulptur und Sockel)', 2009, Mack Archive.

Mack 2013
Heinz Mack, 'Biographische Notizen anlässlich der ZERO-Ausstellungen 2014–2016', December 2013, Mack Archive.

Mack 2018 a
Heinz Mack, 'Bettlager im Krieg und auf Reisen', 2018, Mack Archive.

Mack 2018 b
Maria Valeria Mack, 'Die Auseinandersetzung mit dem Kontinent Afrika aus der Perspektive eines Bildhauers, Malers und Sammlers', in idem and David Zemanek, *Afrikanische Kunst der Sammlung Mack* (Munich, 2018).

Mack/Höpker 1977
Heinz Mack and Thomas Höpker, *Sculpture Safaris: Photographic Interpretations of Artifacts in Nature* (New York, 1977).

Mack/Mack 2011
Heinz Mack and Ute Mack, *Mack. Leben & Werk* (Cologne, 2011).

Mack/Piene 1960
Heinz Mack and Otto Piene, 'Dynamo', in *Nota*, 4/1960, unpaginated.

Mack/Piene 1961
Heinz Mack and Otto Piene (eds.), *ZERO*, Bd. 3, Düsseldorf 1961, Vorlass (living bequest) Heinz Mack, ZERO foundation, Düsseldorf, mkp.ZERO.1.VII.144; reprinted in Pörschmann/Visser 2012, unpaginated.

Martin 2016
Michael Martin, *Planet Wüste* (Munich, 2016).

Meister 2006
Helga Meister, *Zero in der Düsseldorfer Szene. Piene – Uecker – Mack* (Düsseldorf, 2006).

Nannen 1977
Henri Nannen (ed.), *Mack. Expedition in künstliche Gärten* (Hamburg, 1977).

Noll 2020
Chaim Noll, *Die Wüste. Literaturgeschichte einer Urlandschaft des Menschen* (Leipzig, 2020).

Oberbayerisches Volksblatt 1977
Anonymous, 'In den Vorgärten der Wüste', *Oberbayerisches Volksblatt* (Rosenheim), 17 September 1977.

Otten 2003
Marie-Luise Otten (ed.), *Auf dem Weg zur Avantgarde. Künstler der Gruppe 53*, exh. cat. Museum der Stadt Ratingen (Heidelberg, 2003).

Otterbeck 2007
Christoph Otterbeck, *Europa verlassen. Künstlerreisen am Beginn des 20. Jahrhunderts* (Cologne, 2007).

Özbek 2016
Çağla Özbek (ed.), *MACK. Sadece Işık ve Renk / Just Light and Colour*, exh. cat. Sakıp Sabancı Müzesi, Istanbul, 2016.

Poirier 2016
Matthieu Poirier, 'Mack: Spectrum, 1950–2016', in *Mack. Spectrum*, exh. cat. Galerie Perrotin, Paris, 2016, pp. 16–38.

Pola 2015
Francesca Pola, 'Artists Take the Lead: Strategies of Imagination in Italy, 1957–1967', in Caianiello/Visser 2015, pp. 58–113.

Pörschmann 2015
Dirk Pörschmann, '"M. P. UE." DYNAMO FOR ZERO: The Artist-Curators Heinz Mack, Otto Piene and Günther Uecker', in Caianiello/Visser 2015, pp. 17–57.

Pörschmann/Shavemaker 2015
Dirk Pörschmann and Margriet Shavemaker (eds.), *ZERO. Die internationale Kunstbewegung der 50er und 60er Jahre*, exh. cat. Martin-Gropius-Bau, Berlin; Stedelijk Museum, Amsterdam (Cologne, 2015).

Pörschmann/Visser 2012
Dirk Pörschmann and Mattijs Visser (eds.), *4 3 2 1 ZERO* (Düsseldorf, 2012).

Reiche 1974
Maria Reiche, 'Peruanische Erdzeichen', in Kunstraum München e. V. (ed.), *Peruanische Erdzeichen*, exh. cat. Kunstraum München, Munich, 1974, pp. 5–13.

Rennert/von Wiese 1996
Susanne Rennert and Stephan von Wiese (eds.), *Otto Piene. Retrospektive, 1952–1996*, exh. cat. Kunstmuseum Düsseldorf im Ehrenhof (Cologne, 1996).

Restany 1961/2016
Pierre Restany, 'Die Beseelung des Objektes' [1961], in Stiftung Ahlers/Kestner 2016, pp. 57–64.

Richter 2011
Gerhard Richter, *EIS* (Cologne, 2011).

Rosenberg 1952/2005
Harold Rosenberg, 'The American Action Painters (from *Art News*, December 1952)', in David and Cecile Shapiro (eds.), *Abstract Expressionism: A Critical Record* (Cambridge, 2005), pp. 75–85.

Rosenthal 2016
Norman Rosenthal, 'Heinz Mack. An Artist of Union', in Özbek 2016, pp. 24–35.

Rubin 1984 a
William Rubin (ed.), *Primitivismus in der Kunst des zwanzigsten Jahrhunderts*, trans. Peter Stepan et al. (Munich 1984).

Rubin 1984 b
William Rubin, 'Der Primitivismus in der Moderne. Eine Einführung', in Rubin 1984 a, pp. 8–92.

Rüth 2001
Uwe Rüth, 'Heinz Mack und sein Sahara-Projekt', in idem (ed.), *MACK. Licht der Wüste, Licht des Eismeers*, exh. cat. Skulpturenmuseum Glaskasten, Marl, 2001, pp. 17–62.

Saint-Exupéry 1939/56
Antoine de Saint-Exupéry, *Wind, Sand und Sterne* [1939], trans. Henrik Becker (Düsseldorf 1956).

Schmidt 1991
Heinrich Schmidt, *Philosophisches Wörterbuch*, revised by Georgi Schischkoff (Stuttgart, 1991).

Schmied 1975
Wieland Schmied, *Caspar David Friedrich* (Cologne, 1975).

Schmied 1998
Wieland Schmied (ed.), *Utopie und Wirklichkeit im Werk von Heinz Mack*, exh. cat. Liechtensteinische Staatliche Kunstsammlung, Vaduz (Cologne, 1998).

Schmitt 2013
Ulrike Schmitt, *Der Doppelaspekt von Materialität und Immaterialität in den Werken der ZERO-Künstler 1957–67*, PhD diss. University of Cologne, 2013.

Schmitt 2015
Ulrike Schmitt, 'Die Bedeutung der Reliefform im Werk von Heinz Mack', in Robert Fleck (ed.), *Mack. Reliefs* (Munich, 2015), pp. 10–23.

Schneckenburger 2010
Manfred Schneckenburger, 'Skulpturen und Objekte', in Ingo F. Walther (ed.), *Kunst des 20. Jahrhunderts*, vol. 2 (Cologne, 2010), pp. 407–575.

Schulze/Zetzsche 2005
Dietrich Schulze and Viola Zetzsche, *Bilderbuch der Wüste. Maria Reiche und die Bodenzeichnungen von Nasca* (Halle, 2005).

Schwarzer 2005
Yvonne Schwarzer, *Kunst Portrait: Das Paradies auf Erden schon zu Lebzeiten betreten. Ein Gespräch mit dem Maler und Bildhauer Heinz Mack* (Witten, 2005).

Scott 2012
Emily Eliza Scott, 'Desert Ends', in Kaiser/Kwon 2012, pp. 67–91.

Sharp 1969
Willoughby Sharp (ed.), *Earth Art*, exh. cat. Andrew Dickson White Museum of Art, Cornell University, Ithaca, New York, Ithaca 1969.

Sharp 2012
Willoughby Sharp, 'On the "Earth Art" Exhibition at Cornell University, Ithaca, New York, 1969', in Kaiser/Kwon 2012, pp. 37–41.

Sloterdijk 1993
Peter Sloterdijk, *Weltfremdheit* (Frankfurt am Main, 1993).

Sloterdijk 2014
Peter Sloterdijk, 'Lichtung und Beleuchtung. Anmerkungen zur Metaphysik, Mystik und Politik des Lichtes, in Peter Weibel (ed.), *Peter Sloterdijk. Der ästhetische Imperativ. Schriften zur Kunst* (Berlin, 2014), pp. 84–103.

Smithson 1967/96
Robert Smithson, 'Towards the Development of an Air Terminal Site (1967)', in Jack D. Flam (ed.), *Robert Smithson. The Collected Writings* (Berkeley, 1996), pp. 52–60.

Smithson 1968/96
Robert Smithson, 'A Provisional Theory of Non-Sites (1968)', in Jack D. Flam (ed.), *Robert Smithson. The Collected Writings* (Berkeley, 1996), p. 364.

Staber 1968
Margit Staber, *Heinz Mack. Eine Monographie* (Cologne, 1968).

Stachelhaus 1968
Heiner Stachelhaus, 'Licht-Künstler preist Sahara. Heinz Mack verwirklichte einen alten Traum', *Neue Rhein Zeitung*, 17 December 1968.

Stachelhaus 1993
Heiner Stachelhaus, *ZERO. Mack, Piene, Uecker* (Düsseldorf et al., 1993).

Steinbauer-Grötsch 2001
Barbar Steinbauer-Grötsch, 'Ramlat-al-Wahiba, Die Modellwüste', *Spiegel Online*, 14 May 2001, https://www.spiegel.de/reise/fernweh/ramlat-al-wahiba-die-modellwueste-a-133747.html (last accessed on 26 November 2021).

Steingießer 2018
Barbara Steingießer, (ed.), *Taten des Lichts. Mack & Goethe*, exh. cat. Goethe-Museum Düsseldorf (Berlin, 2018).

Stiftung Ahlers/Kestner 2016
Stiftung Ahlers Pro Arte/Kestner Pro Arte (ed.), *ZERO und Nouveau Réalisme. Die Befragung der Wirklichkeit*, exh. cat. Stiftung Ahlers Pro Arte/Kestner Pro Arte, Hannover, 2016.

Thomas 1972
Karin Thomas, *Kunst – Praxis heute. Eine Dokumentation der aktuellen Ästhetik* (Cologne, 1972).

Tolnay 2006
Alexander Tolnay (ed.), *Günther Uecker. Twenty Chapters* (Ostfildern-Ruit, 2006).

Ullrichs 2009
Wolfgang Ullrichs, *Raffinierte Kunst. Übung vor Reproduktionen* (Berlin, 2009).

Varnedoe 1984
Kirk Varnedoe, 'Abstrakter Expressionismus', in Rubin 1984 a, pp. 628–675.

Werkner 1992
Patrick Werkner, *Land Art USA. Von den Ursprüngen zu den Großraumprojekten in der Wüste* (Munich, 1992).

Westenholz 2015 a
Caroline de Westenholz, *1965–1966. 'ZERO on Sea'* (n.p., 2015).

Westenholz 2015 b
Caroline de Westenholz, 'ZERO ON SEA', in Caianiello/Visser 2015, pp. 271–395.

Wevers 2003
Ursula Wevers, 'Liebe Arbeit Fernsehgalerie', in Groos et al. 2003, pp. 23–46.

Wyss 2021
Beat Wyss (ed.), *Mack. Skulpturen 2003–2020* (Munich, 2021).

Xhayet 1968
Marianne Xhayet, 'In Neuwerk entstanden – in der Sahara versandet. Mack-Werke gastierten in Nordafrika – Das Große Abenteuer', *Mönchengladbacher Stadtpost/Rheinische Post*, 14 December 1968.

Xhayet 1975
Marianne Xhayet, 'Mack und Weller in der Wüste', *Rheinische Post*, 1975, clipping in the Mack Archive.

Zell 2015
Thekla Zell, 'Chronology, 1957–1967', in Caianiello/Visser 2015, pp. 428–485.

INDEX OF ILLUSTRATIONS

Unless otherwise noted, all photos are from the Mack Archive.

- □ p. 2 — The artist and his silver flag in a stone quarry, Germany, 1972; photo: Lothar Wolleh: *Portrait Heinz Mack* © Lothar Wolleh Estate, Berlin (The idea for the setting came from Lothar Wolleh and the photo was first published in his book *Art Scene Düsseldorf*, 1971.)
- □ pp. 4–5 — Heinz Mack in the Grand Erg Occidental, Algeria, 1976; photo: Thomas Höpker
- □ pp. 6–7 — The artist overlooks the icebergs in Disko Bay, Greenland, 1976; photo: Thomas Höpker
- □ p. 8 — *The Declination of Light Beams*, Grand Erg Occidental, Algeria, 1976, aluminium, ca. 2×8 m; photo: Thomas Höpker
- □ 01 — Heinz Mack on his first visit to the Sahara, Tunisia, 1955
- □ 02 — Heinz Mack next to his eleven-metre-high *Light Stele* in the desert, Tunisia, 1968; still from the film *Tele-Mack*, camera: Edwin Braun
- □ 03 — *Upside-Down* – mirror experiment, Grand Erg Occidental, Algeria, 1976, shards of concave mirrors, max. height: 80 cm; photo: Thomas Höpker
- □ 04 — *Sail without Wind and Ship – The Secret of the Arctic*, Greenland, 1976, vapour-deposited mercury foil, max. height: 7 m; photo: Thomas Höpker
- □ 05 — *Great Sand Relief* in the Grand Erg Occidental, Algeria, 1976, c. 25×5 m; photo: Thomas Höpker
- □ 06 — *Sahara Reliefs*, Mathildenhof School (today the Astrid Lindgren School), Leverkusen, 1960/61, concrete, height: 13 m; destroyed
- □ 07 — *The Scale of the Desert*, Grand Erg Occidental, Algeria, 1976, aluminium reflectors, each c. 56×220 cm; photo: Thomas Höpker
- □ 08 — Ensemble of *Cubes* in the Arctic, Greenland, 1976, acrylic and mirror glass, Fresnel lenses, aluminium; photo: Thomas Höpker
- □ 09 — *Coloured Weather Balloons over an Iceberg*, Greenland, 1976, panels of fabric, helium-filled balloons, length: c. 6 m; photo: Thomas Höpker
- □ 10 — *Marking of the Earth*, Hubbelrath near Düsseldorf, 1960, lime on a ploughed field, triangle: c. 7×7×7 m
- □ 11 — *Safrane Mirror Plantation*, Tunisia, 1967, crystal mirrors, 50×50 cm each
- □ 12 — The artist with a silver flag, near Kebili, Tunisia, 1968; still from the film *Tele-Mack*, camera: Edwin Braun
- □ 13 — *Fire Ship* on a lake near Mönchengladbach, 1968, pyrotechnics, wooden construction, c. 10×18×8 m; still from the film *Tele-Mack*, camera: Edwin Braun
- □ 14 — Shooting for the film *Tele-Mack* in the Grand Erg Oriental, Tunisia, 1968
- □ 15 & 16 — Heinz Mack, Edwin Braun, Klaus Weber, and Hans Emmerling during the installation of the *Light Steles* in the desert, Tunisia, 1968
- □ 17 — *Light Fans* in the Grand Erg Oriental, Tunisia, 1968, aluminium webs (honeycomb); still from the film *Tele-Mack*, camera: Edwin Braun
- □ 18 — Heinz Mack during the shoot of the film *Tele-Mack*, Tunisia, 1968; camera: Edwin Braun
- □ 19 — *Light Prisms in the Arctic (Model for a Floating Research Station)*, Greenland, 1976, nylon, fibre glass, stainless steel, height: c. 2 m; photo: Thomas Höpker
- □ 20 — *Large Space Arrow* in the Grand Erg Occidental, Algeria, 1976, aluminium, length: 15 m; photo: Thomas Höpker
- □ 21 — Mack arranges the *Caravan of Colours* in the Grand Erg Occidental, Algeria, 1976; photo: Thomas Höpker
- □ 22 — Covering a rock with reflective foil, Algeria, 1976; photo: Thomas Höpker

☐ 23 *Caravan of Colours*, Algeria, 1976, acrylic glass, max. length: 36 m; photo: Thomas Höpker

☐ 24 A sandstorm takes the expedition by surprise, Algeria, 1976; photo: Thomas Höpker

☐ 25 *The Saint-Exupéry Crash – Model of a Monument in the Algerian Desert*, 1976, anodised aluminium, height: approx. 240 cm; photo: Thomas Höpker

☐ 26 A *Light Sculpture* is lowered into the sea from a fishing boat, Greenland, 1976, aluminium, height: c. 120 cm; photo: Thomas Höpker

☐ 27 Balloons with spectral colour sails are released into the sky from a boat, Greenland, 1976, panels of fabric, helium-filled balloons, length: c. 6 m; photo: Thomas Höpker

☐ 28 Mack lowers a *Water Sculpture* into the water, Greenland, 1976, acrylic glass, coloured water, height: c. 120 cm; photo: Thomas Höpker

☐ 29 The *Fire Raft* on the iceberg, Greenland, 1976, pitch torches on wooden structure, height: c. 70 cm; photo: Thomas Höpker

☐ 30 The *Fire Raft* in the Arctic Sea, Greenland, 1976, pitch torches on wooden structure, height: c. 70 cm; photo: Thomas Höpker

☐ 31 *Large Stele* in the Wahiba desert, Oman, 1997, anodised aluminium reflectors, height: 14 m

☐ 32 *Shadow Calligraphy*, Wahiba desert, Oman, 1997, wood, max. height: c. 50 cm

☐ 33 *Design for a Glass Architectural Structure*, Wahiba desert, Oman, 1997, mineralogically vapour-deposited glass, max. height: 1 m

☐ 34 *Golden Pyramid in the Desert Sand*, Oman, 1997, gold-coloured anodised aluminium, height: c. 70 cm

☐ 35 *Untitled* (from the suite of pictures to the *West-Eastern Divan* by Johann Wolfgang v. Goethe), 1998, oil, ink, pastel on handmade paper, 86×61 cm, Private Collection

☐ 36 *2nd Hommage à Georges de La Tour*, Galerie Schmela, Düsseldorf, 1965, 200 candles on reflective foil

☐ 37 *Sand Relief*, 1956/57, Sahara sand on cardboard, gold bronze, 50.5×54.5×5.5 cm, Collection of the artist

☐ 38 *Model for a Sand Wedge in the Desert*, 1970, Sahara sand on wood, 69×96×9 cm, Collection of the artist

☐ 39 *Fire Ridge* project, 1975, photo-collage

☐ 40 *Dream of the Navigator*, Greenland, 1976, metallised Ultraphan film, length: c. 100 m; photo: Thomas Höpker

☐ 41 *Water Cloud* on the Olympic Lake, Munich, 1972, water, pump units, 112 underwater floodlights, 24 floodlights, height: 8–max. 36 m, surface area: 30×14 m; photo: Lothar Wolleh © Lothar Wolleh Estate, Berlin

☐ 42 *Foam Sculpture*, Galerie Diogenes, West Berlin, 1963, water, soap, height: c. 110 cm; photo: dpa

☐ 43 *Ice Sculpture*, Greenland, 1976, aluminium web (honeycomb), frozen water, c. 50×60×13 cm; photo: Thomas Höpker

☐ 44 *Untitled (Chromatic Constellation)*, 2016, acrylic on canvas, 210×223 cm, Private Collection

☐ 45 *Light Prisms in the Arctic (Model for a Floating Research Station)*, Greenland, 1976, nylon, fibre glass, stainless steel, height: c. 2 m; photo: Thomas Höpker

☐ p. 140 *Experiment on the Jardin Artificiel*, Wahiba desert, Oman, 1997, aluminium web (honeycomb)

ACKNOWLEDGMENTS

When I applied for a position at Heinz Mack's studio in 2013, I was fresh out of university and had just completed my master's degree. During the interview, I mentioned to Ute and Heinz Mack that I wanted to do a doctorate. A short time later, they approached me with the idea of writing a thesis on Heinz Mack's *Sahara Project* – it goes without saying that I was immediately enthusiastic and began to study the artist's wonderful, extensive, and multifaceted work in connection with the *Sahara Project*. Since then, Ute and Heinz Mack, as well as their daughter Valeria, have encouraged and supported me in this endeavour: with numerous conversations, unlimited access to literature and all archive materials, with proofreading and critical feedback, with patience, and last but not least with financial support. My heartfelt thanks therefore go first and foremost to the artist and his family, who made my doctorate possible. Moreover, they encouraged me to write this book about the *Sahara Project* on the basis of my dissertation, thematically expanded for a wider audience. I would also like to take this opportunity to thank my colleagues at Atelier Mack: Petra Rickenbach, Sandra Gronenberg, Bettina Weiand, Tatjana Zimfer, Michael Molitor, Roland Steinhauser, and Felix Baltzer.

I wrote my dissertation, *The Sahara Project by Heinz Mack in the International Context of ZERO and Land Art, 1959–1976* at the University of Cologne. I am grateful to my doctoral supervisor, Günter Herzog, and his team at the Central Archive for German and International Art Market Research (ZADIK) for mentoring my work and supporting my research. Special thanks go to Robert Fleck at the Düsseldorf Academy of Art, who accompanied my doctoral thesis critically and helpfully as a reviewer and also contributed the preface to this book. I would also like to thank Christian Spies from the Institute of Art History at the University of Cologne, my third reviewer, as well as Stephan Packard from the Institute for Media Culture and Theatre for chairing my disputation, and the friendly staff of the a.r.t.e.s. Graduate School for the Humanities Cologne for their assistance. The ZERO foundation in Düsseldorf also supported me in the research and publication of the doctoral thesis – my special thanks go to Barbara Könches and the staff members at the time, Tiziana Caianiello and Thekla Zell. I am also grateful to the contemporary witnesses who responded to my questions: Heinz Holtmann and Thomas Höpker, whose wonderful photos from Algeria and Greenland are featured in this book.

This book was made possible with the generous support of NATIONAL-BANK AG. For this and for the constant interest of its Chairman of the Board, Thomas A. Lange, I thank them. I would also like to thank the great team that worked with me on this publication: Jutta Allekotte at Hirmer Verlag, the graphic designer Dominik Lanhenke, the copyeditors Almut Otto and Olivia Parkes, and the translator Gérard Goodrow.

Last but not least, I sincerely thank my family and friends for their encouragement and interest: especially Edith, Anna, and Elli Sotke, Ulrich Böse, the Hillen family, Wina Kraus, Sascha Peters, and Isabelle Niessen.

COLOPHON

Mack – Sahara
From ZERO to Land Art
Heinz Mack's Sahara Project, 1959–1997

Author:
Sophia Sotke

Picture Editing:
Maria Valeria Mack and Sophia Sotke, Studio Heinz Mack

Project Management, Hirmer:
Jutta Allekotte

Copy Editing, German:
Almut Otto, Berlin

Translation from the German:
Gérard Goodrow, Cologne

Copy Editing, English:
Olivia Parkes, Berlin

Graphic Design and Typesetting:
Dominik Lanhenke, Düsseldorf

Production:
Hannes Halder

Pre-Press:
Reproline Genceller, Munich

Paper:
Luxoart Samt 150 g/m2

Typeface:
Argesta, Silka

Printing and Binding:
Eberl & Kœsel GmbH & Co. KG, Altrusried-Krugzell

Printed in Germany

Bibliographic information published
by the Deutsche Nationalbibliothek.
The Deutsche Nationalbibliothek lists this publication in the Deutsche Nationalbibliografie; detailed bibliographic data are available online at http://dnb.de.

ISBN 978-3-7774-3922-8 (English edition)
ISBN 978-3-7774-3919-8 (German edition)

www.hirmerverlag.de
www.hirmerpublishers.com

Cover Illustration:
Heinz Mack, *Large Stele* in the Wahiba desert, Oman, 1997